Colección Támesis
SERIE A: MONOGRAFÍAS, 312

LIFE-WRITING IN CARMEN MARTÍN GAITE'S *CUADERNOS DE TODO* AND HER NOVELS OF THE 1990s

Tamesis

Founding Editors
†J. E. Varey

†Alan Deyermond

General Editor
Stephen M. Hart

Series Editor of
Fuentes para la historia del teatro en España
Charles Davis

Advisory Board
Rolena Adorno
John Beverley
Efraín Kristal
Jo Labanyi
Alison Sinclair
Isabel Torres
Julian Weiss

MARIA-JOSÉ BLANCO LÓPEZ DE LERMA

LIFE-WRITING IN CARMEN MARTÍN GAITE'S *CUADERNOS DE TODO* AND HER NOVELS OF THE 1990s

TAMESIS

© Maria-José Blanco López de Lerma 2013

All Rights Reserved. Except as permitted under current legislation no part of this work may be photocopied, stored in a retrieval system, published, performed in public, adapted, broadcast, transmitted, recorded or reproduced in any form or by any means, without the prior permission of the copyright owner

The right of Maria-José Blanco López de Lerma to be identified as the author of this work has been asserted in accordance with sections 77 and 78 of the Copyright, Designs and Patents Act 1988

First published 2013 by Tamesis, Woodbridge

ISBN 978 1 85566 247 6

Tamesis is an imprint of Boydell & Brewer Ltd
PO Box 9, Woodbridge, Suffolk IP12 3DF, UK
and of Boydell & Brewer Inc.
668 Mt Hope Avenue, Rochester, NY 14620-2731, USA
website: www.boydellandbrewer.com

A CIP catalogue record for this book is available
from the British Library

The publisher has no responsibility for the continued existence or accuracy of URLs for external or third-party internet websites referred to in this book, and does not guarantee that any content on such websites is, or will remain, accurate or appropriate

Papers used by Boydell & Brewer Ltd are natural, recyclable products made from wood grown in sustainable forests

Typeset by BBR, Sheffield
Printed and Bound in Great Britain by
TJ International Ltd, Padstow, Cornwall.

CONTENTS

Acknowledgements	ix
Introduction	1
1. Letters, Diaries and Self-Reflective Writing	15
2. *Cuadernos de todo*: Carmen Martín Gaite's Diaries	50
3. *Nubosidad variable*: Letters and Diaries, Female Friendship through Writing	112
4. *La Reina de las Nieves*: a Personal Search through Diaries and Letters	137
5. *Lo raro es vivir*: Personal Reflections from Historical Research	161
6. *Irse de casa*: Life through the Cinematographic Lens, Writing One's Own Life-Script	180
Conclusion	199
Bibliography	206
Index	218

This book is dedicated to David, Rebecca and Marta with all my love and to my parents Mary y José Luis.

ACKNOWLEDGEMENTS

I would like to thank David Henn for all the support and encouragement he has given me over the years. I am grateful to Catherine Davies and Mercedes Carbayo Abengózar for the advice given to make this a better and more focused work. I would also like to thank some of those who read and commented on the different chapters, especially Gwen MacKeith for her meticulous reading and Gill Rye for the French translations. Special thanks to Ana María Martín Gaite for letting me into the 'Back room' and always welcoming me into her house every time I visit Madrid. Thanks to the Office for Cultural and Scientific Affairs at the Spanish Embassy in London for sponsoring the conference *Carmen Martín Gaite 10 years on*, where I was able to meet some of the most important of my fellow Carmen Martín Gaite scholars.

Parts of Chapter 2 have been presented in conferences and/or published with revisions in books and journals: '*La Reina de las nieves* en los *Cuadernos de todo*', *Espéculo*, forthcoming; 'Carmen Martín Gaite's *Cuadernos de todo*: A Writer's Diary/A Writer's Workshop', in *Beyond the Back Room: New Perspectives on Carmen Martín Gaite*, ed. Marian Womack and Jennifer Wood (Oxford: Peter Lang, 2011), pp. 233–57 and 'The feminism of an antifeminist in Carmen Martín Gaite's *Cuadernos de todo*', *Journal of Romance Studies*, vol. 9, no. 1 (Spring 2009), pp. 47–57.

Finally, I would like to thank my husband and daughters for all the patience and understanding they have shown during my years of research.

INTRODUCTION

Born in 1925, Carmen Martín Gaite was a prolific author who cultivated many different literary genres through the second half of the twentieth century, starting in 1947 with the publication of her first poem, 'La barca nevada', and then her first short story, 'Desde el umbral' the following year in *Trabajos y días* when she was a student at the University of Salamanca.[1] She was subsequently identified as belonging to the group of writers known as the 'Generación del Mediosiglo' or 'Generación del 50'. She worked continuously until her death in 2000, and her unfinished novel *Los parentescos* was published in 2001.

Like many other fiction writers of her generation, Martín Gaite began as a short-story writer, publishing her first collection, *Las ataduras*, in 1960 and *Cuentos completos* in 1978. Her first short novel, *El balneario*, which won the Premio Café Gijón 1954 and was published a year later, can be seen as a literary bridge between her short stories and her novels. Her first novel was *Entre visillos* (1958), winner of the 1957 Premio Nadal, followed by *Ritmo lento* (1963), a finalist in the Biblioteca Breve de Narrativa competition a year earlier. In total she published nine full-length novels, two novellas, *El balneario* and *Caperucita en Manhattan* (1990), as well as some fiction for children.

Her novelistic career was interrupted on several occasions by disenchantment with fiction, indeed she stated in 1971 that 'Todas las historias de ficción que leía o intentaba escribir me parecían repetidas, me aburrían.'[2] These periods of 'silence' allow us to divide her output into three main phases: the 1950s and 1960s, with the publication of the first two novels;

---

[1] In the Biblioteca Virtual Cervantes, it is now possible to read her first short stories and poems published in *Trabajos y días* (Salamanca, 1946–51), 'Desde el umbral' (1948) and 'Historia de un mendigo' (1950), and the poems 'La barca nevada' (1947), 'En mi vejez' (1949) and 'Destello' (1949). See http://213.0.4.19/servlet/SirveObras/46828399437915617422202/p0000010.htm#I_15_.

[2] Carmen Martín Gaite, *La búsqueda de interlocutor y otras búsquedas* [1973] (Barcelona: Destinolibro, 1982), p. 59.

the 1970s, with the appearance of *Retahílas* (1974), *Fragmentos de interior* (1976), and *El cuarto de atrás* (1978), which won the Premio Nacional de Literatura; and the 1990s, which saw the publication of her final novels, *Nubosidad variable* (1992), *La Reina de las Nieves* (1994), *Lo raro es vivir* (1996) and *Irse de casa* (1998). Although *El cuarto de atrás* is a novel which took the author in a new direction in her career, the death of her parents in 1978, especially that of her mother,[3] and most importantly the death of her daughter in 1985, meant that she did not publish another novel until the 1990s, despite continuing to publish other work. During those years and until the release of *Nubosidad variable* in 1992, she took refuge in children's literature and focused her energies on finishing some of the work that had been years in preparation, namely *El cuento de nunca acabar* (1983) and *Usos amorosos de la postguerra española* (1987).

Martín Gaite never stopped researching and writing during her periods of novelistic 'silence'. Her investigation into Don Melchor de Macanaz (1670–1760) started in 1962, after she had written *Ritmo lento*, and culminated in the publication in 1970 of *El proceso de Macanaz: Historia de un empapelamiento*. Subsequently, and encouraged by her investigation into Macanaz's biography and the world in which he lived, Martín Gaite published a volume of cultural history, *Usos amorosos del dieciocho en España*, in 1972.

She also published many articles in newspapers and magazines, as well as working as a literary critic for *Diario 16* from 1976 until 1980, compiling some of these articles into collections such as *La búsqueda de interlocutor y otras búsquedas* (1973) and *Agua pasada* (1993). In addition, Martín Gaite published monographs such as *El cuento de nunca acabar*, *Usos amorosos de la postguerra española*, *Desde la ventana: Enfoque femenino de la literatura española* (1987) and *Esperando el porvenir: Homenaje a Ignacio Aldecoa* (1994).

The 1980s saw the publication of a number of children's stories: *El castillo de las tres murallas* (1981), *El pastel del diablo* (1985)[4] and *Caperucita en Manhattan* (1990). Her volumes of poetry include *A rachas* (1976) and *Todo es un cuento roto en Nueva York* (1986), and among her

---

[3] As Martín Gaite stated in 1980, 'Mi madre murió en diciembre de 1978 ... Y desde entonces he andado con los rumbos un poco perdidos, aunque parece que ya los voy recobrando': 'Retahíla con nieve en Nueva York', in *Agua pasada* (Barcelona: Anagrama, 1993), pp. 26–32 (p. 31).

[4] These two stories were published together in *Dos cuentos maravillosos* (Madrid: Siruela, 1992).

theatrical works are *A palo seco (Monólogo en un acto)* (1985) and *La hermana pequeña* (1999). She also collaborated in the writing of scripts for films and television series. Some were adaptations of her short stories, such as *Emilia, parada y fonda* (1976), based on 'Un alto en el camino' (1958), and *La conciencia tranquila* (1956; never filmed), based on the short story of the same name. Other scripts were for television series such as *Santa Teresa de Jesús* (1983) and *Celia* (1993). She also wrote the script of one episode, 'Salamanca', for the series *Esta es mi tierra* (1983). Furthermore, Martín Gaite translated into Spanish selected works only previously published in Portuguese, Italian, French and English.

Finally, Martín Gaite possessed another artistic talent: she enjoyed drawing and creating collages. This material was incorporated in some of her other work, for example the illustrations for *Caperucita en Manhattan* or the collages which appeared on the covers of some of her novels and monographs.

Carmen Martín Gaite's work has been comprehensively studied over the last thirty years, having first attracted interest in 1980, when she travelled to the United States as an invited writer at Barnard College in New York City. *From Fiction to Metafiction: Essays in Honor of Carmen Martín Gaite* (1983), edited by Mirella Servodidio and Marcia L. Welles, was the first critical volume, containing a total of fifteen articles as well as an interview with Martín Gaite and an essay written by her especially for the volume, 'Retahíla con nieve en Nueva York'. This was followed by Joan Lipman Brown's *Secrets from the Back Room: The Fiction of Carmen Martín Gaite* (1987), for which Martín Gaite wrote an autobiographical text, 'Un bosquejo autobiográfico'.[5] *Cuadernos de todo* (2002) reveals that both volumes were planned during her stay in New York, as will be discussed further in Chapter 2.

After American recognition, Spain followed suit. Although Martín

---

[5] 'Un bosquejo autobiográfico' was later reprinted in *Agua pasada*, which is the version referred to throughout this book. Elsewhere, the author comments on her reception in America: 'He estado en América muchas veces, pero he escrito poco de América, porque creo que para hablar de las cosas tienes que haber alcanzado la sabiduría que da el contacto cotidiano. En América, empezando con la labor crítica de la prof. Joan Lipman Brown, se me ha estudiado mucho. El texto *From Fiction to Metafiction* ..., con los trabajos de R. Gullón y de G. Sobejano, entre otros, representó el inicio, de España, de una valoración diferente de Carmen Martín Gaite': quoted in Emma Martinell Gifre, 'Entrevista con Carmen Martín Gaite', *Espéculo: Revista de Estudios Literarios* (Madrid: Universidad Complutense, 1998), available at: <http://www.ucm.es/info/especulo/cmgaite/entr_cmg.htm>.

Gaite's work had already been recognized by various literary prizes,[6] as well as through articles in literary journals and chapters in books (where in some cases she was the only woman represented in a collection),[7] it was not until 1990 that the first book dedicated to her work was published in Spain. Carmen Alemany Bay's *La novelística de Carmen Martín Gaite* contains a short biographical sketch as well as an analysis of the author's short stories, poetry, essays and her first five novels, with a particularly detailed study of *Entre visillos*. This was followed by Pilar de la Puente Samaniego's *La narrativa breve de Carmen Martín Gaite* (1994), which was the first book to look exclusively at her short stories. It also included, in the opening chapter, an extensive study of Martín Gaite's generational context and Spanish postwar narrative. María de los Angeles Lluch Villalba's *Los cuentos de Carmen Martín Gaite: Temas y técnicas de una escritora de los años cincuenta* appeared in 2000. This work examined her short stories, undertaking a detailed study of structure, narrative voice, time, space, characters and style.

There have also been a number of books edited by Emma Martinell Gifre, some consisting of anthologies of the author's work, others based on conferences in her honour. *Hilo a la cometa: La visión, la memoria y el sueño* (1995), an anthology of Martín Gaite texts, studies the themes suggested in the title. Another of Martinell Gifre's works on the author, *El mundo de los objetos en la obra de Carmen Martín Gaite* (1996), as the title indicates, deals with many of the objects (houses, windows, curtains, rooms, mirrors, furniture, clocks, shoes, bags, newspapers, notebooks, and so on) found in the author's work. Martinell Gifre also co-ordinated two volumes of essays in homage to Martín Gaite: *Carmen Martín Gaite* (1993), based on a conference, 'La Semana de Autor', which took place in Buenos Aires in October 1990 and to which Martinell Gifre accompanied the author. This was followed by *Al encuentro de Carmen Martín Gaite: Homenajes y bibliografía* (1997), resulting from a conference on the occasion of the award to Martín Gaite of the Premio Nacional de Letras Españolas in 1994. Consisting of a series of talks and a round table discussion, with participants such as Josefina Aldecoa, Belén Gopegui, José Luis Borau, Maria Vittoria Calvi and Jorge Herralde, this volume

---

[6] Notably the Premio Café Gijón (1954), Premio Nadal (1957), Premio Nacional de Literatura (1978), Premio Anagrama de Ensayos (1987) and Premio Príncipe de Asturias (1988).

[7] See, for example, Juan Paredes Núñez, *5 Narradores de posguerra* (Granada: Universidad de Granada, 1987).

also includes the transcripts of two talks by Martín Gaite, 'La mirada ajena' and 'La edad de merecer'.

New perspectives on Martín Gaite's work began to emerge in the 1990s. Mercedes Carbayo Abengózar's *Buscando un lugar entre mujeres: Buceo en la España de Carmen Martín Gaite* (1998) studies Martín Gaite's work from a feminist perspective up to the publication of *Lo raro es vivir*. Adrián M. García's *Silence in the Novels of Carmen Martín Gaite* (2000) analyses the idea of 'silences' as a narrative strategy *Retahílas*, *El cuarto de atrás* and *Nubosidad variable*. In addition, the e-journal *Espéculo* presented a monographic edition (web-page) in 1998, co-ordinated by Martinell Gifre, containing a number of articles on Martín Gaite's work, including studies of how her writing was received in France, Germany, Italy and the United States.

Martín Gaite's work has, therefore, been studied from many different perspectives. There have been assessments involving feminist and psychoanalytical theories, metafictional and autobiographical perspectives, as well as appraisals of her as a Realist and Postmodern writer. She has been compared to authors such as Doris Lessing,[8] Miguel de Unamuno and Jorge Semprún,[9] and Juan Goytisolo.[10]

Martín Gaite died on 23 July 2000, and since her death there has been uninterrupted publication of her manuscripts, starting with her unfinished novel *Los parentescos* in 2001. In the same year Plaza & Janés published a collection of Martín Gaite's poems, *Poemas*, which includes a CD of the author reading her poetry. This was followed by her *Cuadernos de todo* (2002), which incorporates the contents of the author's notebooks or diaries, written from 1961 until her death. *Visión de Nueva York*, another of Martín Gaite's notebooks (a scrapbook or collage diary) was published in 2005.

In 2007 Martín Gaite's *El libro de la fiebre* (written in 1949) was published,[11] a book which is fundamental to an understanding of her development as a writer. In this first-person narrative she describes weeks

---

[8] See Linda Chown, *Narrative Authority and Homeostasis in the Novels of Doris Lessing and Carmen Martín Gaite* (New York: Garland, 1990).

[9] See Liliana Soto Fernández, *La autobiografía ficticia en Miguel de Unamuno, Carmen Martín Gaite y Jorge Semprún* (Madrid: Editorial Pliegos, 1996).

[10] See Doris Gruber, *Literarische Konstruktion und geschlechtliche Figuration: Das Erzählwerk Carmen Martín Gaites und Juan Goytisolos im Kontext des Frakismus* (Berlin: Edition Tranvía, 2003).

[11] This work never appeared during the author's lifetime, apart from a couple of fragments published in *Alcalá: Revista Universitaria Española* on 25 January 1952.

of illness as a result of contracting typhoid fever (which at that time was life-threatening, as she explains in 'Un bosquejo autobiográfico'), and writes of the dreams and hallucinations she suffered. In the third part, she looks back at those forty-eight days in bed, reflecting on the book she was writing and how to finish the story, which, in fact, she never completed. This is the only work in which Martín Gaite clearly identifies herself as the protagonist of her narration, and thereby anticipates some of the characteristics of what was going to be her most famous novel, *El cuarto de atrás*.

As well as these posthumous publications, two volumes of talks and articles have been published. *Pido la palabra*, a collection of twenty-five talks given by Martín Gaite and not previously published in *Agua Pasada*, came out in 2002.[12] *Tirando del hilo (Artículos 1949–2000)*, published in 2005, recovered 192 of her articles written between 1949 and 2000 – from the first article, 'Vuestra prisa', written when she was twenty-four years old, to 'De Furtivos a Leo', her last article to be published in May 2000.

The publication of Martín Gaite's *Obras completas* began in 2008. The first volume contains her novels from *Entre visillos* to *El cuarto de atrás* and includes an unpublished manuscript, *La charca* (1955). In 2009 the second volume, also dedicated to her novels, was published and the third volume, published in 2010, presented the short stories, poetry and theatre. They will be followed by four more volumes which will include the essays, as well as some other unpublished manuscripts. In the same way that the early poems and short stories published in *Trabajos y días* show the beginnings of Martín Gaite's literary career, *La charca* and *El libro de la fiebre* might be deemed her apprentice pieces as a novelist. As José Teruel, editor of the *Obras completas*, commented at the launch of the first volume, they are 'un testimonio de primera mano de la vacilante etapa de aprendizaje que supuso su paso del cuento a la entrada en la novela'.[13]

Critics have also been very busy since her death, some publishing the dissertations and theses they had been working on during her lifetime, such as Lissette Rolón Collazo's *Figuraciones: Mujeres en Carmen*

---

[12] Some of the talks in *Pido la palabra*, as well as those that constitute *Desde la ventana* and *Esperando el porvenir*, which Martín Gaite gave in the Fundación Juan March, have been made publicly available and can be found on the Fundación's website: <http://www.march.es/conferencias/anteriores>.

[13] Cited in 'Martín Gaite total: Presentado en Madrid el primer volumen de las obras completas de la escritora, fallecida en 2000', ELPAÍS.com, 2 June 2008, available at: <http://www.elpais.com/articulo/cultura/Martin/Gaite/total/elpepucul/20080602elpepucul_6/Tes>.

Martín Gaite, revistas femeninas y ¡Hola! (2002). José Jurado Morales has published two monographs, *Del testimonio al intimismo: Los cuentos de Carmen Martín Gaite* (2001) (a reworking of his Master's dissertation on Martín Gaite's short stories) and *La trayectoria narrativa de Carmen Martín Gaite (1925–2000)*, published in 2003.[14]

Others works appeared in honour of the author after her death, including in 2000 Biruté Ciplijauskaité's *Carmen Martín Gaite (1925–2000)*. Drawing on her extensive knowledge of contemporary Spanish literature, Ciplijauskaité looks at Martín Gaite's work through her biography, whilst also comparing her fiction with that of contemporary writers and examining influences, such as that of Unamuno, on her narrative output. *Carmen Martín Gaite: Cuento de nunca acabar/Never-ending Story* edited by Kathleen Glenn and Lissette Rolón Collazo and published in 2003, brought together fourteen essays in English and Spanish, together with a section of 'Homenajes' in which friends and fellow writers, Soledad Puértolas, Rosa Montero and Belén Gopegui, show their appreciation of Martín Gaite.

In Spain, Alicia Redondo Goicoechea co-ordinated a collection of seventeen articles in Spanish, titled *Carmen Martín Gaite* (2004), and María José Casorran Marín published *Estudio crítico de 'El cuarto de atrás'* in 2006, written with secondary-school students in mind. Two books by David González Couso, *Una propuesta de lectura para 'Caperucita en Manhattan'* and *Los perfiles Gallegos de Carmen Martín Gaite*, were published in 2008, the latter offering a study of *Las ataduras* and *El pastel del diablo* in relation to San Lorenzo de Piñor, a village in the province of Ourense, Galicia, where Martín Gaite spent her childhood holidays.

Nuria Cruz-Cámara's *El laberinto intertextual de Carmen Martín Gaite: Un estudio de sus novelas de los noventa* (2008) studies different

---

[14] Other countries have also seen the publication of monographs based on doctoral theses on Martín Gaite's work. For example, in France, Anne Paoli published *Personnages en quête de leur identité dans l'oeuvre romanesque de Carmen Martín Gaite* (Aix-en-Provence: Publications de l'Université de Provence, 2000). This work focuses on Martín Gaite's novels from *Entre visillos* to *La Reina de las Nieves* and her characters' search for identity. In Italy, Maria Vittoria Calvi published *Dialogo e conversazione nella narrativa di Carmen Martín Gaite* (Milano: Archipelago, 1990). In Germany, Annette Paatz published *Vom Fenster aus gesehen? Perspektiven weiblicher Differenz im Erzahlwerk von Carmen Martín Gaite* (Frankfurt: Vervuert, 1994), an extract of which was published in Spanish in *Espéculo* as 'Perspectivas de diferencia femenina en la obra literaria de Carmen Martín Gaite', *Espéculo: Revista de Estudios Literarios* (Madrid: Universidad Complutense, 1998), available at: <http://www.ucm.es/info/especulo/cmgaite/a_paatz1.htm>.

levels of intertextuality in the 1990s novels, looking at romance, quest romance, *novela rosa* and psychoanalysis, for example. *A Companion to Carmen Martín Gaite* (2009), by Catherine O'Leary and Alison Ribeiro de Menezes, is a critical companion with one chapter for each of the nine novels, and for each of the following: Short Stories, Essays and Historical Writing, *El cuento de nunca acabar*, Theatre and Poetry, and Children's Literature and *Los parentescos*. *Beyond the Back Room: New Perspectives on Carmen Martín Gaite*, edited by Marian Womack and Jennifer Wood and published in 2011, explores Martín Gaite's work according to the following different sections: Visual, Space, Fairytale, The Fantastic, The Art of Writing, and Cinema.

Apart from these book-length studies, many articles have also been published in the last three decades, most of them looking at Martín Gaite's later fiction.[15] In addition there have been special journal issues dedicated to her life and work. For example, in 2002 a special issue of *Revista de Estudios Hispánicos*, introduced by Patrick Paul Garlinger and titled 'Diálogo crítico sobre Carmen Martín Gaite', included five articles by Garlinger, José Jurado Morales, Andrew Bush, Alicia Andrew and Stephanie Sieburth. In 2007 *Revista Turia* published a monograph with articles by Martín Gaite's manuscript editors, Maria Vittoria Calvi and José Teruel, as well as contributions from friends and colleagues such as José Luis Borau, recalling their stay in New York that coincided with the killing of John Lennon, or María Cruz Seoane, who writes of the times she spent with Martín Gaite in libraries and archives. It also includes an interview with the author's sister, Ana María Martín Gaite. In addition, *Género y géneros II: Escritura y escritoras iberoamericanas* (2006), edited by Ángeles Encinar, Eva Löfquist and Carmen Valcárcel, was the proceedings of a conference held in Madrid in May 2004 and includes a section on Martín Gaite.

Even though *Cuadernos de todo* appeared in 2002, one aspect of Martín Gaite's output that has still not been sufficiently studied, but with the notebooks becomes an easier task, is an examination of her work

---

[15] For a detailed study of the critical work on Martín Gaite see Carlos Uxó's review of the books and articles published about her between 1977 and 1998, 'Revisión crítica de los estudios sobre su obra', *Espéculo: Revista de Estudios Literarios* (Universidad Complutense de Madrid), 1998, available at: <http://www.ucm.es/info/especulo/cmgaite/c_uxo1.htm>; and his 'Cinco años de estudios sobre Carmen Martín Gaite: 1998–2002', in *Carmen Martín Gaite*, ed. Alicia Redondo Goicoechea (Madrid: Ediciones del Orto, 2004), pp. 215–26.

in the context of her own biography.[16] As Calvi indicates, the two were always closely connected:

> El marcado tono intimista de sus escritos, incluidas sus novelas, invita a una lectura autobiográfica de su obra; la autora siempre ha sido consciente de ello, y ha dejado entreabierta la puerta de acceso a su interioridad o, mejor dicho, ha dejado traslucir la imagen de su interioridad que ha querido construir a través de su obra.[17]

In Calvi's words, Martín Gaite's novels allow the reader access to an image of the author's inner world, of her intimate life, or at least the image that she decided to construct of herself.

Intimate and self-reflective narrative and the idea of the writing cure, 'writing ... used as a therapeutic tool',[18] is especially relevant in my study. This book focuses on letters and diaries as well as on other forms of life-writing.[19] In her novels Martín Gaite writes about themes which concern herself and the things to which she feels closest. Themes such as the role of women in Spanish society, motherhood, and especially the theme of the family, come up again and again in her *Cuadernos de todo* and are developed in her later novels. As she states in her notebooks:

---

[16] Critics such as Maria Vittoria Calvi and José Teruel, thanks to their work as editors of Martín Gaite's manuscripts, have started looking at her literary work from a more intimate, biographical perspective: see Calvi's introduction to Carmen Martín Gaite, *El libro de la fiebre*, ed. and intro. Maria Vittoria Calvi (Madrid: Cátedra, 2007), pp. 9–83, or her article, 'El autobiografismo dialógico de Carmen Martín Gaite', in *Turia: Revista Cultural*, 83 (2007), 223–35. The notes by José Teruel to Carmen Martín Gaite, *Tirando del hilo (Artículos 1949–2000)*, ed. and intro. José Teruel (Madrid: Siruela, 2006), and his introduction to Carmen Martín Gaite, *Obras completas*, I, ed. and intro. José Teruel (Barcelona: Galaxia Gutenberg/Círculo de Lectores, 2008), pp. 9–54, are also important. Another example of the biographical approach to Martín Gaite's narrative is Teruel's article on *Caperucita en Manhattan*: 'Un contexto biográfico para *Caperucita en Manhattan* de Carmen Martín Gaite', in *Género y géneros II: Escritura y escritoras iberoamericanas*, ed. Ángeles Encinar, Eva Löfquist and Carmen Valcárcel (Madrid: Servicio de Publicaciones de la UAM, 2006), pp. 143–51.

[17] Calvi, 'El autobiografismo dialógico', pp. 223–4.

[18] Stephen J. Lepore and Joshua M. Smith, 'The Writing Cure: An Overview', in *The Writing Cure: How Expressive Writing Promotes Health and Emotional Well-Being*, ed. Stephen J. Lepore and Joshua M. Smith (Washington DC: American Psychological Association, 2002) pp. 3–14 (p. 3).

[19] Sidonie Smith and Julia Watson explain it as: 'We understand *life writing* as a general term for writing of diverse kinds that takes a life as it subject. Such writing can be biographical, novelistic, historical, or an explicit self-reference to the writer': *Reading Autobiography: A Guide for Interpreting Life Narratives* (Minneapolis: University of Minnesota Press, 2001), p. 3.

'Todo lo que somos las mujeres está relacionado con la familia. Por eso escribimos preferentemente de familia'.[20] Indeed, her relationships with her parents and with her daughter are present throughout the *Cuadernos de todo*, and certainly family relationships, as well as the use of letters and diaries, are particularly significant in her later novels. With the publication of *Cuadernos de todo* it is possible to see how many of the themes dealt with in these novels are linked to material in the *Cuadernos* and subsequently to Martín Gaite's life.

Chapter 1 looks at epistolary literature, diary-writing and self-reflective writing. The chapter will consider epistolary literature and women as both the object and subject of writing. It will also discuss the use of diaries, letters, and memoirs in contemporary Spanish women's writing. To analyse the use of diaries and letters in literature, I refer to Foucault's article 'Self Writing', which is part of a series of studies the philosopher developed on 'the arts of oneself' in the Greco-Roman world.[21] In this article Foucault studies two forms of 'ethopoietic writing',[22] the *hupomnēmata*[23] and the *correspondence*. These types of writing and Foucault's study link with the idea of writing as a self-reflective act. Furthermore this chapter will briefly look at the use of letters and diaries in Martín Gaite's narrative, and the connection with her own diaries or *cuadernos*, in order to assess how this literary technique evolved throughout her career towards a more self-analytical, self-reflective and indeed 'self-referential'[24] style of writing.

Yet she not only used these writings as a literary strategy in her own work, she also reflected in her articles and essays on the significance

[20] Cited in 'El *Cuaderno de todo* de Carmen Martín Gaite', *El cultural.es*, 5 December 2001, available at: <http://www.elcultural.es/version_papel/LETRAS/3674/El_Cuaderno_de_todo_de_Carmen_Martin_Gaite/>.
[21] Michel Foucault, 'Self Writing', in *Ethics, Subjectivity and Truth: The Essential Works of Michel Foucault 1954–1984*, ed. Paul Rabinow, trans. Robert Hurley *et al.* (London: Penguin, 1997), pp. 207–22 (p. 207).
[22] Foucault, p. 209.
[23] '*Hupomnēmata*, in the technical sense, could be account books, public registers, or individual notebooks serving as memory aids. Their use as books of life, as guides of conduct, seems to have become a common thing for a whole cultivated public. One wrote down quotes in them, extracts from books, examples, and actions that one had witnessed or read about, reflections or reasoning that one had heard or that had come to mind. They constituted a material record of things read, heard, or thought, thus offering them up as a kind of accumulated treasure for subsequent rereading and meditation. They also formed a raw material for the drafting of more systematic treatises, in which one presented arguments and means for struggling against some weakness ... or for overcoming some difficult circumstance' (Foucault, pp. 209–10).
[24] This is a term used by Smith and Watson when talking about life-writing (p. 1).

of diaries and letters in general, as well as in other writers' work. As a literary critic, Martín Gaite wrote articles for example on *The Genesis of Dr Faustus* (1949) by Thomas Mann; *The Golden Notebook* (1962) by Doris Lessing and *Letters to Felice* (1973) by Franz Kafka,[25] works which use diaries and letters as their narrative framework. As a historical and cultural scholar, she came into contact with many letters, diaries and other manuscripts which served as the basis for drafting the narrative of history. Also, in her role as translator, she chose many works which had life-writing at their core. Works such as *Les Lettres portugaises* (1669), translated as *Cartas de amor de la monja portuguesa Mariana Alcoforado* (2000); *Letters to Merline 1919–1922* (1926), by Rainer Maria Rilke, which she translated as *Cartas francesas a Merline* (1987); *Caro Michele* (1973) by Natalia Ginzburg, translated as *Querido Miguel* (1989), and *A Grief Observed* (1961) by C. S. Lewis, translated as *Una pena en observación* (1988),[26] all show the author's interest in this area. Furthermore, in her books of essays, such as *El cuento de nunca acabar* and *Desde la ventana*, Martín Gaite dealt with epistolary literature and the use of diaries in literature, as well as what she called 'escritura egocéntrica', as self-writing.

In Chapter 2 Martín Gaite's *Cuadernos de todo* will be the first of her works to be analysed in detail. This chapter is divided into three sections: the first will look at the initial *cuadernos* and their importance as the basis for her notebooks. Here the focus will be on the use of these *cuadernos* as somewhere to reflect on society, especially the role of women in Spanish society of the 1960s. I will look at the different themes that are relevant from the first *cuadernos* that are developed in Martín Gaite's later work, such as women's role in society, motherhood and consumerism. This section will also analyse the use of these *cuadernos* as places to 'converse' with the books she was reading at the time. With the study of these first *cuadernos* a link will be made between the notebooks and Martín Gaite's fictional work, showing the way in which she not only used her notebooks to reflect, but also transferred those reflections into her fictional characters.

The second part of Chapter 2 will look at the *Cuadernos* as a 'writer's workshop'. This will focus on the less intimate side of the notebooks

---

[25] See Martín Gaite, *Tirando del hilo*, pp. 151–3.
[26] For more information on her work as a translator, see José Jurado Morales, *La trayectoria narrativa de Carmen Martín Gaite (1925–2000)* (Madrid: Gredos, 2003), pp. 473–4.

and analyse the way Martín Gaite's *oeuvre* developed from the moment it was conceived to the moment it was published, examining the way in which life and literature were always intertwined. The last section of the chapter will consider the notebooks Martín Gaite composed during time spent in the United States as an invited lecturer at various universities. These periods in America were crucial in her career, as it was then that she started receiving acclaim from academic critics and saw the publication, as mentioned earlier, of the first studies of her work. These years enabled Martín Gaite to isolate herself from the many commitments she had in Spain and allowed her to reflect on both her work and herself. This section also looks at the writing of the *cuadernos americanos* as therapy after the death of her daughter, Marta, when writing was her only escape. As her friend María Cruz Seoane explains, after Marta's death Martín Gaite 'Se mantenía a flote agarrándose al salvavidas del trabajo.'[27] And as Teruel points out, America is: 'donde se da cuenta de que avanzar era seguir con la pluma en la mano, y era sentir esa mágica transformación del tiempo inerte en tiempo de escritura.'[28] The pages of the last *cuaderno americano* are a particularly clear example of the therapeutic side of writing and lead into the remaining chapters of this book, which look at Martín Gaite's four novels of the 1990s.

Nubosidad variable (1992), *La Reina de las Nieves* (1994), *Lo raro es vivir* (1996) and *Irse de casa* (1998), will be individually assessed in terms of their use of letters, diaries, and other life-writing material, and the idea that the writing cure is beneficial not only for the characters of the novels, but also for the author herself. As Calvi indicates:

> En Carmen Martín Gaite encontramos, por ejemplo, una estructura recurrente, tanto en obras de ficción como en fragmentos autobiográficos, que combina la retrospección con el diario: esta modalidad comporta la aparición de un yo, narrador y personaje, que reconstruye episodios del pasado, más reciente o más remoto, a través de la escritura; el movimiento oscilante de la memoria, impulsado por un acontecimiento clave, se combina con el día a día, la anotación de los hechos presentes.[29]

The isolation needed to reflect and write is also highlighted in these

---

[27] María Cruz Seoane, 'La historia y las historias en la obra de Carmen Martín Gaite', *Turia: Revista Cultural*, 83 (2007), 214–22 (p. 222).
[28] Teruel, 'Un contexto biográfico', p. 145.
[29] Calvi, 'El autobiografismo dialógico', p. 225.

novels and can be found throughout the pages of *Cuadernos de todo*. As José Teruel comments on the writing process of *Caperucita en Manhattan*: 'con la libertad pasa igual que con la soledad: únicamente metiéndose de lleno en sus fauces puede llegar a regalarnos su fruto.'[30] The loneliness the author felt after the death of her parents in 1978, especially that of her mother, gave rise to a new way of writing in her notebooks. She recorded her dreams with greater intensity than previously. A project entitled 'Cuenta pendiente', in which she looks back at her parents' lives and notes the recurrent dreams in which her parents appeared, are a reminder of Leonardo's notebooks in *La Reina de las Nieves*. Here, the death of the character's parents makes him confront his own life and the recollection of his dreams in writing reveals his fears as well as his family past. The dreams Sofía describes in her 'diary' in *Nubosidad variable*, after her marriage has ended, are also similar to Martín Gaite's dreams, while the letters written by Sofía's friend Mariana link with Martín Gaite's idea of the need for an interlocutor. In *La búsqueda de interlocutor* Martín Gaite talks in terms of a 'sed de que alguien se haga cargo de la propia imagen y la acoja sin someterla a interpretaciones, un terreno virgen para dejar caer muerta la propia imagen, y que reviva en él'.[31] The characters of her 1990s novels will see the image of themselves reflected in their writing, which will enable them to recover and start again.

The protagonists of Martín Gaite's later novels use reflective writing to look back at their lives after having gone through some kind of traumatic experience. This technique of reflecting on the past in order to deal with difficult present times is one of the main characteristic of psychoanalysis and has been described as 'recovering the original memories of a trauma through techniques such as free association, talking, and releasing the appropriate affect associated with the trauma'.[32] This is what has come to be known as the 'talking cure'. Martín Gaite's protagonists use this kind of technique but instead of recovering their memories through talking they will do it through writing, the 'writing cure'. The links between the notebook material in *Cuadernos de todo* and the novels will be revealed and discussed, concluding with the idea of *Cuadernos de todo* and the 1990s novels as mirrors for Martín Gaite, mirrors used to reflect her life in her later years.

With the publication of several of Martín Gaite's manuscripts after

---

[30] Teruel, 'Un contexto biográfico', p. 146.
[31] Martín Gaite, *La búsqueda de interlocutor y otras búsquedas*, p. 17.
[32] Lepore and Smith, p. 4.

her death in 2000, especially *Cuadernos de todo*, new perspectives have opened up in approaches to her work. By accessing those of her notebooks and other manuscripts that have been published it is now possible to investigate and trace the early steps in her literary career, as well as witnessing a more intimate side of Martín Gaite's character.

1

Letters, Diaries and Self-Reflective Writing

Letters and Diaries in Women's Writing

Letters and diaries have often been linked to women's writing. We see female characters in novels writing their diaries, composing letters to lovers or friends, or even imagining those possible letters they would like to send. Indeed, Ruth Perry comments: 'Women seemed to have a special affinity for this personal one-to-one format.'[1] And Elizabeth Goldsmith refers to an observation made by Jean de la Bruyère in 1684: 'Women, he reflects, have a special facility for epistolary expression, giving their letters a natural quality that men have to struggle to achieve.'[2]

Women as writers are scarce until the Renaissance, as the written word was still the privilege of royalty, the upper class and convents. Writing about women as writers in the fifteenth and sixteenth centuries, María Milagros Rivera observes:

> Los géneros literarios que cultivaron fueron la autobiografía (un género inaugurado en la lengua castellana por una mujer, Leonor López de Córdoba), la confesión mística (inaugurada por Teresa de Cartagena), el tratado político, la poesía, la novela sentimental en forma de la vida de Cristo, la novela de caballería y la carta o epístola.[3]

According to Nora Catelli, writing remained a private practice for women: 'Hasta mediados del siglo XVII, en el ámbito anglosajón, tanto en Inglaterra como en la Norteamérica puritana, sólo el diez por ciento del

---

[1] Ruth Perry, *Women, Letters and the Novel* (New York: AMS Press, 1980), p. xii.
[2] Elizabeth Goldsmith, 'Authority, Authenticity, and the Publication of Letters by Women', in *Writing the Female Voice: Essays on Epistolary Literature*, ed. Elizabeth Goldsmith (London: Pinter, 1989), pp. 46–59 (p. 46).
[3] Maria Milagros Rivera, 'Egregias señoras: Nobles y burguesas que escriben', in *La vida escrita por las mujeres, IV: Por mi alma os digo*, ed. Anna Caballé (Barcelona: Lumen, 2004), pp. 17–22 (pp. 19–20).

total de autobiografías, memorias y diarios publicados estaban firmados por mujeres, y lo publicado, casi en su totalidad, era de índole religiosa'.[4]

Anna Caballé shows that the same could be said of Spain, where the majority of female autobiography prior to the seventeenth century was written by nuns like Santa Teresa de Jesús, whose *Libro de la vida* (1565) 'ejerció una influencia importantísima en la vida conventual: se estima que en aquella época pudieron escribirse más de 3.000 textos místicos ... Muchos de ellos fueron escritos por religiosas'.[5] Nonetheless we do find some women outside convents writing about their lives, such as Estefania de Requesens (1501–49), governess of the future King Philip II, with her *Cartes íntimes d'una dama catalana del s. XVI: epistolari a la seva mare la Comtessa de Palamós*, and the letters and dialogues of Luisa Sigea de Velasco in *Diálogo entre dos chicas jóvenes* (1552).[6]

The beginning of epistolary literature dates from the sixteenth century, when the familiar letter starts to be thought of as a literary genre. Verónica Franco epitomizes sixteenth-century Italy, while in the English seventeenth century Aphra Behn, one of the first women to earn her living as a writer, was the author of *Love–letters from a Nobleman to His Sister* (1684–7). In the eighteenth century in England there is Mary Manley with *Court Intrigues in a Collection of Original Letters from the Island of the New Atalantis & c. (*1711), Eliza Haywood with *Love in Excess* (1719), and Lady Mary Wortley Montagu, with her *Turkish Letters* (1724).[7] As Ruth Perry observes:

> Educated women, too, now found it possible to make a living writing stories according to the popular formula, or publishing diaries or letters in a culture which thought it anomalous for a gentlewoman to produce anything more public. Women's writing, of course, was not taken seriously but thought of as a new, pleasant way for women to busy themselves.[8]

---

[4] Nora Catelli, 'El diario íntimo: Una posición femenina', *Revista de Occidente, El diario Íntimo: Fragmentos de diarios españoles (1995–1996)*, 182–3 (1996), 87–98 (p. 91). Hereafter, this issue of the *Revista de Occidente* will be referred to as *RO: El diario*.

[5] Anna Caballé, 'La autobiografía escrita por mujeres: Los vacíos en el estudio de un género', in *Las mujeres escritoras en la historia de la literatura española*, ed. Lucía Nieves Baranda Leturio and Montejo Gurruchaga (Madrid: UNED, 2002), pp. 141–52 (p. 147).

[6] See Rivera, pp. 19–22.

[7] See Perry, pp. 15–16.

[8] Perry, p. 16.

Epistolary literature reached its zenith in the eighteenth century, as revealed in studies such as Gilroy and Verhoeven's *Epistolary Histories*, which characterizes the 'letter as feminine',[9] or that of Perry, who describes women not only as the literary subject but also as the eager reader of the time: 'By the beginning of the eighteenth century, a sizable female audience was beginning to be assumed for fiction of all sorts',[10] even though the publication of letters written by women was still not seen in a good light.[11] As Goldsmith explains, authors from this period saw the possibility of introducing letters written by women into their narratives: 'By the eighteenth century the practice of male authors appropriating the female voice in their fictions had become a popular and innovative narrative ploy.'[12] Famous French examples are *Les Lettres portugaises* (1669)[13] and Choderlos de Laclos's *Les Liaisons dangereuses* (1782), and in English the classic is Samuel Richardson's *Clarissa* (1747–8).

Letters in literature had a favourable reception during the eighteenth century as they supposedly reflected real lives with authenticity. As Perry notes:

> Middle-class readers could identify with characters who sat down to write letters which told of the agonies of love, or reported experiences of travelling, or revealed secrets, or gave advice, or arranged intrigues. ... The language generally used in epistolary fiction was

---

[9] Amanda Gilroy and W. M. Verhoeven, 'Introduction', in *Epistolary Histories: Letters, Fiction, Culture*, ed. Amanda Gilroy and W. M. Verhoeven (Charlottesville: University of Virginia Press, 2000), pp. 1–25 (p. 1).

[10] Perry, p. 18.

[11] 'To publish a woman's letters, even if the purpose of publication was to praise female epistolary style, was in some way to violate her personal integrity. Published epistolary writing by women was therefore rarely signed, and was often in fact produced by male writers "imitating" the way women wrote': Elizabeth Goldsmith, 'Introduction', in *Writing the Female Voice*, pp. vii–xiii (p. vii).

[12] Goldsmith, 'Introduction', p. vii.

[13] Thanks to the effectiveness of the writing, these letters were believed to have been written by a young Portuguese woman in a convent: 'Durante doscientos cincuenta años numerosos lectores en varios países creyeron a pies juntillas en la realidad de una mujer inexistente. El presupuesto que hizo posible este éxito excepcional de la ilusión de no ficcionalidad fue que la expresión totalmente creíble de un amor tan apasionado como el de la monja portuguesa no podía sino ser espontánea y verídica': Claudio Guillén, *Múltiples moradas: Ensayo de literatura comparada* (Barcelona: Tusquets, 1998), p. 227. The letters were actually by the Viscomte de Guilleragues, Gabriel de Laverge. As mentioned in the introduction, Martín Gaite translated these letters under the title *Cartas de amor de la monja portuguesa Mariana Alcoforado* (Madrid: Hiperión, 2000).

common rather than literary, and the characters who wrote news to their families or advice to their friends were all plausible types.[14]

In these novels, the 'editor' would write a preface to demonstrate the letters' authenticity, found or 'inherited', in which the reasons for their publication were also explained. Perry explains the need to use this formula in eighteenth-century literature:

> Fictions ... particularly those in letter form, were often passed off as historically true ... Because of the residual Puritan distaste for 'falsehood', as well as the new craze for scientific objectivity, the contemporary preference for stories of 'real people' dictated that much fiction be framed as first person writing: diaries, journals, travelogues, confessions, memoirs, autobiographies, and letters.[15]

The desire to peep into other people's lives is fulfilled when these letters are presented as written by others and published without their knowledge. Perry notes: 'Because letters reveal the self, reading the letters written and intended for other eyes is the most reprehensible invasion of privacy and consciousness in epistolary fiction.'[16] And it is presumably because of this that it gives us such pleasure. As Martín Gaite comments on the subject of letters and history: 'Cualquier aviso de publicación de un epistolario póstumo despierta una mezcla de avidez y mala conciencia. Es como estarse asomando por la rendija de una puerta para sorprender la intimidad ajena.'[17]

The epistolary novel subsequently went into decline, as Lorna Martens explains: 'the intimate letter itself became passé. In the course of the nineteenth century it became less and less natural to confide the secrets of one's heart to a friend. In the meantime a new genre, the secret journal, began to displace the letter in its function'.[18] Nora Catelli gives a precise date and reason for this:

> No cabe duda de que la fecha clave aquí es 1800 y que el diario llamado 'íntimo' reconoce sus orígenes en Francia alrededor de ese

---

[14] Perry, pp. 13–14.
[15] Perry, pp. x–xi.
[16] Perry, p. 130.
[17] Carmen Martín Gaite, *El cuento de nunca acabar* [1983] (Barcelona: Anagrama, 1988), p. 248.
[18] Lorna Martens, *The Diary Novel* (Cambridge: Cambridge University Press, 1985), p. 100.

año. ... Y no por casualidad ese mismo año 1800 ... supone un cambio en las costumbres de vivienda y trabajo de la clase media y la consagración de un modelo de mujer laica, encerrada en el círculo familiar, esposa y madre: el ángel del hogar.[19]

She goes on to note that there is a also change in the kind of women who write diaries. They are 'mujeres confinadas. Pero ya no en celdas, sino en la vida familiar, en el círculo domestico'.[20] The number of published women writers grew considerably:

> El hecho incuestionable es que la incorporación de la mujer a la literatura – que, de modo general en el mundo occidental, tiene lugar en el siglo XIX – transforma la literatura universal. ... El siglo XIX cambia la dirección literaria del 'yo' al 'tú', y quien había sido siempre receptor se convierte en emisor.[21]

The feminine model in the nineteenth-century novel continued to portray women as wives and mothers. María de Carmen Simón Palmer observes: 'En España la sociedad premió a las escritoras que no se dejaron corromper por corrientes extranjeras, y que escribían tras realizar sus tareas domésticas y dejar a sus hijos acostados'.[22] In fact, the restricted position of Spanish women writers during the nineteenth century is accurately portrayed by Rosalía de Castro in her 'Carta a Eduarda',[23] where one female author writes to another discouraging her from her vocation, due to the fact that, as the letter-writer observes (Rosalía explains how she found the letter inside a wallet in the street and decided to publish it as she thought its content to be truthful to reality), women writers will never be taken seriously if they try to write like men.

The beginning of the twentieth century witnessed a proliferation of published letters, diaries and autobiographies. Notable among the women writers is Gertrudis Gómez de Avellaneda, a Cuban poet who lived in Spain for most of her life. She wrote a number of letters to her lover

---

[19] Catelli, 'El diario íntimo: Una posición femenina', p. 92.
[20] Catelli, 'El diario íntimo: Una posición femenina', p. 93.
[21] María Pardo, 'La vida vislumbrada', in *La vida escrita por las mujeres, III: La pluma como espada*, ed. Anna Caballé (Barcelona: Lumen, 2004), pp. 15–40 (p. 19).
[22] María del Carmen Simón Palmer, 'La mujer y la literatura en la España del siglo XIX', *Centro Virtual Cervantes*, available at: <http://213.4.108.140/obref/aih/pdf/08/aih_08_2_069.pdf>, p. 595.
[23] Rosalía de Castro, 'Carta a Eduarda', in *Obras completas*, I, ed. Marina Mayoral (Madrid: Turner, 1993), pp. 655–9.

Ignacio de Cepeda between 1839, the year they first met, and 1854, and after meeting him also kept a journal, which represents an interesting example of a diary with epistolary characteristics. The dated entries describe moments of the day, places she visited and people she met, as one might expect from a diary, but each time with Cepeda as her interlocutor, just like the letters. Gómez de Avellaneda gave the notebook to Cepeda and it was kept together with her letters, and on Cepeda's death this material was inherited by his widow, who published them in 1907 under the title *Autobiografía y cartas (hasta ahora inéditas) de la ilustre poetisa Gertrudis Gómez de Avellaneda*; later editions appeared simply as *Diario de amor* (1914) and *Diario íntimo* (1945).

The letters written by Emilia Pardo Bazán to Benito Pérez Galdós are an interesting example of correspondence between writers as they not only used their letters to talk about their friendship and love but also to reveal their projects and literary successes. As Carmen Bravo Villasante comments in the prologue to the letters: 'La lectura de los epistolarios de escritores es sumamente reveladora no sólo de su personalidad literaria y humana, sino por las posibilidades que ofrece de esclarecer su obra.'[24] Pardo Bazán also left a short autobiography, the 'Apuntes autobiográficos', published in the first edition of *Los Pazos de Ulloa* (1886). Caballé comments on the audacity of this eighty-page work: 'Si ya constituía atrevimiento insólito dedicarse por entero a la creación literaria ... mayor era la osadía mostrada por la novelista gallega al intervenir intensamente en las polémicas y controversias estéticas de su tiempo o bien al exponer, sin modestia alguna, su proceso de formación como escritora'.[25]

Another important letter-writer is Rosa Chacel. *Cartas a Rosa Chacel* (1992) was published during her lifetime, and consists of letters from friends and fellow writers, covering the period 1938–88. After her death in 1994, *De mar a mar: Epistolario Rosa Chacel – Ana María Moix* (1998) published the complete correspondence between the two writers.[26]

---

[24] Emilia Pardo Bazán, *Cartas a Benito Pérez Galdós*, prologue and ed. Carmen Bravo Villasante (Madrid: Ediciones Turner, 1975), p. 1.

[25] Anna Caballé, 'Memorias y autobiografías escritas por mujeres (siglo XIX y XX)', in *Breve historia feminista de la literatura española (en lengua castellana) 5: La literatura escrita por mujer (Del s. XIX a la actualidad)*, ed. Iris Zavala (Barcelona: Anthropos, 1998), pp. 111–37 (p. 117).

[26] The editor of the letters, Ana Rodríguez Fischer, also comments on the similarities between Chacel's letters and her diaries: 'En las cartas de Rosa Chacel no sólo hay coloquio. Hay en ellas mucho soliloquio ... Y así a través de esas páginas nos llega también la expresión de variadísimos estados de ánimo, pensamientos figuraciones, e incluso la cuidada plasmación del mundo onírico. Son estos pasajes los que aproximan el

Zenobia Camprubí's epistolary has also been published, the first volume consisting of some 700 letters written to Juan Guerrero Ruiz, with whom she corresponded from 1917 until his death in 1954.[27] Again, these letters provide an important historical record of the life of Spanish writers in exile and their relationship with those who stayed in Spain.

Laura Freixas, in her introduction to a special 1996 issue of *Revista de Occidente* on the intimate diary in Spain, discusses the birth of the writer as diarist in the nineteenth century:

> Amiel ignora si su diario se publicará algún día, pero Constant, Stendhal, Lord Byron, Walter Scott, Carlyle, Tolstoi, Emerson ... saben o suponen que así será, y los Goncourt, Katherine Mansfield, Virginia Woolf, Anaïs Nin, Simone de Beauvoir, André Gide, Witold Gombrowicz, Julien Green ... ya escriben su diario con la intención explícita de publicarlo.[28]

These diarist-writers had a great influence on the work of twentieth-century Spanish writers, who, as Freixas also explains, knew many languages and were capable of reading other writers' work in the original text, especially French and English. In the case of Carmen Martín Gaite (who read and translated Portuguese, Italian, English and French literature), we know of her identification with Katherine Mansfield's or Franz Kafka's diaries by reading her own notebooks and diary pages.[29]

While few intimate diaries were published in Spain until well into the twentieth century, in other countries the publication of diaries, such as those by Virginia Woolf, Katherine Mansfield or Anaïs Nin, or memoirs, like those of Simone de Beauvoir, became widespread. In Europe, intimate diaries written by people who lived through important historical events were very popular both during and after the two world wars. Although in the First World War we find a great number of letters and diaries written by soldiers on the front line, in the Second World War it is women who

---

epistolario chaceliano a su personal alcancía': Ana Rodríguez Fischer, 'Prólogo', in Rosa Chacel, *De mar a mar: Epistolario Rosa Chacel – Ana María Moix*, prologue and ed. Ana Rodríguez Fischer (Barcelona: Península, 1998), pp. 9–17 (p. 15).

[27] See: Zenobia Camprubí, *Epistolario I: Cartas a Juan Guerrero Ruiz 1917–1956*, ed. Gabriela Palau de Nemes and Emilia Cortés Ibáñez (Madrid: Publicaciones de la Residencia de Estudiantes, 2006).

[28] Laura Freixas, 'Auge del diario ¿íntimo? en España', in *RO: El diario*, 5–14 (pp. 5–6).

[29] See: Carmen Martín Gaite, *Cuadernos de todo*, ed. and intro. Maria Vittoria Calvi (Barcelona: Areté, 2002), pp. 216 and 458.

start telling their stories through their diaries. Anne Frank's diary has made it possible to learn about the terrible circumstances many Jewish families had to go through before and during the war. Similarly, in Great Britain, diaries and letters written by women such as Vera Brittain, Ellen Wilkinson, E. M. Delafield and Nella Last in the 1930s and 1940s are invaluable sources for studying social history.

In Spain during the Civil War few diaries were published on everyday living conditions. However, there is one example of a diary produced by a writer, Concha Espina, *Esclavitud y libertad: Diario de una prisionera* (1938), which she defines as 'una especie de rezo'.[30] In this document, Espina describes the days spent in her house in Luzmela where she found herself imprisoned by Marxist, republican soldiers from the beginning of the war until 31 August 1937. Since then, diaries written by writers in exile have included Silvia Mistral's *Éxodo: diario de una refugiada española* (1940), Victoria Kent's *Cuatro años en Paris (1940–1944)* (1947), Federica Montseny's *El éxodo: pasión y muerte de españoles en el exilio* (1969), Rosa Chacel's *Alcancía: Ida* (1982), María Zambrano's *Delirio y destino: Los veinte años de una española* (1989) and Zenobia Camprubí's *Diario I: Cuba (1937–1939)* (1991).

Of course, the twentieth century also saw many important works of fiction featuring substantial autobiographical elements using diaries, notebooks, and letters as part of the narrative. In Spain fictional diaries and memoirs written by women also appear, including Rosa Chacel's *Memorias de Leticia Valle* (1945), Ana María Matute's *Primera memoria* (1959) and Dolores Medio's *Diario de una maestra* (1961). One thing that these titles clearly do is suggest to the reader that what they are about to read is a type of intimate first-person narration.

It should be stated that Spanish epistolary fiction and the publication of intimate diaries and memoirs has not been as rich and important as in some other countries. As Patrick Paul Garlinger indicates, 'In comparison to the French and English canons, Spain cannot lay claim to a quantitatively rich epistolary history',[31] and in the case of diaries, Laura Freixas comments: 'Hasta por lo menos este siglo la historia del diario íntimo en España ha sido la de una llamativa ausencia.'[32] Enric Bou explains

---

[30] Concha Espina, *Esclavitud y libertad: Diario de una prisionera* (Valladolid: Reconquista, 1938), p. 6.
[31] Patrick Paul Garlinger, *Confessions of the Letter Closet: Epistolary Fiction & Queer Desire in Modern Spain* (Minneapolis: University of Minnesota Press, 2005), p. xxvi.
[32] Freixas, 'Auge del diario ¿íntimo?', p. 5.

that fear of reprisals for keeping possibly incriminating documents may have made the practice of keeping diaries rare for most of the twentieth century: 'La cultura hispana se encuentra en la periferia en cuanto a la práctica del diario, pero las circunstancias no han ayudado en exceso a su proliferación y prestigio.'[33] Another possible reason for the diary being less widespread until recent years is the Catholic practice of confession. Women, especially, used the confessional as the place to relieve their day-to-day worries. As Maurice Blanchot observes: 'Los siglos más cristianos ignoran este examen que no tiene como intermediario el silencio. Se nos dice que en el protestantismo favorece esta confesión sin confesor.'[34]

Yet there have been changes in recent decades, with a proliferation of 'intimate' diaries and the use of diaries and letters in novels. Freixas notes: 'A partir de 1980 florecen los *Diarios*, ya sean íntimos u obras de ficción, ya sean textos recientes o títulos antiguos rescatados o reeditados.'[35] Certainly, after Franco's death a number of writers and political figures published their memoirs of the war and postwar years, for example Federica Montseny with *Mis primeros cuarenta años* (1987). Indeed, Carmen Martín Gaite comments in her most famous novel, *El cuarto de atrás* (1978), that the number of memoirs published during those years was overwhelming: 'Desde la muerte de Franco habrá notado cómo proliferan los libros de memorias, ya es una peste.'[36] And as noted by Alicia Redondo Goicoechea, it was not only professional writers who described their experiences under the dictatorship. Women who were politically active during the years before, during and after the war, and who, in many cases, had to live in exile, were also publishing their memoirs: 'La mayoría de estas autoras [escritoras feministas, comunistas, opositoras al régimen] empezaron a contar sus vidas más o menos noveladas a partir de la muerte de Franco en 1975'.[37]

Diaries and letters nowadays enjoy great freedom and openness, freedom which in past centuries was limited by stylistic restrictions, critiques and censorship. Although in Spain most published diaries are written by male

---

[33] Enric Bou, 'El diario: Periferia y literatura', *RO: El diario*, 121–62 (p. 122).
[34] Maurice Blanchot, 'El diario íntimo y el relato', *RO: El diario*, 47–54 (p. 52).
[35] Freixas, 'Auge del diario ¿íntimo?', p. 10.
[36] Carmen Martín Gaite, *El cuarto de atrás* [1978] (Barcelona: Destino, 1996), p. 128.
[37] Redondo Goicoechea, 'Las autoras frente al espejo: Imágenes y modelos', in *Lo mío es escribir: La vida escrita por las mujeres, I*, ed. Anna Caballé (Barcelona: Lumen, 2004), pp. 11–53 (p. 39).

authors, it has become more common to see female writers' diaries in bookshops. In fiction, a great number of novels also use diaries and letters as vehicles to develop the narrative. For example, Lucía Etxebarria's *Un milagro en equilibrio* (2004) takes the form of a letter-diary memoir that the protagonist writes to her daughter. In Carme Riera's *La mitad del alma* (2004), the mother's letters are interwoven with the daughter's diary, written while she looks for answers about a moment in her mother's life that she was unaware of.[38] Works such as Laura Freixas's *Último domingo en Londres* (1997), where the letters and diaries of four friends alternate in the narrative, give the reader different points of view for their story. Soledad Puértolas has written two autobiographical texts, *Recuerdos de otra persona* (1996) and *Con mi madre* (2001), and in Josefina Aldecoa's *Porque éramos jóvenes* (1986), the letters written to David channel the story. In Rosa Montero's *La función Delta* (1981), the diary and memoirs of the protagonist, who is ill with cancer, alternate.

Other texts have a clearer autobiographical root, for example, Rosa Regàs's *Ginebra* (1987) and *Diario de una abuela de verano* (2004). In 2001 Cristina Fernández Cubas published *Cosas que ya no existen*, a collection of short stories which the author says she does not want to call 'memoirs' and which she instead describes as a 'libro personal' or 'libro de recuerdos'.[39] Memoirs, true or partially fictional, have also seen a revival in the last few years. Josefina Aldecoa wrote her memoirs, releasing *En la distancia* in 2004 after having published *Confesiones de una abuela* (1998). Rosa Montero's *La loca de la casa* (2003), Laura Freixas's *Adolescencia en Barcelona hacia 1970* (2007) and Esther Tusquets's *Habíamos ganado la guerra* (2007) or *Confesiones de una vieja dama indigna* (2009) also serve as examples.

In Esther Tusquets's *Correspondencia privada* (2001), the author published four letters, the first written to her mother, 'Carta a la madre' (reprinted from Laura Freixas's 1996 anthology *Madres e hijas*), and a further three to former loves or lovers: 'Carta a mi primer amor', 'Carta a

---

[38] Kathleen M. Glenn, on the subject of Carme Riera's narrative, comments: 'Se ha afirmado, con notable desprecio, que mientras los hombres escriben libros, las mujeres garabatean cartas. Sin embargo, Riera, como muchas de sus contemporáneas – Rodoreda, Mayoral, Montero, Carmen Martín Gaite, Montserrat Roig y Ana Maria Moix – reivindica el valor literario de la carta': 'Voz, marginalidad y seducción en la narrativa breve de Carme Riera', in *Literatura y feminismo en España (S.XV–XXI)*, ed. Lisa Vollendorf (Barcelona: Icaria, 2005), pp. 339–52 (p. 348).

[39] Cristina Fernández Cubas, *Cosas que ya no existen* (Barcelona: Lumen, 2001), pp. 12, 13.

Eduardo' and 'Carta a Esteban'. Carme Riera's *Tiempo de espera* (1998), first published in Catalan as *Quadern d'una espera*, tells of the author's pregnancy, while in *Cuestión de amor propio* (1988) [*Questio D'amor Propi* (1987)], a single letter constitutes the novel.

While many contemporary authors use the diary or letter as a strategy to present their characters to the reader, to make them, in some ways, more human, it should be noted that Carme Riera sees this as mere commercialism. In an interview given in 1982 she commented:

> Yo me sé la receta para un best-seller de mujeres ... Puede ser, por ejemplo el diario de una escritora, hecho con un poco de feminismo pero no mucho, algo de sentimentalismo, un punto erótico, pero muy leve, algunas relaciones confusas, porque lo del aborto ya está un poco pasado, y un lenguaje sencillito, muy denotativo.[40]

Letters and Diaries in Carmen Martín Gaite's Work

Although the narrative forms of letters and diaries have many features in common, there are a number of significant differences between the two. First, and most significantly, is that letters are conceived in relation to an addressee, to a reader, while diaries are written, in principle, without an interlocutor and not intended for publication. This is what Jamile Trueba Lawand defines as distant conversation: 'una conversación por escrito con alguien que está ausente',[41] although, as Porter Abbott explains, 'Fictive diarists commonly address their remarks to someone – friend, lover, God, the diary itself'.[42] Looking at the use of diaries and letters in fiction, Martens finds a natural evolution from the epistolary to the diary novel:

> The epistolary novel was the structural ancestor of the diary novel. It initiated a line of development in narrative technique that the diary novel continued, ... one need think only of the 'dear diary'

---

[40] Cited by Rosa María Pereda in 'Carmen Riera, "Yo me sé la receta para un 'best-seller' de mujeres": Se presentó su novela "Una primavera para Domenico Guarini"', *El País*, 3 February 1982, available at: <http://www.elpais.com/articulo/cultura/ORTEGA/_SOLEDAD_/NO_USAR/Carmen/Riera/receta/best-seller/mujeres/elpepicul/19820203elpepicul_6/Tes/>.

[41] Jamile Trueba Lawand, *El arte epistolar en el renacimiento español* (Madrid: Támesis, 1996), p. 24.

[42] H. Porter Abbott, *Diary Fiction: Writing as Action* (Ithaca, NY: Cornell University Press, 1984), p. 10.

convention to realize to what extent intimate diary keeping was influenced by letter writing.[43]

Indeed, the privacy or intimacy of the diary is what Abbott defends: 'The term "diary" evokes an intensity of privacy, cloistering, isolation, that the "letter" does not'.[44]

In his essay 'Self Writing', Michel Foucault makes a distinction between letters and diaries, but at the same time categorizes them both as 'self-examination' tools:

> As Seneca points out, when one writes one reads what one writes, just as in saying something one hears oneself saying it. The letter one writes acts, through the very action of writing, upon the one who addresses it, just as it acts through reading and rereading on the one who receives it. In this dual function, correspondence is very close to the *hupomnĕmata*, and its form is often very similar.[45]

However, at the same time he finds that the difference between correspondence and the diaries written in Ancient Greece, or *hupomnĕmata*, centres on the presence of the writer:

> The letter makes the writer 'present' to the one to whom he addresses it. And present not simply through the information he gives concerning his life, his activities, his successes and failures, his good luck or misfortunes; rather, present with a kind of immediate, almost physical presence.[46]

In her *Cuadernos de todo*, Martín Gaite comments on the freedom of writing diaries without the intention of publishing them: 'Los diarios tienen a veces una frescura que jamás podrá tener la obra deliberadamente hecha para publicar',[47] while Anaïs Nin asserts that 'Starting a diary, and writing in it "is as easy as breathing."'[48]

Letters and diaries had always been part of Martín Gaite's narratives

---

[43] Martens, *The Diary Novel*, p. 56.
[44] Abbott, p. 11.
[45] Michel Foucault, 'Self Writing', in *Ethics, Subjectivity and Truth: The Essential Works of Michel Foucault 1954–1984*, ed. Paul Rabinow, trans. Robert Hurley *et al.* (London: Penguin, 1997), pp. 207–22 (p. 214).
[46] Foucault, p. 216.
[47] Martín Gaite, *Cuadernos*, p. 455.
[48] Quoted in Curtis W. Casewit, *The Diary: A Complete Guide to Journal Writing* (Allen, TX: Argus Communications, 1982), p. 14.

from the early part of her career as a writer. As she notes in *El cuento de nunca acabar*, a letter was for her one of the easiest ways to write, as one only needs to sit down and start describing the place from where one is writing for other thoughts to start streaming out.[49] The best way to write a letter is in complete solitude, as she explains in her *Cuadernos de todo*: 'así se escriben las cartas buenas, como las que yo escribía en estado de trance, cuando todo el silencio de la casa me arropaba y se volvía música'.[50] From her very first short stories, letters – either written or received – are present. In some cases they form an important part of the narrative. In others, there are simple mentions of not much obvious importance, but they always serve to indicate contrasts or reflect on the situation of the protagonist. So, in 'Ya ni me acuerdo' (1962),[51] the letter that the country girl writes to the film-maker suggests a contrast between urban and rural life. In 'Las ataduras' (1959),[52] Alina writes a postcard to her parents telling them about her happiness; although the reader can see how different reality is, there is once more a contrast between truth and lies, between life in a Galician village and in a city like Paris. In 'Un alto en el camino' (1958),[53] the lack or the prohibition of letters from abroad suggests the censorship of the postwar period. In another story, the idea of not having an interlocutor for the letters is what makes them part of the story so, in 'Los informes' (1954),[54] the maid looking for work in the city thinks of her recently deceased mother who will not be there to receive her news.[55] Elsewhere, a promised letter which is never written makes us aware of class difference: in 'La chica de abajo' (1953),[56] the daughter of a concierge awaits the letter that her friend promised to write before she moved to another town.

The use of diaries as a narrative strategy emerges in Martín Gaite's first novel, *Entre visillos* (1958), which is divided into chapters with first-person or third-person narration. With a good number of characters, it is mainly narrated by the voices of two protagonists, Natalia and Pablo

---

[49] Martín Gaite, *El cuento de nunca acabar*, pp. 33–4.
[50] Martín Gaite, *Cuadernos*, p. 216.
[51] Carmen Martín Gaite, *Cuentos completos* [1978] (Madrid: Alianza, 1989), pp. 73–88.
[52] Martín Gaite, *Cuentos completos*, pp. 89–135.
[53] Martín Gaite, *Cuentos completos*, pp. 136–48.
[54] Martín Gaite, *Cuentos completos*, pp. 294–308.
[55] Later in life, Martín Gaite reflected on the same idea after her parents' death. See 'Un bosquejo autobiográfico', in *Agua pasada* (Barcelona: Anagrama, 1993), pp. 11–25 (p. 24).
[56] Martín Gaite, *Cuentos completos*, pp. 274–93.

Klein, who, through their diaries and first-person reflections, give a point of view from their different social positions. Natalia's diary opens the novel, while Pablo's closes it. Natalia presents an internal point of view, as a young woman who has to fight repression and lack of freedom in the provincial Spain of the 1940s and 1950s. Natalia's diary gives her a voice which other female protagonists lack,[57] their conversations being mere background noise. Natalia, however, is capable of putting her thoughts into writing and thereby crosses the barriers of silence imposed by society. As Joan Lipman Brown comments, 'Only Natalia shows promise of formulating and expressing her own ambitions.'[58] Natalia's diary serves as the repository of the circumstances the protagonist is going through and as a way of relieving her frustration and incomprehension of the society she has to live in. Even so, Natalia is still too young to be able to reflect on her past in the way that the protagonists of Martín Gaite's 1990s novels will do.

Natalia shows diary to her best friend, Alicia,[59] but feels ashamed of this, as the difference in social class between them impels her friend to understand the things she writes about, which are, in Natalia's opinion, too vain. As Alicia comments: 'nuestra vida va a ser muy distinta. Basta ver las cosas que escribes tú, y lo que piensas y eso. Verás cómo luego, dentro de un par de años, no seremos amigas ya, no lo podremos ser.'[60]

Pablo's narrative, on the other hand, gives an external point of view, the point of view of a foreigner who finds the repression and the rules which drive Spanish society difficult to understand. Pablo holds the reins of the novel, being the narrator of seven of the eighteen chapters, interwoven with Natalia's diary and the voice of the extradiegetic narrator, who is witness to the conversations of the rest of the characters. His story serves as a contrast to that of the townsfolk and, when he decides to leave, his return home does not suggest much hope for future life in a provincial town. In Natalia's case, at the end of the narrative some things have

---

[57] With the publication of the manuscript *La charca* (1955), it is interesting to see how the author did not include Natalia in the first drafts of her novel, but that the inclusion came after her daughter's birth in 1956.

[58] Joan Lipman Brown, 'The Challenge of Martín Gaite's Woman Hero', in *Feminine Concerns in Contemporary Spanish Fiction by Women*, ed. Roberto C. Manteiga, Carolyn Galerstein and Kathleen McNerney (Potomac, MD: Scripta Humanistica, 1988), pp. 86–98 (p. 88).

[59] An action that twenty years later will be echoed in *El cuarto de atrás* when C. explains how she used to show her diary to her childhood friend (pp. 57, 195).

[60] Carmen Martín Gaite, *Entre visillos* [1958] (Barcelona: Destino, 2002), p. 221.

changed and she seems to be strong enough to confront her father, even though her future is still uncertain: 'De lo de mi carrera no le he dicho nada. Me he dormido muy tarde haciendo diario'.[61]

Julia, Natalia's sister, writes to and receives letters from her boyfriend, who lives in Madrid. These letters are their only way of communicating, as every brief encounter they have is full of confrontations and regrets. The letters show their love and Julia's taste for melodrama: 'Sobre la A cayó una lágrima. La dejó empapar el papel y luego la corrió un poco con el pañuelo. Hacía bonito'.[62] They also show the difficulties of a relationship at a distance, where the time-lapse between the letter written and the letter received makes it difficult to understand each other's feelings. There are other letters in the narrative, such as that sent by Elvira to Pablo, 'casi una declaración de amor',[63] in which she is able to say things that she will never be able to repeat in front of Pablo.

Ritmo lento appeared in 1963, and could be classified as a psychological novel in which the protagonist, David Fuentes, reflects on his life and the circumstances which have caused him to end up in a psychiatric hospital. Using a form of psychoanalytical therapy, the psychiatrist encourages him to talk about his past. Indeed, David seems to be writing his past, although it is unclear whether he is actually taking notes or only thinking about that past. At times, the protagonist makes references to his notebooks or to notes he is taking or needs to take.[64] He speaks, for example, of the papers he has in front of him, which were soaked by the rain when he left the window open.[65] On another occasion he comments on the notes he took, in notebooks which remind us of Martín Gaite's:

> En aquel cuaderno, que empecé llamando 'el cuaderno fichero', terminé por anotar todas las incertidumbres provocadas en mí por el tema del empleo del tiempo y relacionadas de algún modo con él, las cuales anotaciones al cabo se desbordaron de su condición marginal e invadieron todo el ámbito del cuaderno. Así que cuando este primero se gastó, me vi obligado a sustituirlo por otro y aquel por uno más.[66]

---

[61] Martín Gaite, *Entre visillos*, p. 230.
[62] Martín Gaite, *Entre visillos*, p. 110.
[63] Martín Gaite, *Entre visillos*, p. 95.
[64] Carmen Martín Gaite, *Ritmo lento* [1963] (Barcelona: Anagrama, 1984), p. 37.
[65] Martín Gaite, *Ritmo lento*, p. 89.
[66] Martín Gaite, *Ritmo lento*, p. 101.

At the same time as the protagonist reflects on his past, he makes a critique of the situation in Spanish society, especially women's roles in the 1960s, a clear parallel with the author's own critique in her first *Cuadernos de todo*. Also, letters appear in the narrative to mark key moments in David's life. In fact, as David mentions in his prologue, the very first chapter opens with the arrival of a letter written by his former girlfriend, Lucía, and it is through a detailed analysis of this letter that David starts taking the reader into his world. At the end of the book, his father's letter is a cry for help to which David responds too late, finding his father dead from an overdose after returning from the psychiatric hospital. This way of opening and closing the novel gives letters an important presence in the narrative. Although the letters, as well as the self-reflective cure David is undergoing, will not change his personality, this is the first novel in which Martín Gaite used self-reflective writing to great effect, but its lukewarm reception seems to indicate that readers were not ready for this kind of psychoanalytical reflective novel. Nonetheless, some of the characteristics of this male protagonist were developed decades later in *La Reina de las Nieves* (1994) where the protagonist, Leonardo, is able to 'save' himself through his self-reflective writing.

After *Ritmo lento*, bored with fictional characters,[67] Martín Gaite decided to spend time researching Spanish history and cultural history. First, she studied the life of Melchor de Macanaz, producing *El proceso de Macanaz: Historia de un empapelamiento* in 1970 (later reissued as *Macanaz, otro paciente de la Inquisición* in 1975). Then, using material researched for her doctoral thesis, 'Lenguaje y estilo amorosos en los textos del siglo XVIII español' (1972), she published in the same year *Usos amorosos del dieciocho en España*. This work looks at the extra-marital customs of Spanish women in that century, examining, for example, the 'situación y papel de las mujeres en la sociedad',[68] 'los albores de la sociedad de consumo'[69] and 'el problema del aburrimiento femenino',[70] themes which can also be found in her notebooks and later novels. Subsequently, *El conde de Guadalhorce, su época y su labor* (1977) was commisioned by the Ministerio de Obras Públicas and, in the *Cuadernos de todo*, there is a logbook (or *cuaderno de bitácora*) on the

---

[67] See introduction, p. 1.
[68] Carmen Martín Gaite, *Usos amorosos del dieciocho en España* (Madrid: Siglo XXI de España Editores, 1972), pp. 2–3.
[69] Martín Gaite, *Usos amorosos del dieciocho*, p. 21.
[70] Martín Gaite, *Usos amorosos del dieciocho*, pp. 21–2.

day-to-day development of the research for this work between 27 April and 30 May 1976, so adding yet another dimension to her 'diaries'.

The influence of the years Martín Gaite spent researching in archives and libraries, and the many letters read during that research, would have been important to her when using diaries and letters as a means of threading the narrative in her later novels. Indeed, in *La búsqueda de interlocutor* (1973), the she comments on reading Macanaz's letters: '¡Cuánto escribió en su vida Don Melchor de Macanaz! Cartas y más cartas ... cartas farragosas y justificatorias desde distintos tiempos y países'.[71] She also refers to the most important moment in the research, when Macanaz 'talked' to her for the first time:

> En una de aquellas cartas demenciales y obsesivas de su vejez, escrita en París, me parece, Macanaz, una mañana, me habló por primera vez directamente. ... se quedó mirando al futuro de sus papeles, tuvo miedo a la caducidad de cuanto estaba diciendo, miedo a estar hablando en el vacío para nadie. Era la primera vez que yo lo veía así y me sobrecogió.[72]

She comments on what reading his letters, written from exile, meant for her: 'además de darme noticias de aquella injusticia, que era lo que en principio me había intrigado, me empezó a dar noticias también de su alma, de sus obsesiones, de su envejecer.'[73] And she continues describing her feelings as she read the letters: 'Me enteré del daño que le estaba haciendo aquella soledad de la que no quería darse cuenta ... de hombre que habla para nadie. ... Llegué a sentir que se dirigía a mí personalmente.'[74] These studies of Macanaz's activities would have some influence on the novels the author wrote later, especially in *Lo raro es vivir* (1996), where the protagonist Águeda is, like the author in the 1960s, researching the life of a historical character, Luis Vidal y Villalba, with a 'vida ... novelesca'[75] similar to that of Macanaz.

---

[71] Carmen Martín Gaite, *La búsqueda de interlocutor y otras búsquedas* [1973] (Barcelona: Destinolibro, 1982), p. 62. A number of talks and articles from the 1990s were added to the 2000 edition, *La búsqueda de interlocutor* (Barcelona: Anagrama, 2000).

[72] Martín Gaite, *La búsqueda de interlocutor y otras búsquedas*, pp. 69–70.

[73] Quoted in Federico Campbell, 'Carmen Martín Gaite: La búsqueda de interlocutor', in *Conversaciones con escritores* (Mexico D.F.: CONACULTA, Dirección General de Publicaciones, 2004), pp. 231–40 (p. 238).

[74] Campbell, p. 238.

[75] Carmen Martín Gaite, *El proceso de Macanaz: Historia de un empapelamiento* (Madrid: Moneda y Crédito, 1970), p. xix.

After her works on political and cultural history, Martín Gaite turned again to the publication of fiction, with novels that had been developed during her years in the archives. The first was *Retahílas* (1974), in which the author uses dialogue as the narrative thread. Here two characters, Eulalia and Germán, aunt and nephew, talk during one night about their lives. Waiting for the death of Eulalia's grandmother, both characters reflect on their present lives and the way they have reached this point. The chapters alternate, threading both stories through their shared memories, or through their doubts about certain events in their past. The dialogue used by Martín Gaite resembles a succession of monologues, as neither aunt nor nephew interrupts the other's speeches, starting their own monologue only when the other asks a question which is then answered. At the same time, these monologues resemble a series of letters: the way they are written simulates a reply to a letter, as if there has been time to formulate a written response. As Brown comments: 'The characters express themselves as if they actually were talking, although the format of their alternating discourses resembles the sending and answering of letters.'[76]

Also, the language used is closer to written language, even though Eulalia comments on the difficulty of putting in writing the dialogue they are engaged in that night: 'fíjate el esfuerzo que supondría escribir esto mismo que ahora te voy diciendo.'[77] In fact, the length of the chapters, of the monologues or 'retahílas', makes it impossible to read them as a dialogue between two real-life people. As well as the dialogue-monologue-letter between Eulalia and Germán, there is the constant presence of the grandmother's trunk. This trunk, which the grandmother brought all the way to Galicia from Madrid to have next to her until her death, is full of letters, photographs and papers which constitute her whole life, her memories. Occasionally Eulalia comments on the responsibility that inheriting those papers means to her, as she will not know what to do with them.[78]

The two also talk about letters burned in moments of elation. This idea is repeated in other works by the author, who admits to having burned letters and papers in the same way as her characters. Germán tells Eulalia

---

[76] Joan Lipman Brown, *Secrets from the Back Room: The Fiction of Carmen Martín Gaite* (Valencia: University of Mississippi, 1987), p. 120.

[77] Carmen Martín Gaite, *Retahílas*, afterword by Montserrat Escartín Gual [1974] (Barcelona: Destino, 2003), p. 74.

[78] Martín Gaite knew years later what it was to inherit papers, letters and photographs from loved ones, first with her father's papers and then with her daughter's. See *Cuadernos*, pp. 474, 612–13.

of the night when, with his ex-girlfriend, they decided to burn all their love letters, choosing St John's day – the night when in Spain the 'hogueras de San Juan' are celebrated. In contrast with the grandmother's papers which she takes with her to her deathbed, the strange pleasure of reading letters written in other moments of their lives is what Germán wants to erase: 'es una sensación muy rara volver a leer cosas tuyas que escribiste en un trance determinado, revives ruidos, colores, si te dolía o no la cabeza'.[79] As will be seen in *Fragmentos de interior* (1976), this way of clinging to the past, rereading old letters, can be very detrimental, impeding any continuation towards the future. This kind of renewal through the destruction of past manuscripts, which have a different meaning for later generations, suggests the times Spain was going through in the 1970s, when new generations were looking for change in a society that had been at a standstill for so long.

Letters play an important role in *Fragmentos de interior*, especially for two of the characters in the novel: Agustina, Diego's ex-wife and the mother of Jaime and Isabel, and Luisa, the girl who comes from the country to work as a maid in Diego's house. Agustina takes refuge in the letters written by Diego when they first met. She does not want to confront her present situation and even writes to Diego every day, as one of the maids comments: 'Hay temporadas que le da por escribirle dos al día y son todas iguales.'[80] Agustina spends her days in bed reading and drinking gin with Diego's letters all around her, and some of these letters appear in Chapter 4 of the novel.[81] Agustina is a character living in the past who does not want to admit to reality and who tells the same story over and over again to whoever is available to hear it. She is what her daughter calls 'un espécimen puro de narración única'.[82] This need to cling to the past through the letters serves as a contrast with Germán's indifference when destroying his love letters, and with the burning of documents and other papers that C. describes in *El cuarto de atrás*. Since these two novels were written just before and after Franco's death, the reader is again invited to think of the need for renewal that Spain was experiencing.

Diego seems to represent the author's alter ego. He used to be a

---

[79] Martín Gaite, *Retahílas*, p. 155.
[80] Carmen Martín Gaite, *Fragmentos de interior* [1976] (Barcelona: Destino, 1996), p. 88.
[81] Martín Gaite, *Fragmentos*, pp. 41–2, 44–5.
[82] Martín Gaite, *Fragmentos*, p. 54.

researcher, who in his youth travelled to Coimbra thanks to a grant.[83] He is also a writer, who, like Leonardo's father in *La Reina de las Nieves*, never gets to finish his novel. In addition he is a parent who has a very good relationship with his daughter,[84] and in Chapter 5 we see how father and daughter are able to talk freely and how the father feels comfortable in his daughter's bedroom, which he thinks is the best room in the house.[85] He is going to use this room to start writing again, which also occurs with Sofía in *Nubosidad variable* (1992), who writes in her daughter Encarna's bedroom. Finally, he is a good letter-writer, as we see through access to his letters to his ex-wife. One of the notes that Diego reads when he decides to sit down and write says:

> La situación de empezar era siempre la misma ... Rebuscar esforzadamente en el interior de uno mismo, después de muchas horas de debatirse en una yerma sábana de hastío y decir con una especie de reiterada compunción: 'Hay que hacer algo, hay que hacer algo por salir'.[86]

And this thought, which Diego never manages to realize, is the one that will be passed on to the protagonists of the 1990s novels, who will be able to escape from the monotony (*hastío*) and sadness (*compunción*) in which they find themselves at the beginning of the novels, after looking within through their reflective writing.

Luisa, on the other hand, reminds us of some of the characters of Martín Gaite's first short stories: a young woman coming from the country to work as a maid in a house in the capital. She escapes some of the 1950s and 1960s parameters in the way that, for her, working as a maid provides an excuse to travel to Madrid to find her lover Gonzalo, a film-maker whom she met in her village and to whom she writes passionate letters. Luisa has just one letter from Gonzalo, the single one he has written to her and which can be read in Chapter 8.[87] She discovers that Gonzalo

---

[83] See Martín Gaite, *Fragmentos*, p. 54. It is well known that Martín Gaite had a grant to study in Coimbra, her first journey abroad. She mentions this in *El cuarto de atrás*, p. 42 and also 'Un bosquejo autobiográfico', p. 17.

[84] The author comments on her relationship with her daughter: 'Mi hija es muy amiga, nos reímos mucho juntas y nos lo contamos todo' ('Un bosquejo autobiográfico', p. 23).

[85] Martín Gaite, *Fragmentos*, p. 61.

[86] Martín Gaite, *Fragmentos*, pp. 68–9. This way of encouraging oneself in moments of being stuck will be seen again in *Cuadernos de todo*.

[87] Martín Gaite, *Fragmentos*, p. 101.

never received the letters which she wrote daily, as he had moved house. She collects those letters and in a scene which reminds us of Agustina on her deathbed, Luisa reads the letters she wrote not that long before. Rereading the letters makes her wake up and decide to return to her village (after finding out that she is not pregnant), a resolution that suggests the difference between the generations living in Spain in the 1970s.

El cuarto de atrás (1978) has been described by Patrick-Paul Garlinger as 'an epistolary novel without letters.'[88] The blue letter which appears and disappears throughout the narrative gives rise to memories which add to the protagonist's story, similar to the memories described by Germán in *Retahílas*. As well as bringing memories from the past, old letters are a reminder of the inexorable passing of time and the arrival of old age, and that is why, as C. explains, she burned a large pile of papers and letters one day after reading a poem by Antonio Machado:

> Me vi disparada a la vejez, condenada al vicio de repasar para siempre cartas sin perfume, con la tinta borrosa de tanto manosearlas y llorar sobre ellas y me entró un furor por destruir papeles como no recuerdo en mi vida; me levanté y me puse a sacar cartas y a vaciar el contenido del baulito, lo apilé todo ahí en el pasillo y lo fui tirando a la caldera de la calefacción sin mirarlo, una hora estuve y a cada puñado crecían las llamas, sabe Dios cuántos tesoros caerían.[89]

After *El cuarto de atrás*, Martín Gaite did not publish another novel until the 1990s, even though during those years she never stopped working as a literary critic and essayist, and also published three books for children. Diaries are also important in one of those books for children, *El castillo de las tres murallas* (1981), with Serena writing of her dreams in a green velvet notebook[90] (similar to the one Martín Gaite had when she was a child), which will help Serena's daughter to understand her mother better.

Fundamental to the study of diaries, letters and reflective writing in Martín Gaite's work is *El cuento de nunca acabar* (1983). In this well-received collection of essays Martín Gaite draws on years of reflection on the theme of narration, integrating incidents which happened to her during the years she was preparing the book. In the third prologue, she comments on the easiness of writing letters:

---

[88] Garlinger, *Confessions*, p. 36.
[89] Martín Gaite, *El cuarto de atrás*, pp. 46–7.
[90] Carmen Martín Gaite, *El castillo de las tres murallas*, illus. Juan Carlos Eguillor [1981] (Barcelona: Lumen, 1991), p. 6.

> Me parece muy sintomático, por ejemplo, el hecho de que en trances de acidia y empantamiento, lo que menos pereza dé sea ponerse a escribirle una carta a un amigo, al primero que se nos pase por la cabeza. Porque, claro, en una carta no se tiene por desdoro empezar describiendo la habitación de la fonda desde la cual elaboramos el mensaje ni si se oye el pitido de un tren a través de la ventana, ni si el empapelado de la pared es de florecitas amarillas con una greca malva en el remate. Circunstancias que, al ser consignadas en primer lugar, desplegarán su poder de convocatoria y hasta podrán llegar a marcar el texto de la carta misma, con lo cual acabarán contándose cosas que ni por lo más remoto se habían formulado en el propósito inicial y que surgen entrelazándose tan estrechamente con la descripción situacional que luego, en el texto resultante, será difícil separar lo que el remitente piensa y añora y ha venido a hacer a esta ciudad de lo que está viendo y oyendo.[91]

This technique will be used by the two protagonists of *Nubosidad variable*, making it, in their narrative, part of the rules they made up in their youth. Martín Gaite also refers to letters in the chapter called 'Río revuelto', where, as the title indicates, she mixes up a number of ideas in rough form, something also seen in *Cuadernos de todo*, referring to narration in a more or less direct way. In one of the sub-chapters titled 'Literatura epistolar', she describes the emotion of receiving a personal letter and the way in which this emotion is recreated for readers of epistolary literature: 'hay una curiosidad irreprimible por meter las narices en correspondencias ajenas, por soñar que es uno aquel destinatario. (Tampoco lo es ya – por supuesto – el que relee, al cabo de los años, una carta vieja dirigida a ese otro que él era)'.[92] There is also a reference to the relationship between letters and history, as was mentioned previously in the discussion of *Macanaz* and *Usos amorosos del dieciocho*, and how epistolary material was an important part of her years of research in the archives: 'Los archivos están plagados de cartas, que nos ayudan a componer, fragmentariamente, el rompecabezas de la historia'.[93]

In *El cuento de nunca acabar*, more than in any other book, the soul of the author's notebooks is apparent. Prologue 5 is titled 'Mis cuadernos de todo' and in it Martín Gaite describes how these *cuadernos* became part of her life, a theme which will be dealt with in detail in the next chapter.

---

[91] Martín Gaite, *El cuento de nunca acabar*, pp. 33–4.
[92] Martín Gaite, *El cuento de nunca acabar*, p. 247.
[93] Martín Gaite, *El cuento de nunca acabar*, p. 247.

In *El cuento* there are quotes taken from the notebooks and in some cases, as in the third prologue, the author writes as if she were composing a diary: 'Se me han ocurrido estas cosas porque hoy he estado ayudando a mi hija, que se examina de primero de letras'.[94] She even follows the diaristic form of writing the date: 'Todavía no son las doce. Pongo la fecha: 21 de junio de 1974'.[95]

The difficulties of writing, a theme which also recurs in Martín Gaite's notebooks, has a place in these essays. Such moments are what she calls 'bache de empantanamiento'.[96] She includes in them not only thoughts she had after thinking of writing *El cuento*, but also reflections already written in her first *cuadernos de todo*.

Desde la ventana (1987) is a compilation of essays based on talks given by the author at the Fundación Juan March in November 1986,[97] entitled 'El punto de vista femenino en la literatura española.'[98] In these talks the author reflected on women and literature or 'La cuestión de si las mujeres tienen un modo particular de escribir',[99] as she observes it in the opening words of her introduction to the book. There are a few comments on the subject of letters and diaries in literature written by women, as Emma Martinell Gifre notes in the prologue to the second edition:

> En su soledad, hacen [las mujeres] de la carta o del diario su interlocutor que, si bien callado, acepta de buen grado el divagar de su mente, el vuelo de su fantasía, o el estallido de sus sentimientos contenidos. Martín Gaite indica lo propicios que le han resultado siempre a la mujer el diario y las epístolas, formas en las que se encauza su capacidad creativa.[100]

Examples of epistolary literature and diary writing, as Martín Gaite indicates, contribute to 'un punto de vista femenino directo y en carne viva'.[101] Discussing the theme of women and love in literature, the author comments on how the need to give expression to desires makes women

---

[94] Martín Gaite, *El cuento de nunca acabar*, p. 34.
[95] Martín Gaite, *El cuento de nunca acabar*, p. 37.
[96] Martín Gaite, *El cuento de nunca acabar*, p. 48.
[97] See <http://www.march.es/conferencias/anteriores>.
[98] Carmen Martín Gaite, *Desde la ventana: Enfoque femenino de la literatura española* [1987] (Madrid: Espasa Calpe, 1992), p. 33.
[99] Martín Gaite, *Desde la ventana*, p. 25.
[100] Emma Martinell Gifre, 'Prólogo', in Martín Gaite, *Desde la ventana*, pp. 9–21 (pp. 9–10).
[101] Martín Gaite, *Desde la ventana*, p. 116.

write letters to their loved ones: 'Y es verdad que el amor, ya sea divino o humano, puede considerarse como uno de los principales acicates de la escritura femenina'.[102] However, she also points out that although 'Pocas cartas de pasión se conservan escritas por mujeres reales',[103] literature is full of examples of love letters supposedly written by women.

As mentioned, the author also believes that 'Sin duda que la forma epistolar ha debido ser para las mujeres la primera y más idónea manifestación de sus capacidades literarias'.[104] If the ideal interlocutor is not found, the 'you' in the love letter will be invented. An invented interlocutor shows, in Martín Gaite's words, the relationship between letters and diaries: 'El paso del "tú" real al "tú" inventado tiene su correlato literario en la transformación del género epistolar al pasar a otra modalidad también muy grata a la mujer introvertida: la del diario íntimo'.[105] In their personal diaries, women can create their own perfect love and write them letters full of emotion and sentiment. Yet in Spain, as was noted, there are few published diaries written by women. As Martín Gaite explains:

> No es este un género del que queden en España demasiadas muestras auténticas, aunque haya sido explotado como artificio literario, consciente el transcriptor de diarios apócrifos femeninos que es en secreto y entre las cuatro paredes de un recinto cerrado donde la mujer se encuentra más a sus anchas para ensayar, libre de trabas impuestas por la vigilancia ajena, un desagüe a sus capacidades expresivas.[106]

In *Desde la ventana*, Martín Gaite discusses Santa Teresa de Jesús and her *Libro de la vida* and asks herself about the role of the interlocutor in this diary: 'Escrito en primera persona, como podría estarlo un diario íntimo o una carta, las alteraciones de ritmo vienen motivadas por la duplicidad de la emisión, es decir, por la índole tan distinta de los presuntos receptores del mensaje. Porque ¿para quién escribía Teresa?'[107] However, she seems to have an answer to her own question, indicating the importance that first-person narration has for her as a method of self-reflection and self-analysis: 'Teresa de Ahumada, cuando moja la pluma en el tintero, no

---

[102] Martín Gaite, *Desde la ventana*, p. 58.
[103] Martín Gaite, *Desde la ventana*, p. 59.
[104] Martín Gaite, *Desde la ventana*, p. 59.
[105] Martín Gaite, *Desde la ventana*, p. 60.
[106] Martín Gaite, *Desde la ventana*, p. 60.
[107] Martín Gaite, *Desde la ventana*, p. 68.

busca más "tú" que el suyo, más respuesta que la suya'.[108] Another work which Martín Gaite considers is Rosalía de Castro's *Carta a Eduarda*, and her comments on this work recall *Nubosidad variable*, where the interlocutors are two women:

> Lo más interesante de este texto es su tono llano, de charla entre dos mujeres. No en vano se ha elegido el género epistolar, tan propicio al desahogo y a la ironía, para colorear con ejemplos concretos una queja que pierde así toda la altisonancia teórica de los discursos varoniles. Y, como consecuencia su eficacia es mucho mayor.[109]

Desde la ventana finishes with one of the author's dreams in which she is writing a letter to her mother, but instead of using the written word she is using sign language sent through the window of her New York apartment. This dream-letter was published as 'De su ventana a la mía' and demonstrates the importance of the letter as method of communication, even if never written and addressed to someone no longer living.

La búsqueda del interlocutor y otras búsquedas draws us to the search of the interlocutor, real or ideal. The eponymous article contains an idea which the author has explored throughout her career: 'se escribe y siempre se ha escrito desde una experimentada incomunicación y al encuentro de un oyente utópico'.[110] In order to start writing, a person needs isolation (a key theme in Virginia Woolf's essay *A Room of One's Own*, which Martín Gaite mentions in her introduction to *Desde la ventana*) and so she comments: 'nunca habría existido invención literaria alguna si los hombres, saciados totalmente en su sed de comunicación, no hubieran llegado a conocer, con la soledad, el acuciante deseo de romperla'.[111] This isolation and self-imposed excommunication will be a constant preoccupation for her characters in the 1990s novels. Solitude, always present in her reflections, could and should be, in Martín Gaite's words, transformed into a positive state, especially for women who should take refuge in solitude in order to find themselves. Writing in solitude, whether in diaries, letters, novels, short stories, film scripts or cultural and historical essays, is what will bring them closer to reflection.

With *Usos amorosos de la postguerra española* (1987) the author returns to the romantic traditions of Spanish women; here it is her own

---

[108] Martín Gaite, *Desde la ventana*, p. 69.
[109] Martín Gaite, *Desde la ventana*, p. 93.
[110] Martín Gaite, *La búsqueda de interlocutor y otras búsquedas*, p. 28.
[111] Martín Gaite, *La búsqueda de interlocutor y otras búsquedas*, p. 28.

experience, as a woman who lived through postwar Spain, that she is dealing with. She supports her own memories with visits to newspaper libraries to read articles from the postwar period. Letters do not appear in the narrative, even though the cover of the first edition shows a photographic portrait of a dreamy young woman and an envelope drawn in a corner with the sender's address: 'Una romántica. Paseo del Chopo 5. León'.[112] The idea that isolation is fundamental to writing is again presented here and, for example, the author quotes a 1951 article from the magazine *Letras*, written by J. L. de Auria:

> La mujer es ante todo intimidad y vida privada; ... su papel es más bien silencioso, de pura presencia. Si opera lentamente, como un clima, si representa la serenidad callada frente a la ruidosa acción del hombre, es evidente que donde se encontrará a sus anchas, donde dará sus mejores frutos si acaso trata de comunicar sus pensamientos, será en las cartas, documentos íntimos, privados y confidenciales por excelencia.[113]

This silence fomented by postwar society meant that letters and diaries were the only places where young women were able to unburden their thoughts: 'A la jovencita de postguerra le encantaba escribir cartas'.[114] They particularly liked to send letters to Agony Aunts, the only people who could understand their worries:

> La complicidad que se establecía mediante aquella correspondencia fomentaba el gusto por lo secreto ... Las periodistas anónimas encargadas de aquella sección fija eran conscientes, sin duda, de que sus consejos, aunque fueran de repertorio, iban a ser recibidos como agua de mayo por cada una de aquellas desorientadas y borrosas muchachas a quienes se llamaba 'querida amiga', y que lo que necesitaban sobre todas las cosas era que alguien les hiciera caso.[115]

There is a special mention of the correspondence, during the war, between women and men on the frontline who had never met before: 'la guerra había fomentado las confidencias epistolares ... mediante la

---

[112] Carmen Martín Gaite, *Usos amorosos de la postguerra española* (Barcelona: Anagrama, 1987).

[113] Carmen Martín Gaite, *Usos amorosos de la postguerra española* (Barcelona: Anagrama, 1994), p. 175. Further references to this work will be to this edition.

[114] Martín Gaite, *Usos amorosos de la postguerra*, p. 175.

[115] Martín Gaite, *Usos amorosos de la postguerra*, p. 175.

institución de las madrinas de guerra, encargadas de consolar ... a un soldado del que podían acabar enamorándose sin haberlo visto nunca'.[116] And near the end of the work Martín Gaite describes the custom of sending back love letters once the relationship had ended: 'había la costumbre de que se devolvieran los regalos y las cartas que se hubieran podido escribir. Muchas veces esta petición, que solía partir de la novia, era un pretexto ... para reanudar el rosario amoroso de reproches y disculpas'.[117]

Carmen Martín Gaite experienced a spectacular resurgence in the 1990s, this decade being her most prolific in terms of number of novels published and the extent of her readership. Her 1990s novels reveal a noticeable degree of projection of the author into her characters, for all her protagonists show some similarities to her, either with regard to her obsession with the redecoration of her house (with a marked critique of consumerist society and the unnecessary need to renovate and hoard), the books they read, the writing of diaries and letters, or being afflicted by writer's block. Even though it is not exactly true that all her characters keep a *cuaderno de todo*, it remains the case that writing is an important part of their lives. All her protagonists look to other characters in novels or fairy tales with whom they can identify, making these works intertextual and metafictional novels in which writing or the difficulty of writing is brought to the fore. These novels use diaries, letters and reflective writing as narrative forms, either for the protagonists to be able to understand their present situation, or to show others their need for self-discovery. The protagonists of the 1990s novels, in contrast to those of her other novels, spend many hours in complete solitude, giving free rein to their thoughts, reflecting on their lives and their future and, in every case, altering their lives as a result. These protagonists find in their writing a means of therapy which allows them to analyse their deepest traumas, make decisions and so change their lives.

Reflective Writing: The Writing Cure

In her *Cuadernos de todo* Martín Gaite affirms that 'La mujer escribe para liberar su alma, hace un camino solitario y partiendo de cero (a tientas) hacia el autoanálisis'.[118] And, as Ciplijauskaité comments, 'El recurso de la primera persona sirve, además, como el modo más adecuado para

---

[116] Martín Gaite, *Usos amorosos de la postguerra*, p. 153.
[117] Martín Gaite, *Usos amorosos de la postguerra*, p. 207.
[118] Martín Gaite, *Cuadernos*, p. 605.

la indagación psicológica. La narrativa adquiere puntos de contacto con procedimientos psicoanalíticos.'[119] Following up the theme of women as writers of diaries and letters, Perry's study gives a number of suggestions about the psychoanalytical function of that kind of writing for, as will be seen, as women write they reflect constantly on their lives. Reflection is fundamental to Martín Gaite's characters of her 1990s novels. Isolation and solitude are key themes in her literary work and are also present in her *Cuadernos de todo*. As Perry points out, these are central to the character's self-examination:

> The isolation of the characters is essential to the epistolary formula because it throws the characters back into themselves, to probe their own thoughts, their own feelings. ... What the characters enact in their seclusion is at the core of the epistolary novel: a self-conscious and self-perpetuating process of emotional self-examination.[120]

Or, as Martín Gaite says, 'Para escribir hay que partir de la soledad. Por eso las mujeres, cuando se enfrentan a ella sin paliativos, están más dotadas que nadie para explorar esa condición que – de ingrata como padecida – puede pasar a ser riqueza como explorada'.[121] In the case of letters, as Perry continues, this reflection is transmitted to the interlocutor: 'In epistolary fiction, then, writing letters is a way of at least sharing oneself with another, and perhaps even creating a version of the self for the occasion.'[122] This will be seen, for example, in the relationship between Sofía and Mariana, the friends in *Nubosidad variable*.

On the other hand, as Caballé observes, diarists need not only solitude but also a moment of crisis, or an experience of some kind of depression or lack of communication in order to feel the need to pick up the pen:

> Se ha repetido en numerosas ocasiones que la noche y la soledad, cierta tristeza de ánimo, las dificultades e insatisfacciones de la vida resultan ser las condiciones más favorables a la escritura diarística. ... Tal vez lo contrario no tenga demasiado sentido: los estados de euforia y bienestar reclaman ser vividos intensamente y en eso agotan su potencial realizador, mientras que la falta de correspondencia

---

[119] Biruté Ciplijauskaité, *La construcción del Yo femenino en la literatura* (Cádiz: Servicio de Publicaciones de la Universidad, 2004), p. 170.
[120] Perry, p. 117.
[121] Martín Gaite, *Cuadernos*, p. 607.
[122] Perry, p. 135.

entre lo íntimo y lo ajeno es el mimbre más adecuado para tejer la meditación que, de una manera u otra, requiere el hecho de escribir un diario.[123]

Martín Gaite's characters of her 1990s novels are seen trying to recover from some event in their lives, which has been the catalyst for their writing, and to understand themselves better, taking night and solitude as their companion. All of her characters go through a moment of crisis in their lives which makes them stop and think about their present situation; isolation, solitude, and the need to communicate will trigger reflection. Thus Leonardo, in *La Reina de las Nieves*, after leaving prison finds out about his parents' death; Sofía and Mariana in *Nubosidad variable*, meet at a party after having lost contact during their youth; her mother's death (and the birth of her own daughter) is what brings Águeda to write about her life in *Lo raro es vivir*; her second husband's death is for Amparo Miranda, in *Irse de casa* (1998), what triggers her need for self-analysis. In every case, these events will make the protagonists take decisions for the first time in their lives, and writing will help them to understand their situation and be able to go on. They are in Perry's words: 'People whose urge to communicate takes the form of writing.'[124]

Cuadernos de todo reveals how some events in Martín Gaite's life were also catalysts for her writing. There are the pages written in the USA after her daughter's death; the recurrent dreams after her parents died; the impossibility of continuing with some projects after the death of a friend. But what is apparent in every one of these moments, is the relief that writing about these feelings brings to the author. As Rita Felski observes: 'El diario ... está frecuentemente originado por un momento de crisis particularmente de la autora del mismo. El texto aparece totalmente inmerso en la experiencia de ésta y, por el hecho de seguir el ritmo vital.'[125]

There are other authors who use diaries in such a way. For example, Elena Soriano wrote *Testimonio materno* after her son's death, observing that 'Este libro no pertenece a ningún género literario determinado. Es un híbrido de varios diferentes ... Apuntes deshilvanados, sin fecha.'[126]

---

[123] Anna Caballé, 'Ego tristis (El diario íntimo en España)', *Revista de Occidente, El diario Íntimo: Fragmentos de diarios españoles (1995–1996)*, 182–3 (1996), 99–120, p. 100.
[124] Perry, p. xii.
[125] Quoted in Isolina Ballesteros, *Escritura femenina y discurso autobiográfico en la nueva novela española* (New York: Peter Lang, 1994), p. 123.
[126] Elena Soriano, *Testimonio materno* (Barcelona: Plaza & Janés, 1986), p. 9. In this

Another example is Lolita Bosch, who published *La persona que fuimos* in 2006, a book she began only a few days after her painful separation from her boyfriend:

> No es que esas cosas te curen, sólo dejan que te expliques lo que ha pasado. Cuando después de una larguísima relación te quedas sola, es como si te hubieran soltado en el vacío y sólo quieres explicarte qué ha pasado, por qué estás ahí, sola, así que escribes.[127]

Others, such as C. S. Lewis, wrote diaries to overcome the death of a loved one. *A Grief Observed* (1961), written after Lewis's wife died, was translated by Martín Gaite and published in 1988 under the title *Una pena en observación*.[128] So when the writers or the protagonists take the story of their life in their own hands they reach a moment of understanding: 'entender su vida y su personalidad desde una percepción individual, sin necesidad de confirmación externa.'[129] When this kind of reflective writing is taken up by women it has been seen by some critics as subversive, as women go from being the objects of their stories to being the narrators and the protagonists of those stories. As Margaret McLaren observes:

> Since the 1970s, there has been an explosion of women's autobiography. Women's autobiography has a special place in the feminist canon. It is significant for at least two reasons; it allows the woman to speak for herself, and it draws on her own experience. Autobiography is a form of self writing that demonstrate the self's active self-constitution.[130]

Or as Ciplijauskaité notes, with regard to the contemporary feminine novel: 'En muchas de estas novelas la protagonista no sólo es mujer, sino

---

book the author analyses certain problems, especially drug-related, confronting young people in Spanish society, which will also be seen in some of Martín Gaite's novels.

[127] Cited by Laura Fernández, 'Lolita Bosch explora «la intimidad» en un libro autobiográfico', *El Mundo*, 6 October 2006, available at: <http://www.elmundo.es/papel/2006/10/06/catalunya/2034149.html>.

[128] This book was given to Martín Gaite by one of her students at Vassar College during the autumn of 1985, after her daughter's death. See José Teruel, 'Un contexto biográfico para *Caperucita en Manhattan* de Carmen Martín Gaite', in *Género y géneros II: Escritura y escritoras iberoamericanas*, ed. Ángeles Encinar, Eva Löfquist and Carmen Valcárcel (Madrid: Servicio de Publicaciones de la UAM, 2006), pp. 143–51, p. 145.

[129] Joanne Frye, quoted in Ballesteros, p. 30.

[130] Margaret A. McLaren, *Feminism, Foucault and Embodied Subjectivity* (Albany, NY: State University of New York Press, 2002), pp. 151–2.

además escritora: se trata de una emancipación en dos niveles diferentes. Al autoanálisis se une el problema de la expresión. ... un camino hacia la auto-realización.'[131] On the subject of diaries and memoirs Verónica Luna makes the point:

> Debido a su carácter de intimidad, como una interacción del 'yo' con el mundo, como una división entre lo público y lo privado, muchos personajes se refugiaron en la privacidad del diario para expresar su verdad ante la vida y su tiempo. ... Éstos no sólo servían para descargar la memoria sino también como un instrumento de autocontrol y conocimiento de sí mismo, asumiendo su práctica una especie de examen de conciencia.[132]

And Ballesteros, with regard to Spanish feminine writing, says: 'El diario es el espacio que favorece el psicoanálisis.'[133]

In some novels the protagonists are writing on the advice of their psychiatrist, or, in the case of Alas's *La Regenta*, Ana Ozores is fostered by her spiritual tutor. In *Nubosidad variable*, the psychiatrist, Mariana, advises her friend Sofía to write. This type of writing is what María José Palma Borrego has called 'relato de cura femenino', noting that 'En general, podemos decir que el "relato de cura femenino" introduce en la autobiografía femenina una temática especifica, a saber, la confrontación de un "sujeto femenino" hembra con la muerte y su reconstrucción como sujeto de deseo.'[134] However the 'reconstrucción como sujeto de deseo' will surely not be the only goal these women want to reach. Their main goal is to take control of their own lives.

Marlene Schiwy gives a list of psychologists and psychiatrists who encourage their patients to write a diary, to help them from one session to the next, recovering in that way certain memories and reaching an understanding of their present situation. Schiwy also recommends the practice even if one is not formally a patient: 'You don't have to be in

---

[131] Biruté Ciplijauskaité, *La novela femenina contemporánea (1970–1985): Hacia una tipología de la narración en primera persona* (Barcelona: Anthropos, 1994), p. 13.

[132] Verónica Luna, 'Diario, memorias y crónica', *Correo del Maestro*, 122 (2006), available at: <http://www.correodelmaestro.com/anteriores/2006/julio/anteaula122.htm>.

[133] Ballesteros, p. 32.

[134] María José Palma Borrego, 'La autobiografía psicoanalítica femenina o el "relato de cura" femenino', in *Autobiografía en España: Un balance. Actas del Congreso Internacional celebrado en la Facultad de Filosofía y Letras de Córdoba del 25 al 27 de octubre de 2001*, ed. Celia Fernández and María Ángeles Hermosilla (Madrid: Visor, 2004), pp. 533–40 (p. 534).

therapy to experience the powerful healing benefits of keeping a diary. Through consistent and honest journal writing, you can become your own therapist.'[135] Even though writing a diary cannot be compared to psychoanalysis, what is evident, in Martín Gaite's characters and in her own diaries, is how writing will help through being a *tabla de salvación*, or as a writing cure in moments of difficulty. But not only writing will help in such moments: reading what one has written will give the diarists an external perspective on their feelings, helping them to understand their problems more clearly, to look at them in perspective and be able to take decisions on the steps needed to change their situation.

It is not just diaries that help to overcome these situations for, as Foucault observes, letters written in moments of isolation can also be of benefit: 'The letter one writes acts, through the very action of writing, upon the one who addresses it, just as it acts through reading and rereading on the one who receives it.'[136] He goes on to say that this type of writing, correspondence, was the first kind of 'narrative of the self'; in the letter one 'reviews one's day', in Foucault's words, a clear practice of 'self-examination.'[137] Books such as Lepore and Smith's *The Writing Cure: How Expressive Writing Promotes Health and Emotional Well-Being* (2002) show a series of alternative treatments for not only psychological concerns but also for physical illnesses such as cancer. Perhaps one of the best literary examples of the use of psychoanalysis and writing as therapy is Marie Cardinal's *Les Mots pour le dire* (1975), an autobiographical work in which the author, having spent years under psychiatric treatment, decides to try psychoanalysis and writes a novel based on her experience. According to Gunnthórunn Gudmundsdóttir, 'All of Cardinal's descriptions of writing talk of joy, freedom, and independence. It is a continuation of the importance she places on words in her autobiography and how, as in psychoanalysis, one can use them to cure oneself.'[138]

Entering the 'inside', as Béatrice Didier calls it, helps the writers to find themselves and be born again: 'Ce retour au-dedans est plus ou moins clairement assimilé à une seconde naissance. ... Cette deuxième naissance, d'autre part, est une naissance à la parole, ou du moins à l'écriture du journal, transcription du discours intérieur. Ainsi s'opère la

---

[135] Marlene A. Schiwy, *A Voice of Her Own: Women and the Journal-Writing Journey* (New York: Fireside, 1996), p. 120.

[136] Foucault, p. 214.

[137] Foucault, p. 219.

[138] Gunnthórunn Gudmundsdóttir, *Borderlines: Autobiography and Fiction in Postmodern Life Writing* (Amsterdam: Rodopi, 2003), p. 135.

découverte de l'identité et du "je"'[139] ['This return to the inner world is very much like a second birth. ... However, this second birth is a birth effected through words, or at least through writing the journal, it's the transcription of an inner discourse. This is how discovery of identity and the self works'].[140] As will be seen, diary and letter-writing, as well as other kinds of writing of the 'I', will help Martín Gaite and her characters to draw painful periods of their lives to a close and to start anew.

Conclusion

Letters and diaries have an important function as channels to make women's voices present at moments when it would be difficult to be heard. Letters and diaries have, over the centuries, been closely linked to women and their writing. The idea of taking an expression of writing which relates to women and turning it into a form of feminine writing could be seen as subversive, as some critics such as Patrick Paul Garlinger have suggested:

> The longstanding link between letters and women's writing – a means of keeping women from the masculine-dominated domain of literature, some might argue – has been revalorized in contemporary feminist studies as a mode of rescuing and recuperating the suppressed voices of women. ... In recent studies of epistolary fiction, Anee Bower and Diane Cousineau have upheld the longstanding notion that the letter can function as a space for women writers, where writing can become a means of reconstructing oneself as a subject.[141]

Or in Ciplijauskaité's words, 'Escribir se vuelve igual a crearse.'[142] In the same way, in Martín Gaite's work it becomes evident that writing the self is fundamental, especially for women, for taking control of their own stories. As Ballesteros would put it, 'La mujer se convierte en sujeto de discurso, rompiendo con la tradición discursiva masculina que la relega generalmente al papel de objeto de la representación.'[143]

Writing a diary can serve as therapy, the writing cure. Reflecting on

---

[139] Beatrice Didier, *Le Journal intime* (Paris: Presses Universitaires de France, 1976), pp. 90–1.
[140] Didier translations by Gill Rye.
[141] Garlinger, *Confessions*, pp. 32–3.
[142] Ciplijauskaité, *La novela femenina*, p. 20.
[143] Ballesteros, p. 5.

Katherine Mansfield's diaries, Carmen Martín Gaite says that 'Estoy segura que la meditación es el mejor remedio para la enfermedad de mi espíritu, para su falta de dominio sobre sí mismo',[144] and with regard to the writing of one's own life, she concludes that 'Contar alivia de ese peso insoportable con que nos abruma lo meramente padecido, nos convierte en protagonistas, nos ayuda a sobrevivir y a rechazar'.[145] In *Nubosidad variable* Mariana asks Sofía to write and this self-reflective writing helps her to go through difficult times, and in the case of Leonardo of *La Reina de las Nieves* it is possible to see the fascination the author felt for the diary as a cure.

The epistolary novel takes the reader closer to 'real' characters, while the publication of diaries puts the reader in contact with the more human side of the public persona. These types of narrative, real or fictional, lead the reader to the interior of people, to their deeper thoughts and feelings, and at the same time these types of writing allow writers to view themselves from the outside, reflected as they are in their text as if it were a mirror. As Didier comments:

> Le journal peut créer un phénomène de dédoublement ...; il peut donc être à lui seul, par rapport à l'écrivain, cet autre dont le regard est un miroir. ... Miroir, reflet, regard, sont des termes qui reviennent souvent sous la plume des diaristes, parce qu'ils répondent à une réalité.[146]

> [The diary (or journal) can create a doubling effect ...; in relation to the writer, it (the diary) can itself therefore be the other whose gaze functions as a mirror. ... Mirror, reflection, gaze, are terms which are often repeated by the diarist's pen, because they relate to reality].

In Spain well into the twentieth century women did not publish their diaries, while epistolary or diary novels were normally published by men. There has been a great increase in the number of female authors publishing either autobiographical novels or their own diaries and memoirs since the 1980s, and while this new phenomenon is seen by some as a formula for creating a best-seller, it may actually be that the reason for those kinds of novel becoming best-sellers is the way they portray women taking control over their own lives. In Martín Gaite's case, not only will her characters

---

[144] Martín Gaite, *Cuadernos*, p. 458.
[145] Martín Gaite, *El cuento de nunca acabar*, p. 122.
[146] Didier, *Le Journal intime*, p. 113.

take control of their lives through their reflective writing, but they will also be seen as mirror shards which reveal the author. Even though she used letters and diaries as part of her narrative strategy throughout her whole career, it was not until the 1990s that Martín Gaite's protagonists employed this kind of self-reflective writing to bring about changes in their lives. The protagonists of the 1990s novels are much more aware of the psychotherapeutic benefits of writing about one's life, exploiting this type of writing to its limits and exploring the possibilities that it provides as an escape from their predicaments. This study will show how, in some ways, through the writing of her characters Carmen Martín Gaite also reached her own *tabla de salvación*.

2

Cuadernos de todo: Carmen Martín Gaite's Diaries

Introducing *Cuadernos de todo*

Cuadernos de todo (2002) is a compilation of the notebooks or diaries Carmen Martín Gaite began in 1961, when her daughter Marta gave her a notebook on her birthday with the title 'Cuaderno de todo' written on the first page, and which, according to the author, gave her the freedom to write 'todo lo que quepa'.[1] The author recounts the story of the gift in one of the prologues to *El cuento de nunca acabar* (1983):

> Mi hija, que tenía entonces cinco y medio, me pidió un duro porque quería hacerme un regalo, y yo, desde la terraza de casa, la vi bajar a saltitos las escaleras de una calle por donde no pasan coches y donde a veces la dejábamos salir a jugar con otros chicos del barrio. Había una papelería allí cerca y en seguida la vi volver muy ufana con el cuaderno nuevo en la mano. Era – y es, porque lo tengo aquí delante – un bloc de anillas cuadriculado, con las tapas color garbanzo, y en el extremo inferior derecha la marca, Lecsa, entre dos estrellitas, encima del numero 1.050, todo en dorado. Cuando me lo dio, me gustó mucho ver que había añadido ella un detalle personal al regalo. En la primera hoja había escrito mi nombre a lápiz con sus minúsculas desiguales de entonces, y debajo estas tres palabras: 'Cuaderno de todo.'[2]

From that day on, she gave the title *cuaderno de todo* to the rest of her notebooks.

Cuadernos de todo consists of thirty-six notebooks plus a chapter called 'Fragmentos inéditos y notas fugaces', selected by Maria Vittoria Calvi from the eighty-plus notebooks and papers that Ana María Martín Gaite

---

[1] Carmen Martín Gaite, *Cuadernos de todo*, ed. and intro. Maria Vittoria Calvi (Barcelona: Areté, 2002), p. 27.
[2] Carmen Martín Gaite, *El cuento de nunca acabar* [1983] (Barcelona: Anagrama, 1988), p. 43.

handed over after her sister's death. The notebooks cover many different kinds of narration, from the most intimate – what we could describe as her diaries, with dreams, letters and poems – to the most public output, with transcripts of talks she gave or fragments of works she published.

There are notebooks with only four pages, such as *Cuaderno 4*, and others with many more, for example *Cuaderno 13*, with fifty-one. The latter is a *cuaderno de limpio*, which the author used to copy quotes from old notebooks, while at the same time making notes of ideas and thoughts for new projects. In this notebook there are also some old drawings which the author cut and pasted to save them from oblivion. Some *cuadernos* consist of two or more notebooks, due to the small quantity of pages used in them: these are *Cuadernos 6, 8* and *9*. Another, *Cuaderno 4*, consists of odd scraps of paper. At the end of the collection, 'Fragmentos inéditos y notas fugaces' consists of notes from many different notebooks, including two unpublished manuscripts: the first is a play, 'A pie quieto, Comedia en un acto',[3] written in 1953 and the second is 'Fin de año',[4] an unfinished drama from 1958.

The first three notebooks, as well as having the words *Cuaderno de todo* written on each cover, with the number, are some of the longest. The remaining notebooks, although presented in chronological order, are sometimes superimposed, in some cases revealing notes completed several years after they were started.[5] 1974, for example, is one of the most prolific years and there are six *cuadernos* in the collection which carry that date.

The structure of the entries does not follow an exact pattern. In many cases there are no dates, although we have an approximate idea of the time when they were written thanks to dated entries elsewhere in the same notebook, or through commentaries about the books Martín Gaite is reading or notes she is making. As well as written notes, *Cuadernos de todo* contains her drawings and collages, telephone numbers quickly written, or small personal reminders, and many of those notes or drawings are reproduced in facsimile.

The entries vary enormously in size. On the one hand there are brief

---

[3] Martín Gaite, *Cuadernos*, p. 643.
[4] Martín Gaite, *Cuadernos*, p. 650.
[5] Ana María Martín Gaite comments on her sister's lack of method when using a notebook: 'Podía empezar un cuaderno con una novela, pero, si estaba en la cama, por no andar buscando otro papel, le daba la vuelta y escribía un artículo, y por el medio igual iba un poema': cited in Juan Carlos Soriano, 'Ana María Martín Gaite: "Nadie, ni siquiera yo, conoció del todo a Carmiña"', *Turia: Revista Cultural*, 83 (2007), 267–79, p. 276.

notes of fleeting ideas which the author wants to capture on paper, such as the first entries with the heading 'Para *El cuarto de atrás*'[6] containing just a single sentence, or the six words written to encourage herself: 'Trataremos de reanudar el *Neverending tale*'.[7] On the other hand there are texts which cover several pages, such as that written for *La Reina de las Nieves*, subtitled 'Retahíla en plan chalado',[8] in which she jots down a whole series of ideas for the novel much like the short sentences mentioned above, although in this case the fleeting ideas that go through her mind form a kind of chain. The heading *Retahíla* is used at other moments in the *Cuadernos*, when Martín Gaite lets her thoughts fly freely, spitting them out, as she says: 'Escupir, no digerir, vomitar lo que se ve'.[9] Most of the longer entries consist of notes taken for *El cuento de nunca acabar*. In some cases there are notes copied from earlier notebooks, for example those on pages 301–9, where, as she explains, she is copying notes taken in *Cuadernos 1, 2* and *3*: 'Procuraré no limitarme a copiarlas sino ampliarlas a la luz de ese nuevo propósito'.[10] Another example of these entries is 'El interlocutor de la narración egocéntrica',[11] or 'Para *El cuento de nunca acabar*',[12] where the reflections on narration persist in her mind for several days when she was writing the notebook, from 24 October to 4 November 1974.

An important feature of the *Cuadernos* is the notes made with ideas for a novel or an essay, such as those already mentioned with regard to *El cuento*. Some notes consist of only two or three sentences, while others may form a large part of one chapter of the published work. It is interesting to see how the novels evolved from the moment Martín Gaite had the initial idea to the time they were published, as well as how, on some occasions, the story remains unchanged, almost word for word.[13] What is really impressive is her capacity to work on different projects at the same time: novels, short stories and essays. Bearing in mind that, as well as writing, she was translating, giving talks, papers and classes in different

---

6   Martín Gaite, *Cuadernos*, pp. 177, 192.
7   Martín Gaite, *Cuadernos*, p. 312.
8   Martín Gaite, *Cuadernos*, p. 559.
9   Martín Gaite, *Cuadernos*, p. 534.
10 Martín Gaite, *Cuadernos*, p. 301.
11 Martín Gaite, *Cuadernos*, pp. 323–8.
12 Martín Gaite, *Cuadernos*, p. 251.
13 Although as Calvi explains in her 'Criterios de selección y de edición', many of the pages which refer to manuscripts of published work have not been included in this volume: Maria Vittoria Calvi, 'Introducción', in Martín Gaite, *Cuadernos*, pp. 9–16 (p. 14).

universities, this provides a clear idea of the productive capacities of Martín Gaite, who continued working right up until her death.

She observes that many other authors had used their notebooks and diaries to jot down ideas, impressions, feelings: 'Me parece algo tan natural eso de ir apuntando cosas, impresiones, como para fijarlas y que quede algo de lo que has visto o pensado.'[14] Hers are notebooks or diaries where life and work are completely interconnected, as is the case with those of Katherine Mansfield or Franz Kafka, with which Martín Gaite was familiar and which she mentions in her notebooks. Thus, in August 1974 she writes: 'Escribir de un tirón paga más. Así escribió Kafka la noche del 22 de septiembre de 1912, cuando yo no había pensado siquiera en nacer. ¡Qué valentía de *élan* hacer eso! Así se escriben las cartas buenas'.[15] One entry in Kafka's diaries reads: 'September 23. This story, *The Judgment*, I wrote at one sitting during the night of the 22nd–23rd, from ten o'clock at night to six o'clock in the morning.'[16] In fact, this influence can be seen in the novel Martín Gaite was working on at the time, *El cuarto de atrás* (1978) which according to the narrative was composed during one night.[17]

Carmen Martín Gaite's notebooks have a great affinity with those of Katherine Mansfield, especially in the feelings Mansfield expresses as a writer: her moments of elation or depression, as well as the need to write:

> No sé hasta qué punto es o no lícito escribir un diario, pero reconocerse en él tanto como yo lo he hecho en el de K.M. atenúa la posibilidad de opinión. Estoy segura que la meditación es el mejor remedio para la enfermedad de mi espíritu, para su falta de dominio sobre sí mismo.[18]

The ups and downs of writing are what link writers' notebooks and diaries. Mansfield notes that 'I am sure that this Sunday is the worst of all my life.

---

[14] See Marie-Lise Gazarian Gautier, 'Conversación con Carmen Martín Gaite en Nueva York', in *From Fiction to Metafiction: Essays in Honor of Carmen Martín Gaite*, ed. Mirella Servodidio and Marcia L. Welles (Lincoln, NE: Society of Spanish and Spanish-American Studies, 1983), pp. 25–33 (p. 29).

[15] Martín Gaite, *Cuadernos*, p. 216.

[16] Franz Kafka, *The Diaries of Franz Kafka 1910–1913*, ed. Max Brod (London: Secker & Warburg, 1948), pp. 275–6.

[17] Martín Gaite states how the idea for the novel came during a stormy night when she was suffering from insomnia, similar to the story of the novel. See Gazarian Gautier, p. 29.

[18] Martín Gaite, *Cuadernos*, p. 458.

I've touched bottom',[19] while Rosa Chacel says that she is 'tratando de trabajar. He abandonado las cartas que debía escribir ... No tengo ganas de hacer nada.'[20] Yet these notebooks and diaries enable such writers, as will be seen with *Cuadernos de todo*, to get back to writing, and give themselves encouragement about their writing, as is the case with Chacel: 'Como no tengo valor para escribir sobre nada de lo que verdaderamente me preocupa, me angustia, me atormenta, apuntaré un sueño'.[21]

Cuadernos de todo contains what María Vitoria Calvi calls in her introduction 'diarios en libertad'.[22] These are notebooks that Martín Gaite takes with her everywhere[23] to use when a thought comes to her that prevents her from concentrating on anything else. They are there to record that thought or idea and give some form to it. Putting it down in the notebook, the author is able to pursue a dialogue with the idea:

> Todos debiéramos apuntar nuestras reflexiones. No por lo que valgan, sino porque dan lugar a otras ... tirar de lo que se piensa ... Se suelen achacar los males del mundo a la neurosis, a la angustia. Pero esta angustia no es sino un resultado. Resultado de no entenderse, de ahogar los pensamientos. Yo nunca sufro más que cuando siento la cabeza llena de pensamientos sin cocer, sin formular, y sé que están ahí, pero los disperso a manotazos por no sentir la bulla que forman ... El único remedio racional es abrirles la puerta y darles salida por orden.[24]

Cuadernos de todo could be designated as diaries or as 'dietario',[25] as the work combines intimate writings with intellectual reflections.

---

[19] Katherine Mansfield, *Journal of Katherine Mansfield*, ed. John Middleton [1927] (London: Persephone Books, 2006), p. 38.
[20] Rosa Chacel, *Alcancía: Vuelta* (Barcelona: Seix Barral, 1982), p. 279.
[21] Chacel, *Alcancía: Vuelta*, p. 56.
[22] Calvi, 'Introducción', p. 11.
[23] Martín Gaite wrote in *El cuento de nunca acabar*: 'la costumbre de meter en el bolso mi "cuaderno de todo" de turno, cuando salgo a la calle, ha llegado a hacérseme tan inexcusable que su olvido acarrea en mí la misma desazón que el de las llaves o el monedero' (p. 44).
[24] Martín Gaite, *Cuadernos*, p. 28.
[25] As Freixas indicates: 'Lo que diferencia, según Girard, al diario íntimo del dietario; a saber: en el primero predomina lo afectivo, en el segundo lo intelectual; el primero (conserve o no las fechas) está enraizado en la vida cotidiana, mientras que el segundo resulta intemporal': Laura Freixas, 'Auge del diario ¿íntimo? en España', *Revista de Occidente, El diario Íntimo: Fragmentos de diarios españoles (1995–1996)*, 182–3 (1996), 5–14, pp. 12–13.

As indicated in Chapter 1, it is very close to the Greek *hupomnĕmata* mentioned by Foucault:

> One wrote down quotes in them, extracts from books, examples, and actions that one had witnessed or read about, reflections or reasonings that one had heard or that had come to mind. They constituted a material record of things read, heard or thought, thus offering them up as a kind of accumulated treasure for subsequent rereading and meditation.[26]

And he goes on to explain the need to have the notebooks always 'Near at hand.'[27]

Martín Gaite takes notes of what she hears in the street, of what she reads, and then she rereads her notes later on. In some moments in *Cuadernos de todo* we sense the compelling need to externalize her thoughts, moments of crisis when her notebooks will help the author to start again. On the other hand, the dialogue in her head, which must be written in order to preserve it, can be combined with other thoughts leading her to the writing of a book, a short story, a novel, an essay or a talk. In some pages of the notebooks, though, the dialogue, instead of bringing new thoughts, stops suddenly and is never continued. In this, there is a similarity to the notebooks of Hélène Cixous:

> I might start, for instance, writing on the page, following a line of thought, and suddenly there is a kind of acceleration in my thinking ... Because it can be of a discourse, which organizes itself in sentences. Or it's a sudden flash of metaphor. Or it is a kind of vision which might be compared to a dream.[28]

This type of fast writing seems to be closer to the thinking process of the author as the thoughts do not seem to have been developed before being put onto paper – what Maria Vittoria Calvi has called 'una vertiente más íntima y espontánea'.[29] In some cases these notes are simple thoughts or private notes, written not to be forgotten. In other cases, Martín Gaite is

---

[26] Michel Foucault, 'Self Writing', in *Ethics, Subjectivity and Truth: The Essential Works of Michel Foucault 1954–1984*, ed. Paul Rabinow, trans. Robert Hurley *et al.* (London: Penguin, 1997), pp. 207–22 (p. 209).

[27] Foucault, p. 210.

[28] Hélène Cixous, *The Writing Notebooks*, ed. and trans. Susan Sellers (London: Continuum, 2004), p. 116.

[29] Calvi, 'Introducción', p. 11.

referring to an audience, to a reader as if she needed them to maintain the dialogue: 'Se me dirá: "primero es el comer". Y yo sé lo urgente que es. Nótese que no hablo de soluciones'.[30] In fact, the use of 'se me dirá', is repeated throughout *Cuaderno 1*. This formula, together with other colloquial forms such as 'quiero decir' or 'nótese que digo', creates a sense of real dialogue with a possible interlocutor. As the author explains when talking about her notebooks: 'lo que quería era entretenerme e imaginar que le estaba diciendo algo a alguien, a no sé quién.'[31]

In the first *cuadernos* there is also a 'dialogue' between the author and the books she is reading at the time. She takes notes on material that catches her eye and then comments on it, as if she were giving an answer to the author of the book she is reading, giving her opinion about what she has just read. Compare this with Cixous: 'Sometimes in the notebooks … it is a kind of inner dialogue I have with another work, because when I write I also read … It's a way of hearing another voice than mine. And immediately the dialogue starts'.[32] Sometimes Martín Gaite's 'dialogue' with these books and authors is continued over several pages of the notebooks; at other times a simple comment indicates what she was reading at the time.

Reading *Cuadernos de todo* allows a better understanding of the process of writing as well as the need that Martín Gaite had to write, which made her a writer. In the interview with Gazarian Gautier, she explains: 'Me recuerdo siempre con un lápiz o una pluma en la mano, desde muy pequeña. No es que quisiera ser escritora, es que escribía'.[33] The need to talk and the lack of an interlocutor present at every moment is what makes the writer write, a theme which the author developed in her journalistic articles and in her books of essays: 'Si uno pudiera encontrar el interlocutor adecuado en el momento adecuado, tal vez nunca cogiera la pluma.'[34] This is one of Martín Gaite's firm beliefs and is clearly reflected in her writing. Indeed, in her novels even her characters take the pen with a person in mind, that perfect interlocutor, as will be seen in *Nubosidad variable*. In *Cuadernos de todo* she observes: 'Mi enfermedad consiste en mi silencio. Es forzoso imaginar un interlocutor, no puede uno salvarse de otra manera. Y si la imaginación no es capaz de forjarlo,

---

[30] Martín Gaite, *Cuadernos*, p. 37.
[31] Cited in Gazarian Gautier, p. 29.
[32] Cixous, p. 116.
[33] Gazarian Gautier, p. 29.
[34] Gazarian Gautier, p. 27.

se va uno tragando todo deseo de hablar'.[35] Indeed, *El cuarto de atrás* clearly reveals the way she creates, imagining an interlocutor, to extract everything that is inside. The advantage of creating or inventing an interlocutor is that it will not disappoint the writer, and will help to attain the goal of putting thoughts in writing:

> Inventar un interlocutor no es un escape, en cuanto que ése, inventado, te ayuda a decir lo que querrías decir a todos estos otros a cuyo santuario no llegas, y si llegaras correrías el peligro de perderte en dulces celebraciones que te entorpecerían el cabal discurrir que en común con ellos pretendes.[36]

Martín Gaite presents her theories on writing and its relation to the interlocutor in books such as *La búsqueda de interlocutor y otras búsquedas* (1973) and *El cuento de nunca acabar*. In the former she states that 'Se escribe y siempre se ha escrito desde una experimentada incomunicación y al encuentro de un oyente utópico',[37] noting in the latter that 'El primer interlocutor satisfactorio y exigente venimos a ser, así, nosotros mismos. Nos proclamamos destinatarios provisionales del mensaje narrativo, mientras seguimos esperando, soñando, invocando a ese otro que un día nos vendrá a suplantar'.[38]

According to Martín Gaite, one can understand one's own life and history through literature and writing, this being one of the characteristics of autobiographical writing: 'la autobiografía obliga a parar, a reflexionar, a analizar, a replegarse en una interioridad protegida de la agresividad exterior ... búsqueda de un espacio en el que se impulse el reconocimiento del yo. ... Si por un lado se reflejan las vivencias pasadas, por otro se reflexiona sobre ellas.'[39] This type of autobiographical writing is what Martín Gaite develops in her novels of the 1990s. She gives her characters the time to reflect, in solitude, on their lives in order to be able to 'recognize themselves'. Such thoughts are reflected in her notebook pages, as she encourages herself by observing the blank pages to be filled. Thus she writes: 'Tengo que volver a descubrir el placer de escribir

---

[35] Martín Gaite, *Cuadernos*, p. 212.
[36] Carmen Martín Gaite, *El cuarto de atrás* [1978] (Barcelona: Destino, 1996), p. 122.
[37] Carmen Martín Gaite, *La búsqueda de interlocutor y otras búsquedas* [1973] (Barcelona: Destinolibro, 1982), pp. 28–9.
[38] Martín Gaite, *El cuento de nunca acabar*, p. 119.
[39] Quoted in Lydia Masanet, *La autobiografía femenina española contemporánea* (Madrid: Editorial Fundamentos, 1998), pp. 7, 9.

en mis cuadernitos junto a la vidriera de un café luminoso, el goce de dejar a los pensamientos que se produzcan y lubrifiquen con libertad, ... escribir, criar ámbitos interpersonales, sosegados, cosa previa a cualquier discurrir'.[40]

With her notebooks always at hand Martín Gaite was able to transcribe conversations, the nuances of language of the street. Her narrative style, which is always up to the minute, comes from her observations of people around her. As she comments in *El cuento de nunca acabar*: 'Han viajado conmigo por bibliotecas, cafés, trenes, archivos y autobuses'.[41] Indeed, in *Cuadernos de todo* she also reveals herself writing while travelling on buses, trains and the underground, as well as in hotels and cafés, and at her friends' houses.[42] Biruté Ciplijauskaité indicates Martín Gaite's need to move among different people, walking in the street to be able to take note of everything she hears: '"¿Usted cree que yo escribiría si no utilizara los autobuses?" le pregunta la autora a su entrevistador, Miguel Villena. "Sólo en la calle, y en plena libertad, puede 'capturar el murmullo de la vida cotidiana.'"'[43] At times Martín Gaite even reveals her moments of elation and depression, moments when it seems impossible to continue writing: 'Pero ahora no puedo reposar en nada de lo que escribo; por eso enmudezco días y más días. Todo lo que escribo no puedo verlo más que como retazos, tentativas que no hacen sino acuciar mi desazón'.[44]

But Martín Gaite never gives a more specific idea of her state of mind in her notebooks, at least not in the published *Cuadernos de todo*. For example, she does not refer to her feelings after Franco's death, leaving that to her novels. She does not talk of her separation from her husband and the fear of solitude: some of her protagonists will be the ones to express those feelings. Nor does she write about her daughter's death, but we can feel her broken spirit when confronted with a blank piece of paper after the loss. In a way, her novels and the characters written

---

[40] Martín Gaite, *Cuadernos*, p. 204.

[41] Martín Gaite, *El cuento de nunca acabar*, p. 44.

[42] From the headings of many of the diary entries it is possible to see where Martín Gaite actually is at the time of writing. One interesting example is found in *Cuaderno 12* where, having written many pages on the theme of narration, she stops to comment: '¡Qué puesta de sol estoy viendo desde el circular (26 de octubre) por la calle de Segovia abajo!' (p. 256). Since *el circular* was one of the buses Martín Gaite used to take in Madrid, this type of commentary and the headings allow the reader to witness the moments and places where she was writing her notebooks.

[43] Biruté Ciplijauskaité, *Carmen Martín Gaite (1925–2000)* (Madrid: Ediciones del Orto, 2000), p. 34.

[44] Martín Gaite, *Cuadernos*, p. 142.

in them were what Martín Gaite used to channel some of her pain and frustration. Through the characters of the 1990s novels especially, the reader is able to experience the difficulties Martín Gaite must have felt at certain times in her life: the death of loved ones, the separations and loneliness that follows.

In this chapter on the *Cuadernos de todo*, I shall begin by focusing on the first notebooks. These *cuadernos* cover a long period, from 1961 to 1967, with a final note in *Cuaderno 3* written in June 1970. The time when she is writing is one of changes in Spanish society and in Martín Gaite's life. Women's new roles in society, motherhood and consumerism are some of the themes which bother the author during the 1960s, and which are not only reflected by her characters in her earlier novels but will also continue throughout her life.

Subsequently, the rest of the *Cuadernos de todo* will be examined with special attention to the use of the notebooks in the development of her published work. In this section I intend to show the close relationship between the *Cuadernos* and her fictional work, between her life and her literature, looking at the way different works appear in the notebooks and are developed. Attention will also be paid to the *cuadernos americanos*, especially as they belong to a period in Martín Gaite's life when she started to be recognized and appreciated outside Spain. Her first lengthy stay in New York in the autumn of 1980 marks the beginning of a period when the author and her work start receiving serious critical attention and acclaim, but which is also a time of solitude and separation from the obligations and commitments she had to deal with in Madrid.[45] The last *cuaderno americano* also gives a very rare picture of the author's need to write after her daughter's death. This *cuaderno* demonstrates to the reader how the author used her *cuadernos* as therapeutical tools, and this links with the subsequent chapters that examine her novels of the 1990s, in which her characters find in writing the cure that enables them to continue with their lives.

The First *Cuadernos de todo* (Beginning 8 December 1961)

In *Cuaderno 1*, as well as explaining its origins, Martín Gaite describes the type of notebook that it is going to be, one in which everything can be included:

---

[45] See Carmen Martín Gaite, *A Fondo*, interview 1981, available at: <http://video.google.com/videoplay?docid=8932946931150749996>.

Pero hoy quiero empezar este cuaderno, siguiendo la dirección que en la primera página ha estampado a lápiz la Torci,[46] como una dedicatoria al regalármelo. Ha puesto debajo de mi nombre las tres palabras siguientes: CUADERNO DE TODO. Para ella, en un cuaderno se puede meter, como en un cajón, todo lo que quepa. Basta con empezar. En este cuaderno, pues, no debo tener miedo de meter lo que sea, hasta llenarlo. La Torci me ha dado permiso.[47]

Her first notebook is full of thoughts and reflections, especially about the family, marriage and women. She is, of course, a woman, a mother, a wife and a writer, writing during a time when the first feminist movements under the dictatorship started to have a voice. This was the period when the Asociación de Mujeres Universitarias was created in 1953, the Movimiento Democrático de Mujeres in 1964,[48] and the Seminario de Estudios Sociológicos de la Mujer was funded by María Lafitte, in 1960.[49] This was a time when the first books on civil and labour rights for women, written by Lidia Falcón at the beginning of the 1960s, were published.[50] A time when laws such as the *Ley de Derechos Políticos, Profesionales y Laborales de la mujer y el niño* were approved, in July 1961,[51] giving women back a number of rights that had been taken away from them after the Civil War.[52] Thus Martín Gaite started writing in her notebooks at a time when feminist theories, like those of Simone de Beauvoir and Betty Friedman, whose books were published in Spain in the mid-1960s, were trying to change the role of women in society. When reflecting on work and maternity in *Cuadernos 1* and *2*, Martín Gaite feels that women have not spent enough time analysing their desires, both as mothers and

---

[46] Her daughter Marta, born in May 1956 and known as 'la Torci' on account of the position in which she slept when she was a baby, has a fundamental part in the pages of the notebooks as she was a companion to her mother until her early death in April 1985, just before she turned thirty. They both lived in the same apartment on Doctor Esquerdo, Madrid, where Martín Gaite lived after her marriage to Rafael Sánchez Ferlosio in October 1953.

[47] Martín Gaite, *Cuadernos*, p. 27.

[48] See Rosa Pardo, 'El feminismo en España: Breve resumen, 1953–1983', in *El feminismo en España: Dos siglos de historia*, ed. Pilar Folguera (Madrid: Pablo Iglesias, 1988), pp. 133–40.

[49] See Amparo Moreno Sardá, 'La réplica de las mujeres al franquismo', in Folguera, *El feminismo en España*, pp. 85–110.

[50] See for example *Los derechos civiles de la mujer* (Barcelona: Nereo, 1963) or *Los derechos laborales de la mujer* (Madrid: Montecorvo, 1964).

[51] See Moreno Sardá, p. 97.

[52] See Geraldine Scanlon, *La polémica feminista en la España contemporánea: 1868–1974* (Torrejón de Ardoz, Madrid: Ediciones Akal, 1986), p. 342.

as workers, believing that maternity and family were still important in women's lives and that she needed to defend them. And, as Debra Ochoa indicates, 'Martín Gaite, like Julia Kristeva ... expressed an anxiety about the possibility that the second wave of feminism could create a reversed sexism.'[53]

Like many other Spanish women (including writers), Carmen Martín Gaite denied her status as a feminist. For her, feminism has a negative sense: 'Yo soy antifeminista. Yo aspiro a la libertad. Las feministas hablan de libertad, pero la llevan como una pedrada para arrojársela a la cara a los demás.'[54] Discussing in the *Cuadernos* the disenchantment women were experiencing, Martín Gaite distinguishes three periods: '1.ª época: aceptación, sumisión; 2.ª: euforia, rebeldía (feminismo), afirmando tener lo que no se tiene (por revancha); 3.ª (que apunta ahora): descontento, una especie de pérdida de fe en los ideales'.[55] She links the idea of rebellion and revenge to feminism, seeing as a consequence the disenchantment women suffer after gaining a certain amount of freedom. At the same time, Martín Gaite published articles which together with what she wrote in her notebooks reveal her ideas about the situation of women in Spanish society of the time. Articles such as: 'Las mujeres liberadas', published in *Triunfo*,[56] or 'Personalidad y libertad', published in *Medicamenta*,[57] portray women who start to find freedom through work and separation from their husbands, but have not thought about their new situation and its consequences.

Many critics have cited her writing as an example of feminist, not simply feminine, writing. Articles such as 'Carmen Martín Gaite: A Feminist Author',[58] or 'Significación social de las novelas de Carmen Martín Gaite en cuanto al desarrollo de la conciencia feminista en la España del siglo XX',[59] emphasize the importance of the author as a

---

[53] Debra J. Ochoa, 'Martín Gaite's *Visión de Nueva York*: Collages of Public and Private Space', in *Beyond the Back Room: New Perspectives on Carmen Martín Gaite*, ed. Marian Womack and Jennifer Wood (Oxford: Peter Lang, 2011) pp. 81–97 (p. 84).

[54] Cited by Montserrat Escartín Gual in 'Noticias de Carmen Martín Gaite y *Retahílas*', in Carmen Martín Gaite, *Retahílas*, afterword by Montserrat Escartín Gual [1974] (Barcelona: Destino, 2003), pp. 169–232 (p. 194).

[55] Martín Gaite, *Cuadernos*, p. 75.

[56] Martín Gaite, *La búsqueda de interlocutor y otras búsquedas*, pp. 123–31.

[57] Martín Gaite, *La búsqueda de interlocutor y otras búsquedas*, pp. 107–11.

[58] Phyllis Zatlin Boring, 'Carmen Martín Gaite: A Feminist Author', *Revista de Estudios Hispánicos*, 3 (1977), 323–38.

[59] Mercedes Carbayo Abengózar, 'Significación social de las novelas de Carmen Martín Gaite en cuanto al desarrollo de la conciencia feminista en la España del siglo XX',

feminist writer. Others, such as 'Replegando la voz: Carmen Martín Gaite y la cocina de la escritura',[60] not only present her as a feminist author; she is also criticized for not being a committed feminist author. The most adequate term to describe Martín Gaite's ideas on feminism would be Alicia Redondo Goicoechea's 'feminismo polifónico', which the critic sees as a feminism that is 'liberador, que defiende la diferencia ... dentro de una igualdad de derechos que reconozca la maternidad'.[61]

Women's Role in Society

In her first *cuadernos*, the author seems to be criticizing not the condition of women in society, but those who wish to change their condition with no real belief in what they want to take on, and without believing in what they are going to do. There is clearly a condescending tone in the way she talks about women who called themselves feminists:

> La polémica entre los sexos va siendo un tema demasiado reiterado, sobre todo si se tiene en cuenta algo evidente: que ni los hombres ni las mujeres por mucho que polemicen llegan a entenderse entre sí. ... Mientras hagan [las mujeres feministas] todo lo que hacen en función de 'no ser menos que los hombres' no habrán abandonado su condición satélite y será como si no hubieran pensado en nada ni trabajado en nada.[62]

Martín Gaite's critique of feminist women is mainly directed at those who demand complete equality with men. As Kristeva notes in 'Women's Time', at times such women forget their feminine or maternal attributes when demanding that equality.[63] However, Martín Gaite could be seen as a feminist writer in that she defends understanding between genders, proclaiming difference, coexistence and dialogue between men and women as the only solution to the problem. She observes:

---

in *El papel de la literatura en el siglo XX: I Congreso Nacional Literatura y Sociedad*, ed. Fidel López Criado (A Coruña: Servicio de Publicaciones, 2000), pp. 361–75.

[60] Jacqueline Cruz, 'Replegando la voz: Carmen Martín Gaite y la cocina de la escritura', in *Sexualidad y escritura (1850–2000)*, ed. Raquel Medina and Bárbara Zecchi (Barcelona: Anthropos, 2002), pp. 249–69.

[61] Alicia Redondo Goicoechea, 'Introducción literaria: Teoría y crítica feministas', in *Feminismo y misoginia en la literatura española. Fuentes literarias para la historia de las mujeres*, ed. Cristina Segura Graíño (Madrid: Narcea, 2001), pp. 19–46 (p. 41).

[62] Martín Gaite, *Cuadernos*, p. 33.

[63] Julia Kristeva, 'Women's Time', in *The Kristeva Reader*, ed. and intro. Toril Moi (New York: Columbia University Press, 1986), pp. 187–213 (p. 193).

> Si cambiásemos impresiones con los demás respecto a las cosas con la misma viveza e interés con que hablamos de personas y escuchamos lo que los otros dicen, iríamos al fondo en lugar de quedarnos en la cáscara; es decir entenderíamos esos cambios y altibajos que condenamos, nos pasman o nos indignan en los demás, y al descubrir el porqué de sus comportamientos sabríamos lo que hay en ellos de fenómeno social que igualmente a los demás alcanza y en qué medida serían evitables muchos errores de convivencia.[64]

The importance of dialogue between men and women is evident in some of Martín Gaite's novels. For example, in *Retahílas* there is a significant connection between aunt and nephew, and their conversation, which lasts a whole night, allows them to talk openly about their feelings and desires. In *El cuarto de atrás* a complete stranger is the one (the literary device) who allows the protagonist to dig into her past and think about her projects for the future.

In *Cuadernos de todo* Martín Gaite not only criticizes feminists but also women in a general way. In *Cuaderno 1*, her 'target' is women seeking independence through paid work: 'Las mujeres que tratan de independizarse hoy día arreglan el problema desde fuera. Imitan los gestos, la actividad, la libertad externa del varón. Sin haber conseguido ni de lejos la interna'.[65] Here, she seems to believe that women simply want to work in order to show men that they are able to; in her words: 'para sentirse más revalorizadas como hembras, como presa aun más deseable'.[66] She sees the only solution as being convinced of wanting to do it for one's own satisfaction: 'Cuando una mujer no pretenda demostrar ni que es muy mujer ni que deja de serlo y se entregue a cualquier quehacer o pensamiento desde su condición sin forzarla ni tampoco enorgullecerse de ella, sólo entonces será persona libre'.[67] She, however, believes in work as a means of satisfaction for one's own self, not simply to convince others: 'Pero es que una persona no tiene que darse a valer. Tiene que hacer bien las cosas que hace, tiene que hacerlas de verdad, entregarse a lo que haga. Tiene que hacer algo, no fingir que lo está haciendo'.[68] The notion of 'darse a valer' is key here. During the Industrial Revolution, when men began leaving the household to work outside the home and earn wages,

---

[64] Martín Gaite, *Cuadernos*, p. 34.
[65] Martín Gaite, *Cuadernos*, p. 45.
[66] Martín Gaite, *Cuadernos*, p. 46.
[67] Martín Gaite, *Cuadernos*, p. 33.
[68] Martín Gaite, *Cuadernos*, p. 46.

the value of money changed the value of work. This undermined the work done by women, especially in the home, where they cared for the children and managed the domestic finances. Referring to the changes in Spanish society as it moved from a rural to an urban population, Moreno Sardá documents how these spatial changes (from country to city) also changed the way work was valued as women also began to incorporate themselves into urban life. With the modernization of the household, housework was devalued, money being the measure by which work was valued:

> En la medida que se incorporaron a la vida urbana, estas mujeres vivieron la desmembración de la familia extensa junto con la modernización elemental de las casas ... y la devaluación del trabajo doméstico, debido a que el dinero se impuso cada vez más como medio imprescindible para la adquisición de los medios indispensables para la subsistencia y, por tanto, como patrón de valoración social (tanto cobras, tanto vales, tanto eres; en consecuencia, toda actividad no remunerada significa actividad devaluada).[69]

Martín Gaite's comments show that she considered that the real issue was in the way society valued work, so that 'El sentirse valorada una mujer tiene gran relación con la independencia económica'.[70] The dependence that women of the 1960s continued to experience was a historical reality maintained by men over the centuries. As Simone de Beauvoir points out, 'History has shown us that men have always kept in their hands all concrete powers; since the earliest days of the patriarchate they have thought best to keep woman in a state of dependence; their codes of law have been set up against her.'[71]

Thus Martín Gaite defends the work done by women in the home by investing it with greater value than was generally acknowledged: 'Yo no digo que una mujer tenga que dedicarse forzosamente a tareas caseras; digo que si las hace debe transcenderlas ... crear algo con él'.[72] She argues for women's housework and caring for the family to be considered as acts of generosity on their part. Also, she would like women to think positively about their work in the home and as an opportunity for reflection: 'se

---

[69] Moreno Sardá, p. 87.
[70] Martín Gaite, *Cuadernos*, p. 74.
[71] Simone de Beauvoir, *The Second Sex*, trans. and ed. H. M. Parshley (London: Picador, 1988), p. 171.
[72] Martín Gaite, *Cuadernos*, p. 81.

ha dado en confundir el sosiego con la inmanencia,[73] la pasividad, la cerrilidad, la pereza mental y demás actitudes viciosas y descarriadas que el sosiego y el silencio han tenido una parte meramente accidental'.[74] That space for reflection which men, she suggests, generally do not have, is what women should embrace instead of rejecting. The idea of woman as immanence or passive being is what Martín Gaite wants women to fight against.

The peace, which Martín Gaite proposes as the enviable preserve of women in the home, can however be experienced by men who decide to abandon 'historical time', the time of 'honor y gloria',[75] and retire to reflect, choosing 'silencio y sosiego'.[76] While some men may actively choose to retire and reflect, women, in Martín Gaite's view, passively suffer this space of silence and *sosiego* as a punishment that has, she believes, its origins in their childhood. Of course, in this Martín Gaite is referring only to women who are sufficiently privileged to have free time to reflect on life, rather than worrying about money and other life concerns. However, in her notebooks she is not alert to this and does not distinguish between social groups.[77]

Motherhood

In many of Martín Gaite's novels there is distinction between women who are mothers and 'independent' women. As Eulalia says to her friend Lucía in *Retahílas*, 'En España, Lucía, no cabe compaginar, lo sabemos de sobra, o eres madre o te haces persona'.[78] After this observation, which Lucía thought was 'una clasificación de libro de texto malo', she goes on to say that 'se podía inventar algo distinto de lo que veíamos a nuestro alrededor, y eso era lo apasionante, una forma de ser madre que

---

[73] The existentialist vocabulary of 'transcendence' and 'immanence' in relation to women is to be found in *The Second Sex*, originally published in French in 1949. As Toril Moi explains: 'Beauvoir's main thesis ... is simple: throughout history, 'woman' has been constructed as man's Other, denied the right to her own subjectivity and to responsibility for her own actions. ... patriarchal ideology presents woman as immanence, man as transcendence': Toril Moi, *Sexual/Textual Politics* (London: Methuen, 1985), p. 92.

[74] Martín Gaite, *Cuadernos*, p. 93.

[75] Martín Gaite, *Cuadernos*, p. 94.

[76] Martín Gaite, *Cuadernos*, p. 94.

[77] Even though poor women from the cities, women from the countryside and women who work in domestic service are represented in Martín Gaite's short stories, with the author revealing their difficulties and contrasting them with the middle-class women she is criticizing, in her notebooks these working-class women hardly have a place.

[78] Martín Gaite, *Retahílas*, p. 106.

no tuviera por qué excluir la de seguir siendo persona'.[79] In *Cuadernos de todo*, Martín Gaite comments extensively on motherhood, a kind of motherhood close to what Lucía refers to in *Retahílas* when she asks, '¿Por qué razón el concepto de madre iba a ir inevitablemente unido a quejarse y suspirar o a tiranizar o a seguir rutinas?'[80]

Martín Gaite considers caring for one's child and facilitating his or her development towards independence as an important part of the role of mothers in society. Yet she criticizes women who live through their children: 'no es "razón de su vida", es decir "objeto de trabajo, atención y reflexión", sino ciegamente su vida'.[81] In effect, Martín Gaite sees the role of the mother as one who facilitates the children's development by giving them freedom to understand the world better, by giving them the tools to reach 'criterio autónomo'[82] or independent judgement. Here, Martín Gaite's point echoes child psychologist Donald W. Winnicott's notion of the 'good-enough mother', who 'starts off with an almost complete adaptation to her infant's needs, and as time proceeds she adapts less and less completely.'[83]

Thus Martín Gaite defends women in their roles as wives and mothers, as she believes that these responsibilities, to be done well, 'requieren mucha generosidad, tiempo y atención'.[84] Of course, the child's need for their mother (or mother figure) in the first years of life is a subject still studied by psychologists. One of the first to use the 'object relation theory' with reference to child development was Melanie Klein, whose *Love, Guilt and Reparation* (1988) contains a compilation of articles published between 1921 and 1945, dealing with child development in the first years of life. Donald Winnicott and Nancy Chodorow also belong to an area of psychoanalysis which studies infancy and family relations from the point of view of the 'object relation theory'. The importance of the mother in the baby's first moments of life, the complete dependence needed for the child to reach independence and play as the first manner of emotional communication, are some of the notions these psychologists work with and which are echoed in Martín Gaite's ideas on motherhood and the parent-child relationship.

---

[79] Martín Gaite, *Retahílas*, p. 106.
[80] Martín Gaite, *Retahílas*, p. 106.
[81] Martín Gaite, *Cuadernos*, p. 80.
[82] Martín Gaite, *Cuadernos*, p. 80.
[83] Donald W. Winnicott, 'Transitional Objects and Transitional Phenomena', *International Journal of Psycho-Analysis*, 34 (1953), 89–97 (p. 94).
[84] Martín Gaite, *Cuadernos*, p. 46.

The theme of the parent-child relationship is fundamental throughout Martín Gaite's career. Her 1990s novels will reveal the need for daughters to reconcile with their mothers, after the latter's death, in order to be able to continue with their own lives, as will be seen in *Nubosidad variable* or *Lo raro es vivir*, while the search and encounter with the mother is privileged in the case of Leonardo in *La Reina de las Nieves*. According to Kimberly Chisholm, 'This examination becomes more focused in the 1990s novels ... As mothers come increasingly to the fore, Martín Gaite details the process by which each enables or fails to enable her child to establish and maintain the subjectivity for which Martín Gaite's filial characters incessantly search.'[85]

The maternal relationship with children is dealt with from *Cuaderno 1*. Martín Gaite reflects on play as important for the child's development and, at the same time, she affirms the importance of letting the child develop its own way of thinking:

> El juego como expresión de libertad. ... Tiene más libertad para jugar y desarrollar sus posibilidades un animal que no debe enfrentarse angustiosamente con el problema del sustento ... pero por otra parte esta protección bloquea a veces su 'ser adulto' y comportarse de un modo autónomo.[86]

Martín Gaite understands the difficulty mothers have in distinguishing between their own independence and that of their children. At the same time, she sees how women may find looking after their children a barrier which prevents them from attaining their own goals: 'Separan lo uno [el cuidado de los hijos] de lo otro [cualquier actividad externa a la casa]. Intuyen que hay otra cosa'.[87] And she asks herself: '¿Qué diferencia esencial existe entre ese trabajo y el que se haga en un colegio, en una academia, en una oficina?'[88] She believes that mothers should give their children, through playing and telling stories, answers to all their questions:[89] 'Hay, por ejemplo, muchas madres activas, progresistas, ... y

---

[85] Kimberly Chisholm, 'Maternal-Filial Mirroring and Subjectivity in Carmen Martín Gaite's *Lo raro es vivir*', in *Carmen Martín Gaite: Cuento de nunca acabar/Never-ending Story*, ed. Kathleen M. Glenn and Lissette Rolón Collazo (Boulder, CO: Society of Spanish and Spanish-American Studies, 2003), pp. 109–27 (p. 109).
[86] Martín Gaite, *Cuadernos*, p. 79.
[87] Martín Gaite, *Cuadernos*, p. 81.
[88] Martín Gaite, *Cuadernos*, p. 81.
[89] Martín Gaite relates how her parents always answered all her questions in 'Un bosquejo autobiográfico', in *Agua pasada* (Barcelona: Anagrama, 1993), pp. 11–25 (p. 13).

sin embargo hacen hijos para luego quitárselos de encima comprándoles tebeos interplanetarios'.[90]

Sometimes, though, she seems to contradict herself, especially when she has to decide whether women know the importance of their place in society: 'Las mujeres saben que la estabilidad de una sociedad reposa entre sus manos de madres'.[91] If women really knew their fundamental role, they would have more consideration for, and pride in, themselves. Yet Martín Gaite comments on the same page: 'Si la consideración de un ama de casa fuera mayor, a las mujeres les gustaría más ser amas de casa'.[92] She seems to wonder how women can sit and simply look at the changing world around them. How can women let others make their decisions for them? Martín Gaite lays the blame for this kind of position on cinema and literature, which endorse romantic love, marriage and children as the only goals in their lives. Thus love and marriage come under attack. She seems to find herself in a moment of crisis when she starts thinking about all the ideas with which the young girls of her generation were indoctrinated. These girls were keen readers of romantic novels (the *novela rosa*) in which love and marriage is presented as the only ambition. Such ideas were developed years later in her book of essays *Usos amorosos de la postguerra española* (1987), where Martín Gaite looks at her generation, young girls of the postwar period, and the way they dealt with love. In *Cuaderno 1* she writes:

> Todas las canciones y novelas de amor hablan de magia y ensueño. Es el amor la culminación de lo inexplicable. Siempre se ha echado mano de mentiras para sostener el amor, se ha rodeado su nacimiento de un aparato fabuloso. Pero tanto esfuerzo obliga a no reconocer que fue en vano.[93]

Family Relationships

Everyday life with the spouse, and sex, are an important part of the disenchantment: 'De verdad el sexo ha tenido siempre el mismo valor: un rato'.[94] The excitement of the first moments of love, the only thing

---

[90] Martín Gaite, *Cuadernos*, p. 37.
[91] Martín Gaite, *Cuadernos*, p. 82.
[92] Martín Gaite, *Cuadernos*, p. 82.
[93] Martín Gaite, *Cuadernos*, p. 52.
[94] Martín Gaite, *Cuadernos*, p. 115.

talked about in romantic novels, finishes, and women then want more; they demand from their husbands that the marriage union be permanent:

> El matrimonio sólo puede servirnos para enseñarnos que la felicidad es fugaz. ... y de aceptar esa realidad es de donde viene la riqueza. ... Y el único esfuerzo positivo de la vida en común debía ser el de librar al otro lo más posible de la propia interferencia y no dejarse a su vez tarar por la suya, ... porque así de verdad serían dos colaborando.[95]

Beatriz Celaya comments on the way Martín Gaite remains silent about any theme related to sexuality, not only in her notebooks, but in her novels and in her book of essays, *Usos amorosos de la postguerra española*: 'el deseo sexual femenino no sólo estaba ausente del discurso franquista, también parece estarlo en el mismo análisis que realiza Martín Gaite muchos años después.'[96]

These years when the author stopped publishing novels and dedicated her time to historical research, perhaps because of the difficulty of writing creatively, were also the years when her marriage was going through a crisis which culminated in separation in 1970. In any case, intimate subjects are something Martín Gaite did not like talking about in interviews or writing about even in her notebooks,[97] consequently it is difficult to know exactly what kind of problems she was going through during those years. Her critiques of women, marriage and sex, though, are good indicators of the author's disappointment with love as presented in the romantic novels that she, like many of her female characters, read as a young girl. The sadness she sometimes writes about may also indicate the crisis she was going through:

> Recuerdo cuando iba al parque hace unos años. Todo se me volvía mirar el reloj. Cerraba los ojos, tomaba el sol, y las conversaciones en torno me resbalaban. Cuándo serán las doce. Cuándo serán las doce y cuarto. No estaba tan triste como ahora, pero siempre estaba

---

[95] Martín Gaite, *Cuadernos*, p. 53.
[96] Beatriz Celaya, 'El amor es una tara: *Cuadernos de todo*, de Carmen Martín Gaite', *Neophilologus*, 91 (2007), 221–41 (p. 234).
[97] Some details about 'la vida privada de otras personas' have been edited so as not to appear in the *Cuadernos*, as Calvi explains in the 'Criterios de selección y de edición' ('Introducción', p. 15).

esperando algún acontecimiento exterior y me consumía. De fuera pensaba que me iba a venir, como el maná, la liberación.[98]

Martín Gaite's dedication to *Usos amorosos del dieciocho* indicates that her husband taught her to live alone: 'Para Rafael, que me enseñó a habitar la soledad y a no ser una señora.' In fact, solitude and isolation are themes repeated throughout her work and are found in the early pages of her notebooks. Solitude, often concerning women but also as suffered by men, is analysed in the *Cuadernos*, where she differentiates between 'soledad en compañía' and 'soledad física'[99] and states: 'Vivir en común debía ser no pedir al otro que llene nuestro vacío sino ayudarle a encontrar su soledad, no estarle tendiendo continuamente la mano'.[100] Indeed, she sees solitude as a positive condition as it helps thinking, it gives freedom. She also criticizes those who do not know what to do with their solitude: 'Dicen: es que "naturalmente" una mujer sola se aburre'.[101] Martín Gaite celebrates solitude: she can see in it a place for reflection, from where it is possible to write, from where one can create oneself before presenting it to others. At the same time, she believes that independence for women has arrived too soon, before they can understand the consequences of their new role in society, and she also suggests that independence can bring the anguish of solitude: 'La mujer emancipada rechaza y sufre la soledad más que nunca, perdida en la confusión de letreros que la circundan. Al aburrimiento de la mujer que hacía media ha sucedido la angustia de la soledad'.[102]

For Martín Gaite the solitude some women experience in their homes can serve as a refuge: 'Una mujer debiera tener más paz y equilibrio que cualquier oficinista, mayor capacidad de autoconstrucción si fomentara su razón, su autonomía'.[103] She believes in change from the inside and does not accept that the changes society brings are enough: women have to understand these changes before taking part in them. She suggests that the use of our intelligence is the only way out of difficult moments, the only way to develop thoughts on a changing society, and the only way for women to escape their state of immanence. She talks of 'inteligencia

---

[98] Martín Gaite, *Cuadernos*, p. 50.
[99] Martín Gaite, *Cuadernos*, p. 55.
[100] Martín Gaite, *Cuadernos*, p. 56.
[101] Martín Gaite, *Cuadernos*, p. 56.
[102] Martín Gaite, *Cuadernos*, p. 94.
[103] Martín Gaite, *Cuadernos*, p. 81.

como instrumento'[104] and also observes that 'La capacidad de reflexión es lo único que puede salvar al hombre de desear las guerras y también de pudrirse en la paz'.[105]

Consumerist Society

Consumerism in capitalist society is another theme which appears repeatedly in Martín Gaite's notebooks and is developed in her later novels. Living standards in Spain had fallen behind over many years, but in the 1960s they rose rapidly.[106] Martín Gaite criticizes the attitudes of women in this capitalist society, asking, '¿Qué tienen las mujeres de ahora que nunca están contentas? Sencillamente que les han hecho tener fe en los ambientes, en los uniformes, en las neveras, en lugar de haberles enseñado a tenerla en sí mismas'.[107] This kind of attitude, she believes, encourages social injustice and class difference:

> Cuando veo a tantas señoras que riñen a sus criadas, que cierran las casas con llave, que se pavonean sobre el malestar de otros seres más inferiores económicamente, que han cerrado la puerta de sus vidas a cualquier interés ajeno a la propia comodidad familiar, a esas gentes que aplican sólo la ternura de puertas adentro, precisamente por lo que el hecho me repugna y me conmueve.[108]

Martín Gaite had already developed these themes of social injustice and class difference in short stories such as 'Los informes' (1954)[109] and 'La tata' (1958).[110]

The ideas which she develops in her notebooks on consumerism, women in the workplace or the mother-child relationship, are those she would like other women to think about. Her critique of women who have nothing to talk about, who do not have the need to get out of the house

---

[104] Martín Gaite, *Cuadernos*, p. 37.
[105] Martín Gaite, *Cuadernos*, p. 32.
[106] For a discussion of *desarrollismo* in Spain, see Alex Longhurst, 'Culture and Development: The Impact of 1960s "desarrollismo"', in *Contemporary Spanish Cultural Studies*, ed. Barry Jordan and Rikki Morgan-Tamosunas (London: Arnold, 2000), pp. 15–28.
[107] Martín Gaite, *Cuadernos*, p. 97.
[108] Martín Gaite, *Cuadernos*, p. 36.
[109] Carmen Martín Gaite, *Cuentos completos* [1978] (Madrid: Alianza, 1989), pp. 300–5.
[110] Martín Gaite, *Cuentos completos*, pp. 259–69.

to communicate with others, cannot be turned against Martín Gaite. She blames women who have no interests outside the house; she envies men who go out to the bar, to the 'tertulia', to discuss things outside the home. The vacuity found in some middle-class women can be seen in some of the characters of Martín Gaite's short stories, for example 'Tarde de tedio' (1970)[111] or 'Retirada' (1974),[112] where the author presents women of the middle class with nothing to do, having maids and nannies who look after their children and spending all day at the hairdresser or waiting for their husbands to take them out.

Her protagonists of the 1990s novels take a different position. They appear on the periphery of this capitalist and consumerist society, watching the other female characters of the novels rush around buying goods to have the most modern of houses. The male characters have joined the consumerist frenzy by marrying women who are more concerned with looks than the intellectual needs of the people around them. Sofía, Mariana, Casilda, Águeda and Amparo do not seek the company of other women to convey their frustrations; instead they find in solitude and reflection their weapon against their problems. These women find in their writing the way to understand themselves in the same way that Martín Gaite uses her *cuadernos* as a place to converse with herself.

Cuadernos para el Diálogo

There is also to be found in the pages of the first notebooks a dialogue with the outside world, not only through the thoughts the author reveals about the world, but also by means of a dialogue with other writers and their ideas. As Foucault indicates in 'Self Writing', Seneca stresses the need to read other texts in order to be able to help one's own thoughts and ideas to develop: 'the practice of the self involves reading, for one could not draw everything from one's own stock or arm oneself by oneself with the principles of reason that are indispensable for self-conduct: guide or example, the help of others is necessary.'[113] Responding to authors such as Bertrand Russell, José Ortega y Gasset or Antonio Machado, Martín Gaite appears to be answering letters written after reading their books, in which she develops those writers' thoughts, as if they were posing questions she needs to answer. Indeed, in *Cuaderno 12* she comments on

---

[111] Martín Gaite, *Cuentos completos*, pp. 152–61.
[112] Martín Gaite, *Cuentos completos*, pp. 162–68.
[113] Foucault, p. 211.

the idea of the first notebooks as a base from which to maintain a dialogue with the authors she reads:

> Mis cuadernos de todo surgieron cuando me vi en la necesidad de trasladar los diálogos internos que mantenía con los autores de los libros que leía, o sea convertir aquella conversación en sordina en algo que realmente se produjera. Los libros te disparan a pensar. Debían tener hojas en blanco entre medias para que el diálogo se hiciera más vivo.[114]

In *Cuaderno 2*, dedicated mostly to this type of diary, there are clear examples of this kind of writing. Thus Martín Gaite comments, inter alia, on Georg Simmel's ideas on *Cultura Feminina*[115] which makes her think about women's disenchantment with their society and the need to make themselves valued. Reading Wilhelm Wundt's *Elementos de psicología de los pueblos*, she reflects on solitude and the need for material goods: 'En el apego a las cosas hay mucho del miedo a quedarse solo, desprotegido'.[116] This kind of dialogue is connected to the themes that concern the author and which appear in her later works. She reveals how her readings are linked to her reflections on the position of women in society when she responds to books such as Thorstein Veblen's *Teoría de la clase ociosa* by discussing women's work in the home and their 'aparente liberacion'[117] through the goods that consumerist society provides. Reading Simone de Beauvoir's *Le Deuxième sexe* makes her think of women's revenge, the necessity of communication in marriage and the need for women to reach transcendence: 'La mujer no ha comprendido que no es la supremacía económica y por ende la de dominio del mundo la que debe envidiar al macho y desear poseer, sino la posibilidad y capacidad de transcendencia'.[118] With regard to solitude, she responds to books such as Erich Fromm's *Psicoanálisis de la sociedad contemporánea*, which makes her think about the need for intimacy and about women working outside the home. On the subject of capitalism she reads Max Weber's *La ética protestante y el espíritu del capitalismo*. Here she expresses her feelings towards capitalist society and the need to reach the unreachable: 'La desesperación viene de que nos han presentado como únicamente

---

[114] Martín Gaite, *Cuadernos*, p. 264.
[115] Martín Gaite, *Cuadernos*, p. 72.
[116] Martín Gaite, *Cuadernos*, p. 76.
[117] Martín Gaite, *Cuadernos*, p. 68.
[118] Martín Gaite, *Cuadernos*, p. 88.

deseable y hermoso lo que no se sabe si se va a poder alcanzar o no'.[119] Reading Evelyne Sullerot's *La presse fémenine*,[120] Martín Gaite reflects on motherhood and the influence of women's magazines. And, on the theme of love, she reads classics such as *Les Liaisons dangereuses*,[121] *Madame Bovary* and *La Regenta*.[122] Influenced by these readings, she wrote articles such as 'La influencia de la publicidad en las mujeres', published in December 1965 in *Cuadernos para el Diálogo*,[123] or 'De Madame Bovary a Marilyn Monroe', published in *Triunfo* after the actress's death in 1962.[124] All of these are themes which she develops later on in her fiction. Some of the books she is reading are also brought into her novels, with the protagonists revealing close relationships with fictional characters that have had a great influence on their lives.

The Writer's Workshop

With *Cuaderno 3* begins another thematic aspect of *Cuadernos de todo*: this is the author's work in progress. Sometimes life and literature are so closely connected that Martín Gaite clearly incorporates her own experiences in her published work, as will be seen with *El cuento de nunca acabar* or *El cuarto de atrás*. At other times the experiences she has gone through, or she is going through at the time of writing, form part of what her characters are experiencing in their lives, and here it is possible to see the 'influence' of the author on her characters.

Even though work in progress can be more easily identified from *Cuaderno 3* onwards, some of the ideas exposed in the two first notebooks do find a place in the pages of her published work and, as has been seen, themes treated in the first *cuadernos* will surface later in her short stories and the novels. Now, novels such as *Fragmentos de interior* and *Retahílas*, as well as her historical study on Macanaz, are seen to be clearly delineated in *Cuaderno 3*.

These entries can be termed the 'writer's workshop', as they reveal how a work starts to take shape in the author's head and is developed slowly on account of personal circumstances and external influences:

---

[119] Martín Gaite, *Cuadernos*, p. 71.
[120] Martín Gaite, *Cuadernos*, p. 82.
[121] Martín Gaite, *Cuadernos*, p. 103.
[122] Martín Gaite, *Cuadernos*, p. 85.
[123] See Martín Gaite, *La búsqueda de interlocutor y otras búsquedas*, pp. 113–21.
[124] Martín Gaite, *La búsqueda de interlocutor y otras búsquedas*, pp. 133–46.

> Siempre he echado de menos, al cabo de mis diferentes invenciones narrativas que culminaron en el resultado de un libro nuevo, no haber llevado, paralelamente al trabajo que iba configurando y creando el libro, un diario donde se diera cuenta de los avatares, interrupciones y altibajos de esa elaboración.[125]

These words, written by Martín Gaite at the beginning of her only *cuaderno de bitácora* (*Cuaderno 16*) dedicated to the development of the Count of Guadalhorce's biography, are repeated on other occasions during her life.[126] But what is revealed in *Cuadernos de todo* is exactly this, a great *cuaderno de bitácora*, revealing how many of her works started and the vicissitudes which led to their conclusion.

In *Cuadernos de todo*, Martín Gaite describes her thoughts and feelings during the time she was preparing her work, or during the period when her books were mere ideas and projects without a title. There are notes which discuss her difficulties as well as her moments of excitement when developing a new idea. Sometimes these projects did not materialize, but elsewhere the very words later published in her novels, essays or talks can be seen.[127] Of all of Martín Gaite's works, the one which receives most space in the *Cuadernos* is *El cuento de nunca acabar*. In this book the bridge between life and literature is continuously crossed, as Martín Gaite writes about her life at the same time as reflecting on the subject of narration. As has been mentioned, it was in prologue 5 of this book that she originally introduced the *Cuadernos* to her public, and so this will be the first work looked at here.

---

[125] Martín Gaite, *Cuadernos*, p. 381.

[126] These same words were used in her article, 'La novela de la novela', on Thomas Mann's *Los orígenes del doctor Faustus: La novela de la novela*, published in *Diario 16* on 7 February 1977. See Carmen Martín Gaite, *Tirando del hilo (Artículos 1949–2000)*, ed. and intro. José Teruel (Madrid: Siruela: 2006), p. 75. In the same way, we find this idea in a text written by Martín Gaite during her first long stay in New York. In this case she changed the words slightly: 'una especie de cuaderno de bitácora para registrar la historia de lo que iba pensando y sintiendo, de lo que me movía a escribir y de cómo el hecho de escribir influía en mi humor y lo modificaba': Carmen Martín Gaite, 'Retahíla con nieve en Nueva York', in *Agua pasada*, pp. 26–32 (p. 30).

[127] There are more notebooks and manuscripts dedicated exclusively to her published work which have not been included in *Cuadernos de todo* due to their length, as Calvi explains in 'Criterios de selección y de edición' ('Introducción', p. 14).

El cuento de nunca acabar (1983)

Martín Gaite's ideas for *El cuento de nunca acabar* were already exposed in *Cuaderno 1* (1961) and continued even after the publication of the book in 1983.[128] Her reflections on the theme of narration, which are those she was working on for *El cuento de nunca acabar*, are also fundamental to the rest of her work. Because of its subject, and its close relationship to her life, she found this book of essays difficult to finish, as she admitted: 'este trabajo, que lleva el título previo de *El cuento de nunca acabar*, amenaza con ser demasiado fiel a su título porque no lo acabo nunca, abierto, como está, por naturaleza, a toda clase de interrupciones'.[129]

El cuento and *Cuadernos de todo* complement each other, for the idea of keeping a diary or *cuaderno de bitácora* for *El cuento* is also stated in the book.[130] *El cuento* needs the *Cuadernos* as a place in which to reflect at all times: Martín Gaite writes in the notebooks any thoughts she had on the theme of narration during the years she worked on it. She also uses *El cuento* when overwhelmed by dejection, as the safety net to keep her writing. Ana María Fagundo calls *El cuento* 'una narración cuya protagonista es la propia autora a la cual vemos pensando, escribiendo, viviendo,'[131] as Martín Gaite does in the *Cuadernos*. Because of the freedom Martín Gaite allowed herself in this work (she comments on the idea of writing a book on narration and how she did not want to follow the pattern other writers have used when writing on the same subject), she permitted herself to write anything that came into her head and employed the title *El cuento de nunca acabar*. Under this heading personal experiences and feelings can be found, as well as theoretical ideas derived from other readings.

The first knowledge the reader has of this work, as noted by the editor of *Cuadernos de todo*, are the notes taken in Teruel in September 1963

---

[128] Calvi comments on the intimate relationship between *El cuento de nunca acabar* and *Cuadernos de todo*: 'Ambas obras comparten el rechazo de los géneros establecidos, la busca de la estética de lo provisional e incierto, que encuentra su razón de ser en las conexiones significativas que relacionan lo cotidiano con lo universal y imperecedero. La escritura se fundamenta en la observación y en el gozo que esta produce': 'Presentación de los *Cuadernos de todo* en Salamanca', *Espéculo: Revista de Estudios Literarios* (Madrid: Universidad Complutense, 2003), available at: <http://www.ucm.es/info/especulo/cmgaite/c_todo.html>.

[129] Martín Gaite, 'Un bosquejo autobiográfico', p. 24.

[130] See Martín Gaite, *El cuento de nunca acabar*, pp. 215–16.

[131] Ana María Fagundo, *Literatura femenina de España y las Américas* (Caracas: Editorial Fundamentos, 1995), pp. 147–8.

on the pleasure of writing a letter, which are included in prologue 3 to *El cuento*. Even though this is the first clear note taken for *El cuento*, the author used other notes made in *Cuadernos 1* and *2*. For instance, in *Cuaderno 1* there is a note titled 'El respeto por la letra escrita'[132] which the author used in the first part of 'Río revuelto', entitled 'Los apuntes'.[133]

Cuaderno 4 includes the story of a walk Martín Gaite took with her daughter during their holiday in El Boalo[134] on 31 July 1964 and which she published in a edited form in the third part of *El cuento*, under the title 'Ruptura de relaciones'. Until then, the author had not given a title to her thoughts and reflections. In fact, it is not until *Cuaderno 11* (October 1974) that the title of the book appears for the first time: '*El cuento de nunca acabar*. (Asunto cuya solución se retarda indefinidamente.) Venir a cuento. Déjate de cuentos. Chisme. Noticia. Correveidile. Enredo, maraña, intriga, historia, hablilla. Dar palabra'.[135] This paragraph also gives a synopsis of the book and its topics indicating that, in *El cuento*, there are reflections on every kind of narration. At that time, October 1974, the author gave a definitive title to the book in *Cuaderno 13*: '20 de octubre. He pensado el título de *El cuento de nunca acabar* para mis reflexiones sobre la narración, ensayo o lo que vaya a ser'.[136]

Cuaderno 12 is one of the most important in the development of *El cuento*. From this moment onwards most entries under this title concerned the idea of narration, whether they were her own ideas, reflections from something she heard or observed in the street, or the development of a thought after reading a book on that topic. Some examples of themes that she develops here are 'Dorian Gray',[137] 'Narración vacía'[138] and 'La literatura epistolar'.[139]

The books she was reading at the time influenced her work enormously. For instance, in *Cuaderno 21*, while reading Katherine Mansfield's diaries and Margarita Nelken's *Las escritoras españolas*, she discusses women writers, their readers and female characters in the novels. In her notebooks these reflections were called 'El narrador testigo',[140] a theme which in

---

[132] Martín Gaite, *Cuadernos*, p. 31.
[133] Martín Gaite, *El cuento de nunca acabar*, p. 233.
[134] Her family has a country house in El Boalo (Madrid) which she used frequently.
[135] Martín Gaite, *Cuadernos*, p. 237.
[136] Martín Gaite, *Cuadernos*, p. 298.
[137] Martín Gaite, *Cuadernos*, p. 179; *El cuento de nunca acabar*, p. 280.
[138] Martín Gaite, *Cuadernos*, p. 252; *El cuento de nunca acabar*, p. 310.
[139] Martín Gaite, *Cuadernos*, p. 339; *El cuento de nunca acabar*, p. 247.
[140] Martín Gaite, *Cuadernos*, p. 460.

El cuento de nunca acabar was titled 'La mujeres noveleras'.[141] Other authors Martín Gaite read during her 'research' on narration included Tzvetan Todorov,[142] Roland Barthes,[143] Felix Schwartzmann,[144] Nicolas Leskov[145] and Marthe Robert, of whom she comments: 'Hoy, hablándole a Lozano de *El cuento* ... me he dado cuenta de que no pretendo elucubrar ni hacer teoría de nada ... Si quisiera elaborar una teoría coherente y correcta como la de Marthe Robert, material tendría más que de sobra'.[146]

Once Martín Gaite gave the title to the project, she worked constantly on it for a long period of time. Ideas about narration had been in her head for many years and, in *Cuaderno 13*, she comments on the use of earlier ideas from her first *cuadernos*: 'Hoy, en la tarde del 27 de octubre de 1974, voy a tratar de pasar a limpio, en este cuaderno tan agradable que me regaló Torán, algunas de las notas que salgan a relucir en mis cuadernos viejos y que tengan que ver con el asunto de la narración'.[147] Once copied into a new notebook, these notes develop into new ones, as was often the case with old *apuntes*. *Cuaderno 14*, written during the first half of 1975, is also full of notes on narration. Here she returns to themes dealt with in other notebooks and develops ideas on 'literatura epistolar',[148] 'la narración amorosa',[149] 'la mujer novelera'[150] or 'la narración tánatos'.[151]

So far, examples have been given of how notes from the *cuadernos* were used in *El cuento de nunca acabar*, but the author's difficulties in actually concluding the project are excluded from the published book.

El cuento was dedicated to Gustavo Fabra, a great friend of Martín Gaite who was her main interlocutor while she was preparing the book.[152] When he died in December 1975, she found it impossible to continue the work without his help:

---

[141] Martín Gaite, *El cuento de nunca acabar*, p. 63.
[142] Martín Gaite, *Cuadernos*, p. 251.
[143] Martín Gaite, *Cuadernos*, p. 265.
[144] Martín Gaite, *Cuadernos*, p. 259.
[145] Martín Gaite, *Cuadernos*, p. 269.
[146] Martín Gaite, *Cuadernos*, p. 276.
[147] Martín Gaite, *Cuadernos*, p. 301.
[148] Martín Gaite, *Cuadernos*, pp. 339, 347.
[149] Martín Gaite, *Cuadernos*, p. 341.
[150] Martín Gaite, *Cuadernos*, p. 345.
[151] Martín Gaite, *Cuadernos*, p. 349.
[152] Martín Gaite talked about Fabra during the book launch in the Ateneo in Madrid on 22 March 1983, as she explains in her note to the second (1988) edition of the book.

> Primera interrupción. Desde que dejé ordenado lo que antecede han pasado seis meses, he perdido el estímulo de mi trabajo que ya parecía surcar las aguas con un ritmo seguro – lo cual no significaba ninguna garantía y me vuelve a asediar la zozobra. Hoy, al fin, 30 de abril de 1976, pienso que tal vez confesarlo aquí y recapitular las causas de este quiebro, ... podrá servirme de punto de partida para arrancar a decir algo nuevamente.
>
> Una de las cosas que han pasado en este tiempo es que en diciembre del año pasado murió repentinamente el amigo con quien yo más había hablado de los avatares de este libro y a cuya memoria se lo querría dedicar, si soy capaz de seguirlo ... Todo lo que antecede lo ha leído él y, a partir de ahora ya se lo estoy dedicando a unos oídos ausentes, a un rostro cuya expresión sólo muy a duras penas consigo evocar y reconstruir.[153]

In the same way that Martín Gaite's protagonists of the 1990s novels used writing as a way of dealing with their traumatic losses or experiences, the author uses her notebooks as a *tabla de salvación* and her work as the space to bring her back from her *zozobra*. Thus, a few pages later, dated June 1976, Martín Gaite starts encouraging herself to continue with the project: 'Al *neverending* no le tengo que tener miedo. Está. Tengo que recordar que puedo contarlo por donde quiera, darme cuenta de cómo interesa a Carlos, a Arcadio, a oyentes nuevos, y eso que está sin elaborar'.[154] Although it is known that her work on *El cuarto de atrás* took over, delaying the conclusion to *El cuento* for later, Martín Gaite still continued to encourage herself: 'Me voy a meter de lleno en el *neverending*. Es la única salida verdadera',[155] she wrote in the Ateneo on 7 January 1977, and new interlocutors did indeed help her to return to the project:

> Estuve en el Ateneo todo el día, previo comer en Alcalá 35. ... En las páginas anteriores quedan muestras de mi trabajo. ... Luego vino a casa Millás y estuvimos hablando del *neverending*. Es muy lúcido y me puede ayudar, en adelante, hablar con él. Tanto a él como a Ricardo les parece sugerente conservar dos letreros laterales del borrador. Esto facilitaría las cosas, esa ligereza de factura (aun cuando amplíe algo) que también Nacho me insta a conservar. Tal

---

[153] Martín Gaite, *Cuadernos*, pp. 368–9.
[154] Martín Gaite, *Cuadernos*, p. 372.
[155] Martín Gaite, *Cuadernos*, p. 397.

vez revise lo ya hecho y lo despiece un poco en este sentido para que, en este caso, el libro tuviera una mayor unidad.[156]

Martín Gaite was still encouraging herself in 1978: 'Insistir, en el *neverending*, en el "encuentro con la literatura"'[157] and, through the long journey from the beginning of the project and until the end, many people encouraged her to finish it. On 10 January 1977 she wrote:

> A lo largo de estos años les he hablado mucho a los amigos de la historia de este libro, que se vincula con mi propia historia (Brigitte, Eduardo, Ricardo, Nacho, Gustavo, Pablo, Aguirre …). Les hablo de algo que no está, les hablo de sus orígenes y de un proceso doloroso. (Y tengo miedo de acabarlo).[158]

Nevertheless, some friends were not that optimistic about its success:

> Domingo 23 de marzo [1980]. Ateneo. Acabo de estar en la tertulia del Lyon con Josefina. Eugenio me desanima para el *neverending*, me viene – como Rafael antaño – con letreros, con clasificaciones de lo que es o no es sustancialmente la narración, habla de la búsqueda de la verdad, de la filosofía. Y yo, la verdad, creo que mi libro, por este camino, no va a gustarle nada.[159]

Ultimately, it was during a long period spent in the United States that Martín Gaite decided to resolve the neverending tale: 'Después de nueve años de trabajar en él, terminé de ordenar los apuntes que componen su última parte la madrugada del primer día de octubre de 1982 en Charlottesville, Virginia. Eran las cuatro de la madrugada y había luna llena'.[160] The months spent in the United States gave the author time, in complete solitude, to be able to finish this book. Solitude is often a fundamental requirement for the writing of the self, as Didier explains: 'La solitude crée une aire de silence et de liberté, au sein de laquelle le moi pourra vraiment exister'[161] ['Solitude creates a space of silence and freedom, in which the self can really exist'], and this solitude was made

---

[156] Martín Gaite, *Cuadernos*, p. 400.
[157] Martín Gaite, *Cuadernos*, p. 440.
[158] Martín Gaite, *Cuadernos*, p. 406.
[159] Martín Gaite, *Cuadernos*, p. 491.
[160] Martín Gaite, *El cuento de nunca acabar*, p. 12.
[161] Beatrice Didier, *Le journal intime* (Paris: Presses Universitaires de France, 1976), p. 89.

possible by having a room of one's own as described by Virginia Woolf, an author whom Martín Gaite discovered while in America.[162] As will be seen later in the section on the *cuadernos americanos*, Martín Gaite's stays in the United States were significant for her, not only because of the recognition from critics (unlike anything she had received in Spain), but also because of the time and space that she enjoyed, and needed, to reflect in solitude. In an interview given on her return to Spain from her first visit to the United States in 1979, Martín Gaite commented:

> El cuento de nunca acabar. No es que lo esté preparando. Es que es un libro que creo que lo he estado preparando desde siempre. Lo que pasa es que ahora, después de mi visita a los Estados Unidos y tras el éxito que ha despertado, me ha vuelto la gana de continuar.[163]

However, while working on *El cuento de nunca acabar*, Martín Gaite was also developing other projects which saw the light of day before *El cuento*, the most important being *Macanaz*, *Retahílas*, *Fragmentos de interior* and *El cuarto de atrás*.

Retahílas (1974)

In the final note of *Retahílas*, the author writes:

> Empecé a tomar apuntes para esta novela en junio de 1965, en un cuadernito que llamo, para mi gobierno, 'cuaderno-dragón' por un dibujo que me había hecho en la primera hoja un amigo que entonces solía decorar mis cuadernos. Terminé su redacción definitiva la tarde del 31 de diciembre de 1973, en mi casa de Madrid.[164]

The first note in *Cuadernos de todo* for *Retahílas* appears in *Cuaderno 3* and was written in Alzola in August 1967.[165] This text was used in the chapter 'E. Dos',[166] although the author had already started taking notes

---

[162] Martín Gaite writes about her 'encounter' with Virginia Woolf and her 'A Room of One's Own' in *Desde la ventana: Enfoque femenino de la literatura española* [1987] (Madrid: Espasa Calpe, 1992), p. 25.
[163] Alicia Ramos, 'Conversación con Carmen Martín Gaite', *Hispanic Journal*, 1 (1980), 117–24 (p. 124).
[164] Martín Gaite, *Retahílas*, p. 166.
[165] Martín Gaite, *Cuadernos*, p. 133.
[166] Martín Gaite, *Retahílas*, p. 59.

for the novel two years previously as quoted above. In November 1965, in *Cuaderno 3*, a note about a mysterious woman appears:

> Ya sé que existe esa mujer. Os lo digo. La he visto – la veo casi siempre que estoy aburrida y me quiero poner a escribir. No puedo dar detalles precisos de su rostro porque está formado de expresiones cogidas a retazos de varias mujeres. ... De pronto lo deja todo y se va a ver a la abuela.[167]

This novel is one of the few which maintains its title, theme and structure, although the dialogues that appear in some notes were changed to monologues in the novel. Notes for the novel appear scattered throughout the notebooks and are sometimes headed by the names of the characters, such as 'Eulalia'[168] and 'Para Germán'.[169] Others have headings that indicate themes in the book, such as 'Dos conversaciones tuve con ella sobre amor',[170] while others simply state 'Para *Retahílas*'.[171] Notes without a heading can be recognized through the names of the characters, or the settings. Martín Gaite does not write about the novel as such, or deal with its structure, or the use of dialogues or monologues: the notes are just put on paper in a form similar to that in the novel. Only in *Cuaderno 7* does she make notes on the novel's development and how to link the different chapters:

> G. Cinco (Armaduras de las familias. Puede acabar con consideraciones sobre lo pseudo hippie que enlaza con G. Seis. Ruina.) E. Seis (Envejecer ... al salir de la peluquería. Futuro de la casa. Enlazar el tema de la ruina con el de la ruina de unos determinados supuestos que dejan de valer como 'chepita en alto').[172]

Themes which can be found in other parts of the *Cuadernos*, such as solitude, liberated women or family relationships, find a place in the dialogue between the characters. At the same time, some of the books the author was reading at the time are mentioned in the conversation, for example *Dorian Gray* or *Les Liaisons dangereuses*.[173] In *Cuaderno 8*

---

[167] Martín Gaite, *Cuadernos*, p. 124.
[168] Martín Gaite, *Cuadernos*, p. 165.
[169] Martín Gaite, *Cuadernos*, p. 153.
[170] Martín Gaite, *Cuadernos*, p. 153.
[171] Martín Gaite, *Cuadernos*, p. 177.
[172] Martín Gaite, *Cuadernos*, p. 180.
[173] Martín Gaite, *Retahílas*, pp. 75, 107.

(1973–4) we find the final notes for *Retahílas*, dealing with the ideas of first love and the first years of marriage, which in turn link to a note taken for *El cuarto de atrás* in the same *cuaderno*.[174] After this the novel was published.

Fragmentos de interior (1976)

During the 1960s *Fragmentos de interior* was also being developed. Although at first Martín Gaite gave a different title to the project, calling it 'Bajo el mismo techo', the characters and settings of what was going to be the novel were distinguishable from the beginning. *Cuaderno 3*, page 99, contains part of the initial version of Chapter 1. Gloria is the first character to be 'introduced', together with the maid (whose name changes from Remedios here to Pura in the novel), and the difficult relationship between them is also presented. On page 121 of the same notebook, the first version of what will be part of Chapter 2 of the novel appears.

However, this novel was set aside for a few years and then taken up again in *Cuaderno 13*, in which Martín Gaite reads through the notes made in her first notebooks in order to continue with *El cuento de nunca acabar*. The theme of the difficult relations between the lady of the house and the maid is reworked, and then in *Cuaderno 15* a letter signed by D. and addressed to Agustina appears, as well as an extract of another. These notes were made in the Ateneo on 3 February 1976, and are headed 'Capítulo IV'.[175] Despite there being no more notes for this novel in the *Cuadernos*, and even though the idea for it first occurred in the 1960s, we do know from Emma Martinell Gifre that Martín Gaite wrote the whole novel in a very short time: 'Martín Gaite escribió la novela en tres meses, de enero a marzo de 1976. ... Sabemos que la novela fue fruto de una especie de reto, mantenido entre Carmen Martín Gaite y un amigo, Ignacio Álvarez Vara.'[176]

El cuarto de atrás (1978)

During the writing of *Retahílas* and *Fragmentos*, and the period of *Macanaz* and *Guadalhorce*, Martín Gaite was also working on the novel

---

[174] See Martín Gaite, *Cuadernos*, p. 98.
[175] Martín Gaite, *Cuadernos*, p. 364.
[176] Emma Martinell Gifre, '*Fragmentos de interior*', in *Carmen Martín Gaite*, ed. Alicia Redondo Goicoechea (Madrid: Ediciones del Orto, 2004), pp. 161–71 (p. 161).

which for many is her masterpiece, *El cuarto de atrás*. A number of different projects occurred to the author during the development of this novel, and when these projects became connected it resulted in a single piece of work which is itself a combination of different literary genres: an autobiographical novel, a historical novel and a fantastical narrative.[177]

The first entry, written in the spring of 1973 with the heading *El cuarto de atrás*, does not bear any relation to the final novel: 'Barcelona vista a través de mis intentos fallidos de asumirla',[178] apart from giving a name to the new project. The next entries (6–7 April 1973) link the project to the idea of memoirs: 'Revivir para *El cuarto de atrás* el momento de ebullición de mis versos, aquel invierno en Valladolid, mis luchas a solas y a ciegas, rechazando la burguesía'.[179] A few lines later, the author writes of 'el aire que me entraba allí en la plaza dando vueltas en la bicicleta'.[180] In October of the same year the idea becomes clearer: 'cuando hablas con pasión o amor siempre echas mano de materiales olvidados, almacenados en el cuarto de atrás',[181] bringing the theme of the past into the project. In fact 'Pesquisa personal',[182] which would develop into *La Reina de las Nieves*, started as a project to recover personal stories mixed with Spanish history, and women's social history in particular. Seen by Martín Gaite as a 'Novela, en cierta manera de ciencia ficción. Onírica. Melibea. Camino de perfección. Alicia a través del espejo. Un P. Klein para quien Salamanca es una familia "agitanada" a lo payo',[183] this project surfaced in several different books, including *El cuarto de atrás*, *Usos amorosos de la postguerra española* and the novel it eventually inspired, *La Reina de las Nieves*. Although 'Pesquisa personal' was indirectly dedicated to Lewis Carroll by means of a reference to *Through the Looking-Glass and What Alice Found There*,[184] it was, of course, in *El cuarto de atrás* that Carroll was formally acknowledged: 'Para Lewis Carroll, que todavía nos consuela de tanta cordura y nos acoge en su mundo al revés'.[185]

---

[177] Carmen Alemany Bay describes *El cuarto de atrás* as being 'A mitad de camino entre las memorias, la narrativa tradicional, el reportaje y la novela de misterio': *La novelística de Carmen Martín Gaite* (Salamanca: Ediciones de la Diputación, 1990), p. 152.
[178] Martín Gaite, *Cuadernos*, p. 177.
[179] Martín Gaite, *Cuadernos*, pp. 191–2.
[180] Martín Gaite, *Cuadernos*, p. 192.
[181] Martín Gaite, *Cuadernos*, p. 198.
[182] Martín Gaite, *Cuadernos*, p. 185.
[183] Martín Gaite, *Cuadernos*, p. 208.
[184] Martín Gaite, *Cuadernos*, p. 281.
[185] Martín Gaite, *El cuarto de atrás*, p. 7.

In *Cuaderno 11* the entries under the heading '*El cuarto de atrás*' refer to past and present, to changes in the way things are seen:

> La luz, el gas, el agua, eran como los humores del cuerpo. En la infancia y la juventud corren sin que los advirtamos, nos servimos de ellos a manos llenas pero no nos molestan ni nos duelen. En la edad madura hay que pagar por ellos, atenderlos.[186]

At the same time, thoughts about writing an autobiography slipped into Martín Gaite's notebooks: 'Tengo que escribir una autobiografía de mi relación con los temas y mi oscilación a la caza de ellos al tiempo que hablo de los temas mismos'.[187] Indeed, when confronted with writer's block, she commented earlier in the notebooks:

> 6 de agosto [1974] noche. Soledad. ... Podía hacer una narración en la dirección de ahondar en los antiguos 'cuéntame' de la Torci,[188] no comprendía que no me acordaba de qué libros leí primero que otros, de qué pensaba, de cómo me vestía, de cómo empleaba cotidianamente mi tiempo.[189]

On 23 January 1976 the author wrote in *Cuaderno 13*: 'Para la novela nueva *El cuarto de atrás*'.[190] Then in 1977 a new project appeared which was swallowed into *El cuarto*, 'Entrevista imaginaria'.[191] The idea of a stranger who would help her to live the dreams of romantic novels, like those written by Carmen de Icaza, took shape. The theme of romantic novels and their influence upon young women like her was also, of course, developed in *Usos amorosos de la postguerra espanola*, as well as in *Retahílas* (there are also comments on romantic novels and the influence of romantic films in the first notebooks). And during the last night of 1976, the author imagines the form her project on the 'Usos amorosos' could take:

---

[186] Martín Gaite, *Cuadernos*, p. 231.
[187] Martín Gaite, *Cuadernos*, p. 234.
[188] The idea of an interlocutor who encourages one to talk had already been developed in *Retahílas*: 'Basta con que un amigo te pida "cuéntame" para que salga todo de un tirón': Carmen Martín Gaite, *Retahílas*, afterword by Montserrat Escartín Gual [1974] (Barcelona: Destino, 2003), p. 74.
[189] Martín Gaite, *Cuadernos*, p. 214.
[190] Martín Gaite, *Cuadernos*, p. 309.
[191] Martín Gaite, *Cuadernos*, p. 312.

> un entrevistador venía y me preguntaba que cómo había pasado el año y lo que había pensado a lo largo de él y cómo era mi infancia y cuales mis lecturas y yo le hablaba de Franco y de su muerte y luego de mis recuerdos de películas infantiles, del Instituto, de los bailes.[192]

That interviewer, however, will appear in *El cuarto de atrás* as the mysterious visitor who helps the protagonist to remember and weave together her work and her life, while also referencing the other book she has been working on, *Usos amorosos de la postguerra española*, that would be published a few years later.

Cuaderno 17 is the most important with regard to the development of *El cuarto*. Starting in December 1976, the first note, entitled 'Las encuestas',[193] was followed by notes on books on memoirs and historical works about the Spanish Civil War. These were followed by one titled 'Para un cuento fantástico',[194] which relates to the 'conversations' the author had with Todorov's book, *Introduction a la Littérature fantastique* (1970). This chain of thoughts was foreshadowing what *El cuarto de atrás* was going to be. One note which shows Martín Gaite's excitement is interspersed with notes about narratives of the fantastic: '(Mira Juan, lo de "naturaleza muerta" no vas a verlo escrito como te esperabas. Te brindo y prometo una sorpresa que va a romper todos los moldes, palabra dada el 22 de diciembre del 76 en el Ateneo a las seis de la tarde)'.[195]

Although contemplating writing a novel of the fantastic, the author was still thinking about 'Pesquisa personal': 'Esto puede enlazar con el tema de *Pesquisa personal*, pero debo narrarlo en forma más simple y escalofriante a la vez. Menos introspección, menos claves para el lector de que estoy escribiendo una novela fantástica'.[196] As mentioned earlier, some of the ideas for 'Pesquisa personal' were taken up in *El cuarto* for her encounter with Todorov had given Martín Gaite much a clearer vision of what the novel should be about, reframing the science fictional aspects more as literature of the fantastic. Earlier in her career she had flirted with the idea of writing a novel of the fantastic, and certainly *El balneario* has some characteristics of this kind of narrative. But, as Martín Gaite observed, fear stopped her from going all the way. In the end she

---

[192] Martín Gaite, *Cuadernos*, p. 396.
[193] Martín Gaite, *Cuadernos*, p. 389.
[194] Martín Gaite, *Cuadernos*, p. 390.
[195] Martín Gaite, *Cuadernos*, p. 391.
[196] Martín Gaite, *Cuadernos*, p. 391.

needed nearly thirty years and experience as a published writer in order to be able to realize her first literary impulse and write a 'fantastic' novel, integrating her own life and experiences in her work. In this way she was able to combine life and literature with all the attendant consequences, producing a novel that would make her known throughout the world. Martín Gaite reflects in her notebooks:

> La llamada de lo fantástico la sentí por primera vez en 1949, en mis intentos fallidos del *Libro de la fiebre*. ... Ahondar en el estilo del *Balneario*, sería ahora que sé muchas más cosas y tengo mejor gusto y pulso más seguro, mi salida de los infiernos. Aquello me ha dado una identidad, dormida en mí, que estaba empezando a olvidar, a enterrar. Ahora desafiaré genialmente. Me tengo, al fin, que atrever. Con aparente ingenuidad y prudencia. Despistando. Se van a quedar fríos. Dinamita pura y – hasta ahora – no había disparado. Ya es hora.[197]

However, a few days after her encounter with Todorov, Martín Gaite seemed to have doubts again and returned to her safety net, *El cuento de nunca acabar*.[198] On 24 January 1977, she writes:

> Vuelvo a estar en blanco. Lo que me falta es el empuje para dejarme a la invención. ¿De dónde viene – cuando baja – ese entusiasmo, ese estímulo? ... Yo sé escribir e incluso he llegado a seleccionar ciertos principios para hacerlo que pueden servirle de norma a otro que no sabe. Pues ¿por qué me he aburrido de ponerme a hacerlo, si tengo temas y me saldría bien?[199]

Cuaderno 18 reveals the manuscript for the beginning of Chapter 1 of *El cuarto* and the dedication to Lewis Carroll, together with a few more notes for the novel and the observation: 'Para el final de *El cuarto de atrás*'.[200] Many of the ideas written in the *cuaderno* are used in the novel, even though some of the words were changed. Indeed, one very important difference is the dialogue between C. and her daughter at the end of the novel, especially the omission of one particular adjective. Whereas in the novel the daughter says: '¡Qué bien!, ¿no?, decías que no eras capaz de

---

[197] Martín Gaite, *Cuadernos*, pp. 391–2.
[198] Martín Gaite, *Cuadernos*, p. 394.
[199] Martín Gaite, *Cuadernos*, p. 408.
[200] Martín Gaite, *Cuadernos*, p. 427.

arrancar con nada estos días',[201] in the *Cuadernos* she wrote: '¡Qué bien! Cuánto me alegro. Decías que estabas deprimida, que no eras capaz de arrancar con nada'.[202] It is very significant that the word 'deprimida' is used in the *Cuadernos* in pages written for herself, but suppressed in the novel that was going to be made public. Martín Gaite's moments of despair are indicated throughout the notebooks, but with her autobiographical novel she must have felt the need to suppress a state of mind which could be taken out of context by the readers. *El cuarto de atrás* is the novel which most clearly presents the author as a fictional character and so, perhaps because of this, Martín Gaite took care in the published work not to be completely open with the reader. In her subsequent novels, written after the deaths of her parents and her daughter, she would 'hide' behind principal characters quite different from herself, even though they revealed some of the author's traits.

The ending of the novel also changed: 'Para el final. Veo desprenderse, entre las esterillas, el sombrero negro y los zapatos que llevaba en la mano el hombre de la playa'.[203] The object left behind by the man in black changed from a hat and the pair of shoes to the golden pillbox, an object which has a greater significance for the novel and for the notion of remembering which runs through it. Furthermore, the blue letter disappeared in the first version whereas in the novel C. finds it under the engraving of Luther and the Devil.[204]

Nubosidad variable (1992)

There are few entries for *Nubosidad variable* in *Cuadernos de todo*. The first link with the novel comes from some papers dating from 1981, which, as Calvi indicates in her introductory note to *Cuaderno 26*, refer to the homonym chapter 'Clave de sombra'.[205] The first note to be found referring to the title 'Para *Nubosidad variable*'[206] comes at the end of *Cuaderno 30*. Written in September 1983, this note seems to be a conversation between mother and daughter, although this is unclear: there are no names or situations that remind us of the novel. The second note appears in *Cuaderno 33* although it was written earlier, in June 1983:

---

[201] Martín Gaite, *El cuarto de atrás*, p. 206.
[202] Martín Gaite, *Cuadernos*, p. 429.
[203] Martín Gaite, *Cuadernos*, p. 431.
[204] Martín Gaite, *El cuarto de atrás*, p. 206.
[205] Martín Gaite, *Cuadernos*, p. 511.
[206] Martín Gaite, *Cuadernos*, p. 553.

> Ir a casa de la abuela Dolores el día de su santo equivalía a tener que reconocer: '¡Ya está aquí la semana santa!'. Y los esfuerzos para convocar a mis hijos a aquella casa ¿en qué iban a redundar? (Frente a mi vislumbre angustioso de tener que convidar a El Boalo.)[207]

This note starts to reflect some of the themes that appear in the novel, at the same time linking Martín Gaite's feelings when confronted by the same situations facing the fictional protagonist. Written in the first person and starting at the beginning of the note with the author's voice, Sofía (the fictional character) remembers family meetings and obligations and how the children are growing up and leaving the home. She thinks about her youth and reflects on the changes in society over the years.

In April 1984, in the same *Cuaderno 33* which she used again a year later, and after having been working on *La Reina de las Nieves*, the author admits to being bored with the novel and adds, 'me hace guiños *Nubosidad variable*'.[208] Following this comment there is a short note in which the protagonist of *Nubosidad variable* reflects on the time one spends looking after one's body, 'empaquetar el cuerpo para luego sacarlo embalsamado a pasear'.[209] This is followed in *Cuadernos de todo* by a version of Chapter I of *Nubosidad variable*. Here we can see that some details have changed, such as the cost of redecorating the bathroom going from the one million pesetas Martín Gaite thought it would cost in 1984, to three million in 1992. Sofía's husband's name also changes, from Gerardo to Eduardo, but there is no explanation for this. The last entry for *Nubosidad variable* is found amongst other notes from different notebooks and other scraps of papers in what Calvi titled 'Notas fugaces'. As the editor explains, this appears in a notebook dated 1989, although the original note came from an earlier *cuaderno*. It refers to the other protagonist of the novel, Mariana, and her relationship to two of the men in her life: 'Mi historia con Raimundo y con M. Reina entra en valor al cesar'.[210] After this, there is a note which explains: 'Este desahogo de Mariana – supongo que más bien breve – será un "bocadillo", antes de que Sofía empiece a contestar a su primera carta'.[211] This observation is one of the few sentences that indicates the direction of the novel.

---

[207] Martín Gaite, *Cuadernos*, p. 585.
[208] Martín Gaite, *Cuadernos*, p. 587.
[209] Martín Gaite, *Cuadernos*, p. 587.
[210] Martín Gaite, *Cuadernos*, p. 664.
[211] Martín Gaite, *Cuadernos*, p. 664.

La Reina de las Nieves (1994)

Although *La Reina de las Nieves* was published two years after *Nubosidad variable*, it was conceived much earlier than *Nubosidad*. As was mentioned above, *La Reina* started its life under the title 'Pesquisa personal', and what began as Martín Gaite's personal *pesquisa* ended up being the quest of the novel's protagonist to find answers to his life and his personal situation.

On 28 April 1974, Martín Gaite wrote ideas in her notebook regarding 'Pesquisa personal': 'Posible incorporación a *Pesquisa personal* de este tramo de vida cotidiana que supone el menester de ir las mujeres a peluquerías',[212] a theme that had already been used in 1970 in one of her short stories, 'Tarde de tedio'. Even though this idea is not incorporated in *La Reina de las Nieves*, what she did use were the notes she took the same day on the idea of drugs as stultification, although in her first note she suggests the concept of society, and coexistence with the partner, as anaesthesia 'empobreciendo sus respectivas neuronas'.[213] The protagonist of *La Reina de las Nieves* needs to escape from his addiction to drugs in order to be able to take charge of his life: 'Droga = anestesia. Quien la toma es porque no se atreve a soñar con posturas extremas ni a inventar nada'.[214] The next day, she enters in another notebook her thoughts on the solution to the protagonist's problems: 'Sólo lo personal, lo trabajosamente inquirido en soledad y esfuerzo le podría devolver la magia del amor y de la vida, por eso se afana en esa secreta pesquisa'.[215] And in the novel, we find the protagonist writing in his notebooks/diaries, in his father's study and in complete isolation, until the moment he finds again a reason to live.

Over the following months, the novel starts taking shape in the notebooks. In *Cuaderno 13* Martín Gaite writes what seems to be part of the first chapter with a dedication 'Para Lewis Carroll'.[216] In this first version of the chapter, the protagonist has already taken his pen to write his thoughts, in order to understand his present circumstances in relation to his past. Also included is the character of the girl who picks him up, in this case from the station instead of from the prison, taking him to what

---

[212] Martín Gaite, *Cuadernos*, p. 185.
[213] Martín Gaite, *Cuadernos*, p. 185.
[214] Martín Gaite, *Cuadernos*, p. 185.
[215] Martín Gaite, *Cuadernos*, p. 207.
[216] Martín Gaite, *Cuadernos*, p. 281. As was pointed out earlier, Lewis Carroll was transferred to *El cuarto de atrás*, published many years before *La Reina de la Nieves*.

seems to be a commune where they live. In the novel, that commune will remain in the protagonist's past (Leonardo refers to it when reading his old diaries) and he jumps out of the car before getting there. One aspect of this first version, which remains one of the most important indicators of the protagonist's need to write, is his memory loss: 'Si ella dice que he dormido en el suelo ya más veces, será verdad, yo no lo sé, no me acuerdo de nada, que me deje en paz'.[217] Also, the name of the girl changes from Carola[218] (the name that Martín Gaite gives to the woman who phones C. in *El cuarto*) to Carlota,[219] then to Ángela, her name in the novel.

On 21 September 1974, Hans Christian Andersen's story appears for the first time in relation to this project: '*Pesquisa personal* tiene que tener algo el tono de cuento prodigioso, de niño de Andersen a quien se le clava el cristalito en el ojo mientras Gerda lo llora sin que él se sepa llorado'.[220] Much later, on 15 May 1978, Martín Gaite wrote what seems to correspond to part of the second chapter of the novel, since it keeps most of the theme and the plot. The arrival of the protagonist at his parents' house after many years of absence is the beginning of this first version. In the novel we read: 'Hace más de siete años que no trasponía la puertecita de hierro que lleva a la fachada trasera, y cuando lo hice fue horrible, una sensación como de hundirse en el vacío.'[221] In the first version in the *Cuadernos*, apart from changing the amount of time the protagonist has been away from home, the feeling of anxiety is already present: 'Hacía tres años que no ponía los pies en aquella casa, y los primeros días fue horrible'.[222] Characters such as the black butler or the grandmother are already there in this first version. The room where he will spend the first days after his arrival, as well as some of the objects (his grandmother's bed, for example) or the chaos that prevails in the room (because of redecorating) are also present.

The idea of writing an erotic novel titled *Los objetos del deseo* had also been considered a few days earlier, '9 de mayo de 1978'.[223] Leonardo

---

[217] Martín Gaite, *Cuadernos*, p. 283.
[218] Martín Gaite, *Cuadernos*, p. 283.
[219] Martín Gaite, *Cuadernos*, p. 288.
[220] Martín Gaite, *Cuadernos*, p. 288.
[221] Carmen Martín Gaite, *La Reina de las Nieves* [1994] (Barcelona: Anagrama, 2002), p. 74.
[222] Martín Gaite, *Cuadernos*, p. 316.
[223] Martín Gaite, *Cuadernos*, p. 313. *Los objetos del deseo* was one of the many projects that Martín Gaite never finished. In this case, under the heading '(Posibles sugerencias para una novela erótica.)' (p. 313), we find three pages with what seems to be the beginning of a novel, and these notes are followed by others taken for *Pesquisa personal*.

took on some of the characteristics of the male protagonist of that project, for example writing his notebooks and the need for isolation in order to write: 'El cuaderno era negro, con tapas duras. La tinta corría bien por él, pero aquella chica enfrente de mí, intrigada, me estorbaba'.[224] The mauve flowers, which appear at the beginning of *Cuaderno 13*, reappear in this new project: 'Escribí debajo del texto que acababa de leer, "Flores malvas"'.[225] This recalls the words written by Martín Gaite four years earlier in the same notebook: 'Estas dos palabras, "flores moradas", las tengo apuntadas en el paquete de pitillos ya vacío que venía fumando esta tarde en el tren'.[226] Also, the train which appears in both notes is transformed into the car the girl uses to pick him up from prison. On 26 April 1980, more than two years after her last notes on *Pesquisa*, Martín Gaite picks up the novel again, incorporating the theme of the connection between past and present, and the reading of his father's letters. Even though she had written in her notebooks on 7 January 1977: 'Pero volver ahora sobre historias frías como *Pesquisa* me haría tener una fidelidad de oficio y forzada a algo que tal vez se haya muerto',[227] Martín Gaite seems to find it difficult to abandon this project completely.

She gives the novel its final title in 1980: 'Notas para *La Reina de las Nieves* (Según voy copiando lo que tengo el 3 de julio de 1980)',[228] giving the title to a number of notes on themes she wants to use in the work. This is followed by part of Chapter 4 which, in both draft form in the *cuaderno* and in the final novel, weaves Andersen's story into the narrative. In each case, as well as incorporating the characters from the fairy tale and transcripts of the story, the protagonist comments on his identification with both children in *The Snow Queen*.

Cuaderno 30 (February 1983–September 1983), picks up the novel again with a version of part of Chapter 1 and the incorporation of 'la señora de la Quinta Blanca'.[229] Although some details change in the

---

Even though Martín Gaite writes about an erotic novel, the reality is that it is not possible to find any eroticism in these notes. The male protagonist writes about his feelings towards a girl sitting opposite him in the train and with whom he had sex the night before, but words such as 'el sexo si no es literatura es pura mecánica' (p. 315) remind us of other words written by Martín Gaite in *Cuadernos* showing her own feelings: 'De verdad el sexo ha tenido siempre el mismo valor: un rato' (p. 115).

[224] Martín Gaite, *Cuadernos*, p. 314.
[225] Martín Gaite, *Cuadernos*, p. 314.
[226] Martín Gaite, *Cuadernos*, p. 282.
[227] Martín Gaite, *Cuadernos*, p. 402.
[228] Martín Gaite, *Cuadernos*, p. 321.
[229] Martín Gaite, *Cuadernos*, p. 548.

novel, such as the name of the old owner of the house or the number of years that the new owner has lived in it, the words are almost identical. The prison, in which the protagonist finds himself at the beginning of the novel, appears in the notebooks for the first time in August 1983. From these notes, which the author calls 'retahílas en plan chalado',[230] a series of ideas appear without apparent connection. Only a few of these found space in the novel, notably the lighthouse, the lighthouse keeper's friend, the different social classes, the lack of freedom money brings and the search for the mother. In the autumn of the same year, Martín Gaite writes about reading the second chapter to a friend. The last notes for the novel appear in *Cuaderno 34* and were made on 8 June 1984.

In the preliminary note to the novel, Martín Gaite explains how work on it was left aside at the beginning of 1985 when her daughter fell ill, and how she was not able to pick it up until much later:

> Esta novela, para la que vengo tomando notas desde 1975, ha tenido un proceso de elaboración lleno de peripecias. La empecé a escribir 'en serio' en 1979, por primavera, y trabajé en ella con asiduidad hasta finales de 1984, sobre todo en el otoño de ese año, durante una estancia larga en Chicago. ... Sin embargo, a partir de enero de 1985, y por razones que atañen a mi biografía personal, solamente de pensar en *La Reina de las Nieves* se me helaba el corazón, y enterré aquellos cuadernos bajo siete estadios de tierra, creyendo que jamás tendría ganas de resucitarlos.[231]

The author felt that this novel was so close to her daughter that, after her death in 1985, she found it impossible to continue writing it. There was a long period when her grief for the loss of her daughter did not allow her to concentrate. However, her long stay in the United States in the autumn of 1985, where she found herself completely alone and with few commitments, allowing her enough time to reflect, was a period when she regained the strength to resume her writing, although she did not publish another novel until the 1990s.

Cuenta pendiente: An Unfinished Project on Life-Writing

In considering Martín Gaite's notebooks as writing cure, one of the most interesting projects is her unfinished *Cuenta pendiente*, which was begun

---

[230] Martín Gaite, *Cuadernos*, p. 559.
[231] Martín Gaite, *La Reina de las Nieves*, p. 11.

as a response to the death of her parents in 1978: 'Mis padres estaban, de fondo, en todo lo que hacía, aunque no lo viera. ¿Cuándo se empiezan a deteriorar las defensas, a asaltarte los fantasmas que has logrado mantener a raya?'.[232] This note was written at the end of *Cuaderno 18*.

On 19 November 1979 (*Cuaderno 22*), under the heading *Cuenta pendiente*, she states with reference to a dream: 'tenía que ver como todos los de este año, con la muerte de mis padres, pero ellos no salían'.[233] The papers and documents are the protagonists of the dream, documents that she, already dead herself in the dream, has to find and collect so that others would be able to 'contar como había sucedido'.[234] A few months after her parents' death, in 'Domingo de Resurrección, 6 de abril',[235] she describes her dreams and memories of her parents in diary form over more than four pages:

> Ya hace más de un año que murieron mis padres, los dos en otoño de 1978 con mes y pico de diferencia, y desde entonces no sólo se me aparecen muchas veces en sueños y me dicen cosas que no entiendo o se me olvidan al despertar, sino que he empezado a padecer durante el día un fenómeno que se va agudizando y que interpreto como una especie de respuesta o complemento a esas pláticas nocturnas: la tendencia a hablar sola.[236]

In these lines, Martín Gaite gives details of her parents, their habits, which they kept most of their lives, the objects which were important in their world, and even the poems written by her father.[237] She even starts thinking about this project as a possible novel: 'porque tal vez el muchacho de mis sueños de anteayer (posible iniciación de *Cuenta pendiente*) sea una transformación'.[238] Although she seems to abandon the idea of the novel, her dreams of her parents still fill the pages of her notebooks. There is, for example, mention of a dream she had in New York on 6 October 1980 in *Cuaderno 25* or the one she has in Madrid on 14 July 1981 in *Cuaderno 27*; another dream she had in New York which featured her mother was published as 'De su ventana a la mía'.[239]

---

[232] Martín Gaite, *Cuadernos*, p. 432.
[233] Martín Gaite, *Cuadernos*, p. 467.
[234] Martín Gaite, *Cuadernos*, p. 467.
[235] Martín Gaite, *Cuadernos*, p. 470.
[236] Martín Gaite, *Cuadernos*, p. 470.
[237] Martín Gaite, *Cuadernos*, p. 473.
[238] Martín Gaite, *Cuadernos*, p. 479.
[239] Carmen Martín Gaite, 'De su ventana a la mía', in *Madres e hijas*, ed. Laura

In the United States Martín Gaite also reflects on the diaries written by her father,[240] which presumably connects with her dream about the papers people leave behind after death.

At the end of 1982, during another trip to America, Martín Gaite resumed the project once more: 'Partir del entorno (de la soledad que destila) para que cada objeto de los que ves o paso de los que das provoque una asociación de ideas no sólo hacia el pasado sino hacia el futuro'.[241] This idea does seem, in fact, very close to the function that remembering fulfills for many of the characters of her 1990s novels. She will use her mother as the interlocutor in her project: 'A mamá: a ti te lo tengo que dedicar lo de *Cuenta pendiente*, a ti te lo digo. ... Buscar por ahí, hablarte de mis apuntes. Necesito que estés tú oyendo, que sea para ti, si no, no se engrasa el engranaje' [26 June 1983].[242] Again in 1983 she dreamt of her father during another one of her stays in the United States (*Cuaderno 32*) and, in April 1984, nearly a year after promising to dedicate the book to her mother, she was still making notes for the project: 'Meterme con *Cuenta pendiente*, tal vez en plan diario, donde se fueran comentando y fechando los extractos de cuaderno donde aparecen notas y apuntes sobre este tema'.[243]

In May 1984, Martín Gaite made notes on the illness and death of her father, and the need to remember every detail in order to relive those memories. She also remembers their final conversation, and recalls images of America which she links to her mother, with whom she talked about the country in an idealized way. Martín Gaite describes the dreams she had after visiting America, and consequently talks of different aspects of the project: 'En este trabajo hay dos vías: la de la emoción y la del cerebro (ahora que ya está todo distante y que no duele, que solamente es oquedad, la puedo llenar con mis angustias de entonces)'.[244] However, the project was completely abandoned after her daughter's death in 1985, although the seed that she planted in these notes bore fruit in Martín Gaite's later novels, in which the protagonists use their notebooks to remember the past, with a view, as she stated in one of her notes, to look towards the future.

Freixas (Barcelona: Anagrama, 1996), pp. 39–44.
  [240] Martín Gaite, *Cuadernos*, p. 503.
  [241] Martín Gaite, *Cuadernos*, p. 541.
  [242] Martín Gaite, *Cuadernos*, p. 584.
  [243] Martín Gaite, *Cuadernos*, p. 586.
  [244] Martín Gaite, *Cuadernos*, p. 601.

The American Notebooks

The time spent in the United States of America as an invited writer, giving talks as well as teaching in different universities and colleges, was very important for Martín Gaite. During these periods she made very methodical notes on her stays. *Cuadernos de todo* contains a total of six 'American notebooks' which cover autumn 1980 (*Cuadernos 25* and *26*); January 1982 (*Cuaderno 28*); winter 1982 (*Cuaderno 29*); winter 1983 (*Cuaderno 32*) and August-September 1985 (*Cuaderno 35*), also known as 'El otoño de Poughkeepsie'.[245] In addition, there is *Visión de Nueva York* (2005), a facsimile edition of a ninety-two-page notebook of collages which covers the period 17 September 1980 to 24 January 1981, some of which had previously been published (in black and white) in *Cuadernos de todo* and, before that, in *From Fiction to Metafiction*. This particular notebook is, in effect, a scrapbook she composed during her first long stay in New York and which started as a 'cuaderno de recortes de prensa, esmaltado de vez en cuando con algún comentario'.[246] It ended up as a book of collages in which she pasted show tickets, hotel bills, photos, theatre programmes and so on.

The *cuadernos americanos* are also the ones which follow a structure more closely akin to that of diary-writing, as in many of them Martín Gaite writes almost daily and notes her experiences of the day. She seems to have more time to reflect on her days as the time spent in the United States gave her the opportunity for the solitude she had missed in Madrid. It is interesting to note that Martín Gaite's first stay in America happened after her parents' death and the last after that of her daughter. This makes these American sojourns particularly important in the development of the notebooks as somewhere for her to think about her life.

In these notebooks, Martín Gaite relates her journeys through the country, her encounters with different people (critics, lecturers, students, other writers and friends),[247] the food she eats and the parties she goes to,[248] the films she watches and the exhibitions she visits, the books she is most impressed with and her personal feelings which go from enthusiasm,

---

[245] Martín Gaite, *Cuadernos*, p. 611.
[246] Carmen Martín Gaite, *Visión de Nueva York* (Madrid: Siruela/Círculo de Lectores, 2005), [p. 21]. The pages of the collages are not numbered, so the logical number of each page is indicated in square brackets.
[247] For example, Martín Gaite, *Cuadernos*, pp. 499, 504, 540, 574, 578.
[248] For example, Martín Gaite, *Cuadernos*, pp. 504, 514.

'¡I love NY!',[249] to real sadness: 'Noto, de repente, la despedida inminente desplomándose sobre mí'.[250] The period when she travels coincides with the presidential elections of 1980 and 1984,[251] the Iran–Iraq War and John Lennon's murder.[252] Shopping in the streets of New York fascinates her and she even includes details of what she buys and the clothes she wears to attend different talks, lectures or presentations, such as for the talk at Wellesley College:

> Viene a recogerme Elena Gascón Vera. Paseo con ella por el Boston viejo; compras en el sótano barato (una combinación rosa Valladolid y un jersey de rayas malva, gris y marrón). ... Luego conferencia sobre la aparición de la mentira. Llevaba la falda de *pied-de-poule* larga y el jersey de esta tarde.[253]

She compares images of the United States to the pictures of Edward Hopper,[254] an artist who will appear in many of her notebook pages: 'Esa que va a meterse a un piso prestado y a sacarle calor a esos objetos, a esa llave, a esa cama donde no dormirá, soy yo la desarra, una mujer de Hopper'.[255] For Martín Gaite this is the artist who best represents American life: 'Sí, New York (Hopper lo supo ver mejor que nadie) es una mezcla de agobio y libertad'.[256] In *Visión de Nueva York* she makes a collage in homage to him, showing her admiration after visiting a Hopper exhibition: 'Hago este collage el 28 de septiembre, early Sunday morning;

---

[249] Martín Gaite, *Cuadernos*, p. 574.
[250] Martín Gaite, *Cuadernos*, p. 542.
[251] Martín Gaite, *Cuadernos*, pp. 505, 622.
[252] In the preface to *From Fiction to Metafiction*, Servodidio and Welles discuss the author's impressions of events such as Lennon's death or the presidential elections during her stay in New York: 'Martín Gaite viewed these slices of "American life" at close range and even joined the throngs of Lennon mourners in Central Park as they sang the litany "Let it be, let it be"' (p. 11). José Luis Borau also writes about this episode, when he accompanied the author outside Lennon's apartment: see 'Al día siguiente', *Turia: Revista Cultural*, 83 (2007), 249–60.
[253] Martín Gaite, *Cuadernos*, p. 505.
[254] Other Spanish writers have made the same comparison, presenting Edward Hopper as the painter who best reflects New York. Antonio Muñoz Molina, in his book *Ventanas de Manhattan* (Barcelona: Seix Barral, 2004), states that Hopper represents 'la realidad de New York retratada' (p. 56). Talking about the Village in New York, Elvira Lindo mentions: 'Saint Mark's Place, una calle tan ligada a las canciones de Lou Reed como a los cuadros de Edward Hopper': 'Nueva York un amor correspondido', in *I love NY: Diez autores en busca de una ciudad*, ed. Antonio Gala (Madrid: Planeta, 2002), pp. 267–97 (p. 294).
[255] Martín Gaite, *Cuadernos*, p. 532.
[256] Martín Gaite, *Cuadernos*, p. 495.

la exposición la vi ayer sábado con Manolo Arroyo y es como para morirse'.[257] Some years later she gave a talk based on one of Hopper's paintings, *Hotel Room*, at the Museum Thyssen-Bornemisza in Madrid, on 14 December 1996.[258]

In most cases, the notebooks present moments of enthusiasm for the people Martín Gaite meets. Her work is being valued and she feels comfortable amongst Americans: 'No me querría ir nunca de New York. Estoy descubriendo la vida, de verdad'.[259] She feels full of optimism: '¡Me gusta tanto estar aquí, veo el porvenir como algo tan alegre!'[260] There is a contrast between the pages written in America, where she finds herself welcomed, and the city she lives in, Madrid: 'Lo de New York es, creo, una cuestión de luz. ... Madrid es que es muy feo, no espabila'.[261] Furthermore, the freedom that solitude gives her in New York also serves to contrast with her life in Madrid, which is full of commitments that do not allow her to work. In fact, a few months before she travelled to New York she wrote: 'Tal vez es que esta temporada Madrid me sienta mal, la casa con su continuo telefonear, generalmente asuntos para Marta y Carlos o recados aburridísimos para mí; tal vez para recobrar el gusto por la libertad necesitaría estar completamente sola'.[262] She found that solitude in her New York apartment.

In *Cuaderno 25*, the first notebook from her time in America, she writes during a long stay in New York in the autumn of 1980. From there she made trips to other cities, such as New Haven, Philadelphia, Maryland, Cleveland, Boston, New Jersey, Oberlin (Ohio) and Mount Desert Rock. After leaving New York, she travelled through Houston, Los Angeles and San Francisco, before ending up at José Luis Borau's house in Santa Mónica (13 January 1981), where she admits to experiencing one of the happiest moments of her life: 'La felicidad, lo más parecido a la felicidad que he probado hace muchos años'.[263]

Most of the entries in this notebook are dated, showing that she was writing every few days at the beginning, and daily between 25 October

---

[257] Martín Gaite, *Visión de Nueva York*, [pp. 32–3].
[258] Martín Gaite, 'El punto de vista, Edward Hopper: *Habitación de hotel*', *Conferencia impartida el día 14 de diciembre de 1996 en el Museo Thyssen-Bornemisza de Madrid* (Madrid: Museo Fundación, Colección Thyssen-Bornemisza, 1997).
[259] Martín Gaite, *Cuadernos*, p. 500.
[260] Martín Gaite, *Cuadernos*, p. 580.
[261] Martín Gaite, *Cuadernos*, p. 505.
[262] Martín Gaite, *Cuadernos*, p. 478.
[263] Martín Gaite, *Cuadernos*, p. 509.

and 3 November. Many of the notes simulate a telegram written so as not to forget the moments she is experiencing:

> *1 de noviembre*. Ingredientes para la paella con Illia y Fernando. Incidente en el supermercado. Excursión a Vermillón junto al lago Eire. Día gris y medio lluvioso.
> El flea market. Vuelta al refugio de Fernando. Illia y yo en el sofá, contándonos cosas mientras que él prepara la paella. Paella divina. Baile con gente disfrazada en la casa española, chimenea encendida.[264]

Martín Gaite encourages herself with regard to her work and the need to take advantage of the periods of solitude which allow her to work better. America becomes the place where dedication to her writing will be her primary concern: 'Es un tiempo precioso este de América. Acordarme de las condiciones tan adversas en que escribí *Entre visillos*, de las ganas que tenía de que dieran las ocho para subirme a aquella buhardilla'.[265] Without family responsibilities, she can have periods of complete concentration on writing. And she has Virginia Woolf and her *A Room of One's Own* (1929) in mind: 'Es mi amiga ahora, desde el verano'.[266] In fact, the first contact with Virginia Woolf's essay came in the United States, as Martín Gaite noted in her book on Spanish women's writing, *Desde la ventana*: 'Recuerdo muy bien el primer texto que despertó mi curiosidad con relación a este asunto y me hizo reflexionar sobre él, fue el ensayo de Virginia Woolf, A room of one's own (Una habitación propia), que leí durante mi primera estancia en Nueva York, en el otoño de 1980'.[267]

Visión de Nueva York was composed in parallel to *Cuaderno 25*, and shows a new side of Martín Gaite as a multifaceted artist. As her friend Ignacio Álvarez Vara comments: 'La afición de dibujar le venía a Calila de siempre. Entre sus viejos cuadernos rescatados, los había de dibujo y salvados de su mano.'[268] But this collage notebook is a particular example of Martín Gaite's love for other kinds of artistic manifestation, given her need to use image more than words in a city like New York: 'aquí me

---

[264] Martín Gaite, *Cuadernos*, p. 507.
[265] Martín Gaite, *Cuadernos*, p. 496.
[266] Martín Gaite, *Cuadernos*, p. 496.
[267] Martín Gaite, *Desde la ventana*, p. 25.
[268] Ignacio Álvarez Vara, 'CMG con NYC de fondo', in Martín Gaite, *Visión de Nueva York*, pp. 125–30 (p. 125).

gustaría ser más un pintor o un fotógrafo que un escritor.'[269] Most of the collages were created during her stay in New York, with the final fifteen produced on her way to José Luis Borau's house in California where she ended her stay.

Many pages reveal a connection between the collages and Martín Gaite's notes in *Cuaderno 25*, even though the images in *Visión de Nueva York* make the reader more alive to her experiences in the United States. *Visión* started with written pages in diary style, integrating some cuttings from newspapers. The first entry covers four pages of the notebook and relates how she decided to start this scrapbook after finding pictures, in two different newspapers, of the two men who 'discovered' America for her. The first was her friend Nacho (Ignacio Álvarez Vara), who encouraged her to visit New York:

> Cuando mi amigo Nacho, allá por el año 74, quería ser periodista, me hablaba mucho de América y me decía que New York se parecía un poco a la Gran Vía de Madrid, y que era una ciudad que estaba seguro de que a mí me podría gustar mucho.[270]

And then Edward Hopper, the artist who clearly best represents her image of New York. In these initial pages she comments on the purpose of this notebook: 'Como homenaje a Hopper, y en recuerdo de Nacho, he decidido, pues, empezar este cuaderno de recortes de prensa, esmaltado de vez en cuando con algún comentario'.[271] Even though newspaper articles and her own writing cover most of the opening pages of the notebook, slowly images start taking over from words and the final New York collages are solely images of newspaper cuttings, bills, cinema and theatre tickets, and photographs.

Cuaderno 25 showed that Martín Gaite was witness to some important events and news reported in American newspapers during her stay, and in *Visión de Nueva York* she composed collages which reflected some of those events, such as John Lennon's murder[272] and the Iran–Iraq War.[273] She followed the Carter–Reagan election,[274] watched their debate[275] and

---

[269] Gazarian Gautier, p. 32.
[270] Martín Gaite, *Visión de Nueva York*, [p. 19].
[271] Martín Gaite, *Visión de Nueva York*, [p. 21].
[272] Martín Gaite, *Visión de Nueva York*, [pp. 81–2].
[273] Martín Gaite, *Visión de Nueva York*, [p. 31].
[274] Martín Gaite, *Visión de Nueva York*, [p. 36].
[275] Martín Gaite, *Visión de Nueva York*, [p. 55].

commented on the election of Ronald Reagan: '¡Buena se nos viene encima! Se salió con la suya el Ronnie'.[276] Just as in other notebooks, Martín Gaite mentions the events organized in her honour, pasting in invitations to parties and the posters for some of her talks. In her spare time she enjoyed going to the theatre, the cinema, nightclubs, the ballet and classical concerts and this is also a major part of the collages, featuring the tickets she used, the programmes for, or the reviews of, the shows she went to. There are reminders of the jazz clubs, such as The West End, with a collage in honour of Alberta Hunter,[277] of visits to churches, such as the Cathedral of St John the Divine to see a concert by Paul Winter & The Winter Consort,[278] or St Paul's Chapel at Columbia University, where she attended an organ concert.[279] Here she comments on all the opportunities New York presents her with: 'Lo quiero todo. Es lo malo de New York, que lo quiere uno todo y que continuamente te salen al paso tentaciones inesperadas. Y yo no sé decir que no a ninguna, y ando de acá para allá, a merced de mis pasos, ¡tan feliz!'[280]

There are images of Edward Hopper's exhibition at the Whitney Museum on 27 September 1980[281] and the visit to the Cornell Thomas Traherne exhibition at the Museum of Modern Art, about which she comments: 'No voy a atreverme a hacer "collage" con un "collagista"'.[282] Both give an idea of her taste in art. Authors such as Virginia Woolf also have a place in the collages with three pages dedicated to the writer and *A Room of One's Own*. As Martín Gaite states in the collage, she read this essay during her stay in America: 'Ahora ... he comprado *A room of one's own*, que he terminado de leer este fin de semana en New Haven y que me congracia con la Woolf ya definitivamente'.[283] There is a drawing of the cover of the book, done by Martín Gaite, on one corner of the collage. This was followed by another collage titled 'HOMENAJE A VIRGINIA WOOLF', which shows images of women, old and young, with the words 'Broadway because I want to be alone'. Martín Gaite also wrote a note which reads: 'Women never have an [sic] half hour that they can call

---

[276] Martín Gaite, *Visión de Nueva York*, [p. 62].
[277] Martín Gaite, *Visión de Nueva York*, [p. 79].
[278] Martín Gaite, *Visión de Nueva York*, [p. 88].
[279] Martín Gaite, *Visión de Nueva York*, [p. 41].
[280] Martín Gaite, *Visión de Nueva York*, [p. 41].
[281] Martín Gaite, *Visión de Nueva York*, [pp. 32–3].
[282] Martín Gaite, *Visión de Nueva York*, [pp. 77–8].
[283] Martín Gaite, *Visión de Nueva York*, [p. 27].

their own' and 'no es oro todo lo que reluce'.[284] Another author admired by Martín Gaite whom she met in New York was Tzvetan Todorov, who gave a talk at Columbia University on 22 November 1980: 'He conocido a Todorov, y me parece, casi seguro, que era el hombre del sombrero negro'.[285]

The people and sights Martín Gaite encounters in the streets are also important. She tends to portray types she would have not been familiar with in Spain, like the steel-drum musician she sees on Fifth Avenue, and whose photograph appears in one of the newspapers she reads:

> El otro día cuando compré con Philip en la 5a Avenida los periódicos que motivaron mi idea de hacer este cuaderno, justo al salir de la librería Rizzoli, vimos a este señor que ahora recorto y pego aquí. Su instrumento es un tambor de acero ... O SEA QUE HE VISTO A ESE SEÑOR, mira por donde.[286]

Her lectures and talks are also included in these collages, with a poster advertising her lecture at Barnard College on 20 October 1980 titled 'El cuento de nunca acabar',[287] and which was used on the cover of *Visión de Nueva York*. This type of collage, with pictures of Martín Gaite herself pasted onto them, are pieces of visual evidence that appear to make her stay in New York much more real. She uses images of herself in other collages, such as the one on Mount Desert Rock, where she believes to have found 'La isla de Bergai',[288] including a photograph of her taken on the 'island'. Bergai was an island invented by the author and her best friend from high school and used as a fantasy 'refuge' from their everyday lives and is, of course, an important feature of the early part of *El cuarto de atrás*. There is also a photo of her by the Statue of Liberty, posing with her daughter Marta. In addition, there are various images of the Statue of Liberty and the notation: 'La libertad siempre da algo de miedo cuando se ve de cerca, ¿no lo sabías?'[289] Martín Gaite also draws herself on some occasions, as in the collage where she writes: 'Ya peinando canas, puso proa a Hollywood, se fue a vivir con un director de cine y (¡lo que es más

---

[284] Martín Gaite, *Visión de Nueva York*, [p. 29].
[285] Martín Gaite, *Visión de Nueva York*, [p. 73].
[286] Martín Gaite, *Visión de Nueva York*, [p. 25].
[287] Martín Gaite, *Visión de Nueva York*, [p. 51].
[288] Martín Gaite, *Visión de Nueva York*, [p. 60].
[289] Martín Gaite, *Visión de Nueva York*, [p. 86].

desfachatez!) inauguró el año 1981 ¡estrenando unos vaqueros!'[290] – a sentence that makes her a character of her own story.

As well as portraying herself as a tourist or a character in a narrative, Martín Gaite's work as a writer is also suggested in the collages, with images of typewriters and fountain pens and comments on the amount of work involved or the money she has been offered for her work.[291] In other collages she warns herself: 'Calila, ándate con ojo, que mucho recortar y pegar, mucho andar callejeando y mucho ir a celebrar la fiesta de la Hispanidad al consulado Español, pero ya llevas más de un mes en New York y con *El cuento de nunca acabar* no te metes en serio.' Yet she writes in the same collage: 'no hagas caso, honey. Tú vive, let it be, déjate al vaivén de los días ...'[292] In fact, she suggests that her present experiences will help her creativity later on:

> La cosecha vendrá luego. Cuando ya no tenga que madrugar y tomarme un NoDoz para llegar despejada a mi clase en Milkbank Hall. Cuando me siente en otro lugar, lejos, a la luz de una lámpara a recordarlo. Sacaré entonces mis cuadernos de todo y ... words will come.[293]

In this quotation, it is also possible to see the importance of her 'diaries' as somewhere to note the present to be used in the future, in other words the use of the diary as a memory aid. In the same way that travel writers often use photographs as well as diaries to remind themselves of the places they have visited and the people they met, Martín Gaite uses her collages filled with photographs, newspaper cuttings, tickets and bills to augment her comments and reflections of her life in America.

Martín Gaite's apartment in New York is also a protagonist in the collages. She uses photos of the apartment and the mess she sometimes finds, with letters and accumulated work on the desk[294] or on the floor.[295] Together with phone calls, these letters keep her in contact with Spain and her family, especially her daughter, and into some collages she pastes images of telephones, and envelopes she has received from her home country. There is, as has been noted, an acknowledged contrast between

---

[290] Martín Gaite, *Visión de Nueva York*, [p. 95].
[291] Martín Gaite, *Visión de Nueva York*, [p. 38].
[292] Martín Gaite, *Visión de Nueva York*, [p. 44].
[293] Martín Gaite, *Visión de Nueva York*, [p. 46].
[294] Martín Gaite, *Visión de Nueva York*, [p. 68].
[295] Martín Gaite, *Visión de Nueva York*, [p. 61].

her life in the United States and her life in Spain, and one collage which expresses these feelings was produced on Christmas Day, when she writes:

> ¿Dónde están aquellas de la Calle Mayor? ¿Qué diría la tía Carmen si levantara la cabeza y viera que he pasado el día sola en mi apartamento de la calle 119, que no he probado bocado porque tenía la nevera vacía y que no echaba de menos nada ni a nadie? MANHATTAN estaba desierto y me gustaba sentirme en una ciudad extraña, olvidada de todos, bloqueada por la nieve. Saboreando la despedida.[296]

As mentioned earlier, these moments of complete solitude, which she cannot enjoy in Spain, are a very special part of her stay in America. Yet she can see the negative side of the isolation that people suffer in New York, with collages portraying women alone peering through windows, or the collage in homage to Greta Garbo, where she pastes extracts about her solitary and difficult life which she found in the *New York Post* after having had a dream in which Garbo appeared: '¡Qué cosas!'[297]

Yet, with regard to her own writing, she continued to be mindful of the project on *El cuento de nunca acabar*. Even so, she was not working on a novel at that moment and the kind of work she was engaged in, giving talks and classes, was satisfying enough for her:

> Acordarme mucho del tiempo mucho más sincopado que voy a tener en Madrid para escribir. ... Lo importante es sacarle placer y tranquilidad a cada hora. Y así, sólo así, de repente un día me pondré con entusiasmo a la máquina, espontáneamente, cuando menos lo decida.[298]

In fact it was not until 1982, during her stay in Charlottesville, that Martín Gaite decided to conclude her *Neverending tale*. She explains in the note to the second edition how her time in America allowed her to finish this project: 'El tiempo no oprimía, pasaba de puntillas por encima de mí, y algunos días, cuando llegaban las ocho de la tarde, me daba cuenta de que me había olvidado de comer. ... Casi nunca sonaba el teléfono'.[299]

Cuaderno 28 (January 1982), which contains only six pages, constitutes

---

[296] Martín Gaite, *Visión de Nueva York*, [p. 90].
[297] Martín Gaite, *Visión de Nueva York*, [p. 30].
[298] Martín Gaite, *Cuadernos*, p. 497.
[299] Martín Gaite, *El cuento de nunca acabar*, p. 13.

what Martín Gaite termed 'una larga "retahíla" neoyorkina'.[300] It is a notebook in which there are reflections on life, with the past and the present merging in her thoughts. She dwells on her youth, on her projects and on the present day. And in this 'retahíla neoyorkina' she begins to recount a chain of images which simulate a dream. This kind of narration continues for nearly four pages and she explains this succession of rapid thoughts and images as 'dejar venir la palabra, todo consiste en eso'.[301]

Written during her stay in Charlottesville in the autumn of 1982, *Cuaderno 29* is again full of notes on her journeys and the talks she gives while there. She writes as if making notes for a travelogue.[302] Indeed, the way she narrates her stay and her trips out of the city is similar to travel writing, with descriptions of the weather, the people she encountered, the parties she attended, and the scenery seen from the train or the car:

> Viaje de vuelta de Mount Desert. Penobscot river cruzado en Bucksport por un alto puente metálico, pintado de verde y seguido por su margen derecha hasta Belfast pasando por Searsport. Luego desde Camden se descubre Penobscot Bay, a las diez, con el sol queriendo salir entre nubes, ¡Dios, qué abanico de belleza, con toda la hondura de panorama marino y las rachas de luz sobre el agua alborotada y gris, entre los árboles amarillos de la costa, islas con pinos a lo lejos![303]

This detailed account of what she sees demonstrates her enthusiasm for observing everything around her, in a country where things seem new and exciting.

Cuaderno 32 describes a stay in New York and journeys to Vassar College, Charlottesville and Philadelphia. It is during this trip that *El cuarto de atrás* was published in English, and the launch of *The Back Room* makes the author think about the way she writes: 'Toda mi literatura oscila entre lo excepcional soñado desde lo cotidiano y al revés. Porque lo excepcional cuando se tiene da miedo y se quiere convertir en rutina, no se aguanta'.[304]

Critics and academics take advantage of her presence to give her their articles on her work for her to read: 'Día 26 [octubre, 1980]. Domingo. ...

---

[300] Martín Gaite, *Cuadernos*, pp. 531–4.
[301] Martín Gaite, *Cuadernos*, p. 534.
[302] Martín Gaite, *Cuadernos*, p. 539.
[303] Martín Gaite, *Cuadernos*, pp. 507–8.
[304] Martín Gaite, *Cuadernos*, p. 572.

Comiendo en el restorán vienés y leyendo el maravilloso prólogo inglés al libro de Joan';[305] 'Estaba muy contenta con el artículo que me dio ayer Linda Levine sobre *El cuarto de atrás*'.[306] Martín Gaite's association with her literary critics of the time was very important to her, and with some of them she had more than just a professional relationship: '¡Qué gusto poder albergar conmigo aquí a Joan! Hemos comido cosas ricas. Hemos hablado sin parar, se ha echado la siesta, nos hemos arreglado como para la fiesta de la Cenicienta'.[307] It is clear that Martín Gaite found in her critics the company she needed in America: 'Vino Marie-Lise Gazarian, quiere promocionarme. Se estuvo tres horas. Llama Philip. Llama Linda. Llama Flora. Llama Marcia. Llama Roberto'.[308] And, of course, her critics were able to get from her the input they needed to publish their articles and promote her work in America.

Martín Gaite's dreams are an important part of her writing at that time, and occasionally these dreams are linked to her times in America: 'Las palabras de todos los desheredados del mundo, con cedilla, … barridas como hojas instantáneas por las calles de New York dan lugar a mi sueño'.[309] Her parents are often present in these dreams, with her father appearing as an actor who has to perform his last role in a play, a dream she writes about on 6 October 1980. Elsewhere, he is the owner of a hotel where she is staying, as she notes on 6 November 1983. Martín Gaite's mother is also present in her thoughts. Visiting a friend in hospital reminds her of the days just before her mother's death. The fact of being in America also makes her think of her mother, as she was the first to encourage her to accept the invitation to participate in a conference at Yale in 1978: 'Ver New Haven desde la autopista lluviosa ya anocheciendo es una visión de la ciudad tan diferente de la que tenía hace dos años, cuando mamá aún vivía y acariciaba como algo irreal la idea de venir al congreso de Yale'.[310]

These images merge with other memories: sometimes the diaries that she is writing blend with the diaries her father used to write: 'para mi

---

[305] Martín Gaite, *Cuadernos*, p. 504. The book she refers to, published a few years later, is Joan Lipman Brown's *Secrets From the Back Room: The Fiction of Carmen Martín Gaite* (Valencia: University of Mississippi, 1987).

[306] Martín Gaite, *Cuadernos*, p. 499; Linda Levine, 'Carmen Martín Gaite's *El cuarto de atrás*: A Portrait of the Artist as Woman', in Servodidio and Welles, pp. 161–72.

[307] Martín Gaite, *Cuadernos*, p. 504.

[308] Martín Gaite, *Cuadernos*, p. 513.

[309] Martín Gaite, *Cuadernos*, p. 569.

[310] Martín Gaite, *Cuadernos*, p. 508.

padre, escribir algo todos los días … se había convertido en una obligación … una tarea no sólo algo enojosa sino también inútil'.[311] Martín Gaite, on the other hand, wants to write a much freer kind of diary: 'Gracias a que no me he propuesto escribir un diario, puedo volver a este cuaderno de forma gratuita y placentera, sin el agobio de no haber anotado a su tiempo tal cosa o la otra'.[312] She reflects on the purpose and content of diaries: 'Los diarios se escriben siempre para alguien. Se da importancia a lo cotidiano'.[313] And about her collage-diary, *Visión de Nueva York*, she writes: 'Yo debo procurar que el mío de collages sea visualmente divertido'.[314] But a diary is not just for enjoyment, it should be understandable to others: 'Anotar en mogollón, los diarios no valen. Cuando yo me muera, ¿entenderá mi hija lo que dice aquí?, ¿lo sabrá poner en orden? No. Lo tengo que poner en orden yo. Orden frente al caos … "¿Qué pensó aquella noche que garrapateaba?", dirá la Torci pero no entenderá mi miedo'.[315] Later, after her daughter's death, these thoughts will be linked with her daughter's diaries, those which she never wrote. Indeed, during her stay at Vassar College, Martín Gaite used a notebook which she had bought for her daughter but which she never used: 'Se había limitado a pegarle dentro una etiqueta donde dice con mayúsculas CUADERNO DE TODO, ni una hoja escribió, nada de nada, se debió poner enferma poco después'.[316]

Cuaderno 35, 'El otoño de Poughkeepsie', was the last of the American notebooks, written during Martín Gaite's stay at Vassar College in the summer and autumn of 1985. It is full of sadness and despair on account of the recent death of her daughter, Marta: 'Son las seis de la tarde, veintiocho de agosto y estoy sola, más sola que lo que he estado nunca en mi vida, rodeada de silencio'.[317] She feels lost: 'estoy perdida en medio de un bosque. Tal como suena, no es una metáfora'.[318] Yet, up to a point, the intense solitude and isolation of this stay help her to overcome her loss: 'Vivir sola completamente en una casa en medio del bosque, donde sólo tres veces en tres días ha sonado el teléfono, es algo

---

[311] Martín Gaite, *Cuadernos*, p. 628.
[312] Martín Gaite, *Cuadernos*, p. 627.
[313] Martín Gaite, *Cuadernos*, p. 503.
[314] Martín Gaite, *Cuadernos*, p. 503.
[315] Martín Gaite, *Cuadernos*, p. 533.
[316] Martín Gaite, *Cuadernos*, p. 628.
[317] Martín Gaite, *Cuadernos*, p. 611.
[318] Martín Gaite, *Cuadernos*, p. 611.

muy balsámico'.[319] Indeed, she interprets her need to write as a lifeboat: 'He sacado del equipaje mis libros y mis cuadernos y los he colocado de forma provisional, sin creerme mucho que me vayan a servir para algo, sin creerme mucho nada de lo que pasa ni de lo que veo. Tal vez por eso mismo necesite apuntarlo'.[320]

This idea of the need to write after her daughter's death, and of writing as *tabla de salvación*, the writing cure, is what Martín Gaite will develop in her 1990s novels, novels in which the act of writing and the need to write are paramount. She starts this notebook by describing the room where she is going to spend her next few months – just as Mariana does when she writes her first letter to Sofía in *Nubosidad variable*. She continues reading and rewriting notes she had taken in Spain a few days earlier – just as Leonardo does when he leaves prison in *La Reina de las Nieves* – words which show her emptiness after Marta's death: 'qué verano tan largo, qué avanzar tan penoso el de las horas arrastrándose por las habitaciones de esta casa donde nunca volverá a oírse la llavecita en la puerta ni su voz llamándome por el pasillo'.[321] These pages also contain some reflections on her life which strongly link Martín Gaite with the characters of her 1990s novels. There are reflections on her notebooks: 'notas que luego no sirven para nada, pero en el momento parece muy urgente tomarlas, no sé cuantos cuadernos tendré metidos en cajones por Doctor Esquerdo con apuntes garabateados a toda prisa'.[322] She also reflects on her daughter's notebooks:

> Aparecen … agendas y cuadernos, papeles y cuadernos, apuntes y cuadernos, muchos sin empezar o con una hoja escrita … amaba los cuadernos bonitos como nada en el mundo, pero luego escribía casi siempre en folios volanderos. Nunca ordenaba nada, nunca tiraba nada, nunca acababa nada.[323]

And she reflects, briefly, on papers in general: 'No sé para qué escribo, si odio los papeles, si lo que más querría es prenderles fuego a todos'.[324] As will be seen, the characters of her 1990s novels write their lives in their

---

[319] Martín Gaite, *Cuadernos*, p. 617.
[320] Martín Gaite, *Cuadernos*, p. 611.
[321] Martín Gaite, *Cuadernos*, p. 612.
[322] Martín Gaite, *Cuadernos*, p. 619.
[323] Martín Gaite, *Cuadernos*, pp. 612–13.
[324] Martín Gaite, *Cuadernos*, p. 613.

notebooks, reread their writing, start novels which are never finished and burn old letters to start anew.

Usos amorosos de la postguerra española, a project which Martín Gaite had already discussed in *El cuarto de atrás*, had been taken to America to serve as a continuation of her writing; this is now going to be resumed and she writes its introduction during her stay at Vassar College. *Caperucita en Manhattan*, meanwhile, was a 'present' from her friend Juan Carlos Eguillor when she was staying in his New York apartment: 'Ha inventado una historia de una niña en Brooklyn. ... Me ha dado los papeles para que yo siga escribiendo por donde quiero, pero es que, desde que he llegado aquí, la historia se ha transformado en otra'.[325] Eguillor, a friend with whom she collaborated on *Diario 16*, helped Martín Gaite to settle in after arriving in New York and before she travelled to Vassar College. Her conversations with him encouraged her to distance herself from the present time as they talked about when they used to work together, just after Franco's death, and the changes Spain had gone through. Martín Gaite describes their conversations and realizes how writing has changed her way of perceiving her present situation:

> he estado releyendo lo que llevo escrito ... veintiocho páginas ... esa peculiar transformación del tiempo de inerte en tiempo de escritura me ha ayudado a lidiar la soledad y a convertir esta habitación vacía en un refugio al que siempre estoy deseando volver, en mi casa.[326]

As she reflects on her writing, she realizes that writing is everything and can be found in every activity she does:

> me parecía haber entendido una cosa muy importante, que meterse a escribir equivale exactamente a salir a dar un paseo, así cuando esté tumbada en la hierba mirando las nubes y notando que respiro con regularidad y acordándome de los que ya no respiran, sintiéndolos conmigo dentro de mi corazón, estoy escribiendo también, más que nunca, y las nubes recogen lo que escribo.[327]

This quotation clearly shows the great importance that Martín Gaite gave to writing during this stay, and also parallels the first dream Sofía writes about in *Nubosidad variable*, where she and Mariana are lying on the grass

---

[325] Martín Gaite, *Cuadernos*, p. 618.
[326] Martín Gaite, *Cuadernos*, p. 623.
[327] Martín Gaite, *Cuadernos*, p. 629.

looking at the clouds go by: 'Estábamos tumbadas en el campo mirando las nubes'.[328] Shortly after, Martín Gaite finishes this last American notebook with a message of hope: 'el sol nace de la confusión'.[329]

Conclusion

Cuadernos de todo is a fundamental work in Martín Gaite's biography. As her diaries, they show a side of the writer which was never seen before. The 1960s, when she started writing her *Cuadernos de todo*, were years of great change for Martín Gaite, a period when she decided to leave fiction aside to concentrate on her work as a researcher. As the mother of a young child she was able to see the importance of mothers to their children's upbringing, as a writer she was engaged in discussions on feminism and consumerist society, and as an intellectual, she read other writers' and thinkers' opinions and put down many of her thoughts in her notebooks. Her *Cuadernos de todo* were the place to think and develop her thoughts; it is possible to see in the notebooks her need to write, to note her ideas and experiences, and to have a 'dialogue' with those thoughts. As Martín Gaite commented, this type of autobiographical writing is the best way to stop and look at one's life. Subsequently, it will be shown how this reflective writing influenced the way she developed her characters in her later novels, characters who will take their pen and paper to write their present, make sense of their past, and confront their future.

After the first, more critical *cuadernos*, being a writer took on greater importance and she used the notebooks as a crucible for her work. The notebooks can be seen as her 'writer's workshop', where it is possible to see how some of her fiction started and developed, often taking many years to come to fruition. These pages not only show Martín Gaite's work in progress, they also reflect the close relationship that she always maintained between life and literature.

Finally, the *cuadernos americanos* show how the periods spent in America were very special for Martín Gaite. Her work was acclaimed and during these visits she had the time needed to concentrate on it, without the responsibilities she had in Spain. 'A room of her own' is what Martín Gaite found in the United States, with the accompanying solitude and isolation needed to collect and transcribe thoughts and reflections. She

---

[328] Carmen Martín Gaite, *Nubosidad variable* [1992] (Barcelona: Anagrama, 2002), p. 11.

[329] Martín Gaite, *Cuadernos*, p. 630.

also used this time to engage in a much more methodical completion of her notebooks. Very descriptive writing is found in the *cuadernos americanos*, much more like a diary than the rest of the notebooks, where she jots down her daily comings and goings as well as her dreams. Other times, as in the 'retahílas', she writes her thoughts as they come, casting them on the paper, reflecting on her past and on the present she is living through. The final *cuaderno americano* is also a clear example of Martín Gaite's use of notebooks as therapy. After her daughter's death, the author was able to reflect on her past in complete solitude, allowing her, through the writing of the *cuadernos*, to recover the will to live and the wish to continue with her writing.

Indeed, the importance of the time spent in America will be seen in some of her later work. It is possible to see an influence on the way her characters write their notebooks, reflecting in complete solitude on their lives. What can also be appreciated is the way the physical presence of New York is employed in a novel such as *Irse de casa*. *Caperucita en Manhattan* is also an obvious tribute to the places Martín Gaite visited in New York and the people she met in its streets, with the main character, Sarah Allen, who lives in Brooklyn and dreams of going to Manhattan on her own, and a grandmother who lives in Morningside.

A final point should be made here. Reading the pages of the *Cuadernos de todo* and seeing the valuable literary information found therein, serves as a reminder of those other notebooks, letters and papers, containing many other thoughts, ideas and projects, which have not yet been published.[330]

---

[330] As well as her published works, future volumes of Martín Gaite's *Obras completas* will make available other unpublished manuscripts, together with letters and 'Libro de la memoria diaria', a diary or notebook written in 1977.

3

Nubosidad variable: Letters and Diaries, Female Friendship through Writing

Nubosidad variable (1992) is the novel in which the author's projection of herself into her characters is most transparent. This is certainly the novel which best presents the use of diaries and letters in Carmen Martín Gaite's work. Apart from the four-page epilogue, the novel is 'written' by two friends, Sofía and Mariana, who meet after many years and decide to rekindle their lost friendship, initially through their writing. This novel has strong metafictional aspects, with the process of writing always in the foreground of the work as the protagonists write and comment on their writing. Life and literature are interlaced, with Sofía as the character who finds it more difficult to distinguish between the two. Towards the end of the novel, Mariana also begins to see her life as part of a novel for which she starts taking notes, developing the people she meets as main or secondary characters in her narrative.[1]

In Chapter I Sofía begins the novel by giving the reader information about their encounter. After years of separation the two friends meet at an exhibition. The first mention of this meeting is at the end of the chapter, when Sofía writes: 'Quién podía imaginarse que, después de los años mil, en ese local rebosante de famosos iba a encontrarme contigo, lo que son las cosas, con Mariana León en persona.'[2] In Chapter II more is learned about that encounter and their relationship through Mariana's letter to Sofía. It is also made clear that Chapter I forms part of the 'homework' Mariana set her friend Sofía at the exhibition:

---

[1] Marcia L. Welles comments in a review of the novel: 'Mariana León had no literary pretensions at all. Before her epistolary adventure, her "work in progress" was a theoretical treatise on eroticism. Gradually fiction supersedes nonfiction: the people she encounters become characters, primary or secondary, and she contrives possible plots': 'Carmen Martín Gaite, *Nubosidad Variable*', *Revista Hispánica Moderna*, 47 (1994), 256–9 (p. 257).

[2] Carmen Martín Gaite, *Nubosidad variable* [1992] (Barcelona: Anagrama, 2002), p. 19.

Contesto, aunque sea en plan telegrama, a la nota que acompaña a tus ocho folios mecanografiados. 'Te mando los deberes[3] – me decías –. Gracias, Mariana. Hace mucho que nadie me ponía deberes de este tipo y lo he pasado muy bien haciéndolos. Si no te aburre, puedo continuar.' No es que no puedas, es que debes, puesto que de deberes se trata.[4]

Even though, when they meet after so many years, they seem to have the same connection they had when younger, they are still not sure if their friendship can survive the years of separation. It is for this reason that they start writing. As Mariana says: 'aún puede ser quebradizo el suelo que pisamos. Esta cautela de lo epistolar me parece saludable'.[5] And as Sofía indicates towards the end of the novel, with reference to Mariana: 'Escribir es un pretexto para volver a verla'.[6] Also, before they meet again, the two protagonists must put their past in order. In Nuria Cruz-Cámara's words:

El re-encuentro de las dos amigas de la adolescencia tiene lugar en un momento en que sus vidas parecen haber llegado a un punto muerto, o mejor, a un punto crítico en que debe tomarse una decisión: avanzar hacia el futuro – tras la toma de conciencia de su pasado y de su presente – o quedarse estancadas en este pasado.[7]

The 'homework' that Mariana sets her friend after their first meeting is transformed into a diary-memoir which Sofía sends to Mariana. After the first part has been despatched, Sofía continues with Mariana as her interlocutor, 'Pensando sólo en Mariana ... escribiendo para ella',[8] even though she no longer sends her what she's written.

The chapters alternate between Sofía's homework and Mariana's letters. Sofía opens the novel and also writes the last chapter. In general, the way Sofía writes simulates the diary form: she writes every day about

---

[3] Homework (or *deberes*) is one of the terms used in psychotherapy when referring to the assignments sent by therapists to their patients. See Stephen J. Lepore and Joshua M. Smith, 'The Writing Cure: An Overview', in *The Writing Cure: How Expressive Writing Promotes Health and Emotional Well-Being*, ed. Stephen J. Lepore and Joshua M. Smith (Washington DC: American Psychological Association, 2002), pp. 3–14 (p. 6).
[4] Martín Gaite, *Nubosidad variable*, p. 33.
[5] Martín Gaite, *Nubosidad variable*, p. 23.
[6] Martín Gaite, *Nubosidad variable*, p. 366.
[7] Nuria Cruz-Cámara, '*Nubosidad variable*: Escritura, evasión y ruptura', *Hispanófila*, 126 (1999), 15–25 (p. 18).
[8] Martín Gaite, *Nubosidad variable*, p. 234.

what has happened and these daily events remind her of other moments of her past. Mariana, on the other hand, uses the epistolary form. She follows letter-writing conventions, with a greeting, 'Querida Sofía',[9] a date and a place of origin, 'Madrid, 30 de abril, noche',[10] as well as a closing and signature at the end of the letter: 'Te abraza con cariño, Mariana'.[11] Nevertheless, both literary approaches vary, and at times we see Sofía communicating with Mariana as if the former were writing a letter: 'Aunque ahora, mientras escribo esto, me pregunto: ¿te encontré en persona o en personaje? (Continuará, Mariana, aunque no sé por dónde)'.[12] Sofía only deliberately leaves the diary form in one of the chapters, Chapter IX, where she opens with 'Querida Mariana',[13] although this style of writing is abandoned halfway through the chapter to return to a kind of writing more similar to diary form, when she writes: 'Esta carta, pues ha dejado de serlo y pasará a engrosar mi cuaderno de deberes'.[14] In the following chapter, Mariana in turn abandons the epistolary form and omits the opening 'Querida Sofía'. Elsewhere, Mariana departs from letter-writing in order to narrate some important moments of her story in a more introspective way.[15]

As Christine Arkinstall comments, Sofía and Mariana use their writing 'towards a recovery of selves',[16] as until this point they have only served as mirrors of others. Through their writing, both protagonists connect the reader to a generation of Spanish women, born during the war or postwar period, who have witnessed great changes after Franco's death, and the PSOE's election to government in 1982. However, as Janet Pérez observes: '*Nubosidad variable* focuses more upon the individual consequences of biographical decisions, even though the individual characters are simultaneously representative of Spanish women of their class and generation'.[17]

---

[9] Martín Gaite, *Nubosidad variable*, p. 20.
[10] Martín Gaite, *Nubosidad variable*, p. 20.
[11] Martín Gaite, *Nubosidad variable*, p. 33.
[12] Martín Gaite, *Nubosidad variable*, p. 19.
[13] Martín Gaite, *Nubosidad variable*, p. 145.
[14] Martín Gaite, *Nubosidad variable*, p. 152.
[15] Mariana abandons the epistolary style in Chapters X, XII and XVI, although in X and XVI Sofía still appears as the addressee of the missive.
[16] Christine Arkinstall, 'Towards a Female Symbolic: Re-Presenting Mothers and Daughters in Contemporary Spanish Narrative by Women', in *Writing Mothers and Daughters: Renegotiating the Mother in Western European Narratives by Women*, ed. Adalgisa Giorgio (Oxford: Berghahn Books, 2002), pp. 47–84 (p. 66).
[17] Janet Perez, 'Structural, Thematic, and Symbolic Mirrors in *El cuarto de atrás* and

Through their writing, Sofía and Mariana discuss past events that only they know about. They are the ones who can reassure each other that their past memories actually happened: 'Pero seguro que tú te acuerdas. Menos mal que existes tú,'[18] Mariana writes. These memories are what Sofía calls 'contraseña para reconocernos'.[19] Like Eulalia in *Retahílas* and C. in *El cuarto de atrás* (and Martín Gaite herself), they are witnesses to historical and social changes as well as great generational changes, and through their writing they try to understand the decisions, or lack of them, which took their lives on such different paths. *Nubosidad variable* has been compared to *Entre visillos*, *El cuarto de atrás* and *Retahílas*,[20] and it can be argued that these two women represent an evolution of the female protagonists of Martín Gaite's earlier novels. As Alicia Redondo Goicoechea indicates: 'Desde sus primeras protagonistas de *El balneario* a las últimas de *Los parentescos*, ... el modelo de mujer propuesto ha ido transformándose paralelamente a las etapas que ha recorrido la autora y la sociedad española.'[21] The themes which the protagonists of *Nubosidad variable* discuss in their writing, especially those which refer to women in society, are, of course, topics that the author deals with in other works. The development of these themes can be seen especially in the pages of her first *Cuadernos de todo*, in which the author reflects constantly on the position of women in Spanish society of the 1960s.

Mother/daughter relationships are very important in this novel, as they are in the subsequent novels of the 1990s. In *Nubosidad variable* Martín Gaite seems to be exploring this kind of relationship especially through the character of Sofía, a character named after her own grandmother.

Sofía's Diary: 'Un ajuste de cuentas con el tiempo'

As was noted earlier, Sofía uses the diary-memoir form for her writing. She calls this type of writing '[un] ajuste de cuentas con el tiempo'.[22] She writes what she calls her 'deberes', referring to situations she is living

Nubosidad variable of Martín Gaite', *South Central Review*, 12 (1995), 47–63 (p. 55).

[18] Martín Gaite, *Nubosidad variable*, p. 258.
[19] Martín Gaite, *Nubosidad variable*, p. 232.
[20] See Pilar de la Puente Samaniego, '*Nubosidad variable*', *Anales de Literatura Española Contemporánea*, 18 (1993), 404–6; and Kathleen M. Glenn, '*Nubosidad variable*', *Hispania*, 76 (1993), 297–8.
[21] Alicia Redondo Goicoechea, 'Las autoras frente al espejo: Imágenes y modelos', in *Lo mío es escribir: La vida escrita por las mujeres, I*, ed. Anna Caballé (Barcelona: Lumen, 2004), pp. 11–53. (p. 17).
[22] Martín Gaite, *Nubosidad variable*, p. 298.

through in the present and remembering, through this present, a past which relates to these situations, reflecting at all times on her experiences of the past or the present. As Smith and Watson explain: 'remembering involves a reinterpretation of the past in the present',[23] and this is what Sofía is doing throughout the novel. These memories are like flashbacks which, as Sofía observes, she pastes onto the collage of her life: 'Tengo que atender a este flash back, lo tengo que pegar en el collage, aunque sea con saliva'.[24] For the collage, she uses other documents which help her recover her past:

> Usaré la técnica del collage y un cierto vaivén en la cronología. Aparte de la versión aportada por tu carta ... cuento con otros elementos que me pueden servir para refrescar la memoria: varias cartas de amor y de ruptura ... retazos de un diario que empecé a raíz de la muerte de mamá y ... unos apuntes, que paso a poner en limpio, tomados hace pocos días.[25]

The encounter reminds them of a saying they used when they were young, and which Sofía wrote in her diary of the time: 'la sorpresa es una liebre, y el que sale de caza, nunca la verá dormir en el erial'.[26] This is one of the expressions which form part of what they call their 'léxico familiar'.[27] Another such saying is one their literature teacher used to address to Sofía to encourage her to continue writing, and which Mariana

---

[23] Sidonie Smith and Julia Watson, *Reading Autobiography: A Guide for Interpreting Life Narratives* (Minneapolis: University of Minnesota Press, 2001), p. 16.

[24] Martín Gaite, *Nubosidad variable*, p. 45.

[25] Martín Gaite, *Nubosidad variable*, p. 153. Later on, in Chapter XI, she uses her godmother's letter sent from Paris, giving her advice about the break-up with her friend: 'Tengo aquí delante de los ojos dos cartas de mi madrina, que no copio para que este relato no se vuelva tan largo como aquel invierno. Pero su lectura me está ayudando a reconstruir la sensación de zozobra y desarraigo que acompañaron a mi insensible espera del amor' (p. 204).

[26] Martín Gaite, *Nubosidad variable*, p. 18.

[27] Natalia Ginzburg's autobiographical novel, *Léxico familiar* (*Lessico Famigliare*, 1963) was known by Martín Gaite, who wrote a critique of the Spanish translation for *ABC Literario* on 10 June 1989. See Carmen Martín Gaite, '*Léxico familiar*, de Natalia Ginzburg', in *Tirando del hilo (Artículos 1949–2000)*, ed. and intro. José Teruel (Madrid: Siruela, 2006), pp. 422–4. She also published other articles about the Italian author, for example 'El murmullo de los cotidiano', published in *Saber leer*, June–July 1991 (in *Agua pasada* (Barcelona: Anagrama, 1993), pp. 205–8), and an homage published in *ABC*, 9 October 1991 (*Agua pasada*, pp. 348–51). In addition, she translated two of Ginzburg's novels: *Caro Michelle* (1973), an epistolary novel, translated as *Querido Miguel* [1989] (Barcelona: Acantilado, 2003) and *Tutti nostri ieri* (1952), translated as *Nuestros ayeres* (Barcelona: Círculo de Lectores, 1996).

uses in her first letter: 'Siga usted, señorita Montalvo, siga siempre'.[28] These words bring memories and stir emotions in Sofía when reading her friend's letter: 'Encima de la frase de don Pedro Larroque, que revives al hacerla suya ... concretamente encima del "siempre", se me ha caído una lágrima'.[29] Mariana also comments on how she felt when Sofía's parcel arrived: 'Ya al coger el sobre abultado y ver mi nombre manuscrito por ti me dio un vuelco el corazón y noté que me estabas devolviendo algo olvidado'.[30] Along with these feelings, both friends also experience the desire to continue with their written communication after so many years of separation.

Sofía mentions a great number of characters, calling them 'trocitos de espejo', all of which are important for an understanding of her life. These 'trocitos de espejo' are referred to at the beginning of the epigraph to *Nubosidad variable* in a quotation from the introduction to Ginzburg's *La città e la casa*, an epistolary novel published in 1984: 'Cuando he escrito novelas, siempre he tenido la sensación de encontrarme en las manos con añicos de espejo, y sin embargo conservaba la esperanza de acabar por recomponer el espejo entero'.[31] The image of the shards or fragments of a mirror is repeated throughout the novel, with the different characters and their stories being the pieces which will form the complete mirror at the end of the book. Martín Gaite comments:

> La escritura femenina alude a un mundo fragmentario y mezclado que, según metáfora de Natalia Ginzburg, nunca podrá quedar reflejado en un espejo de cuerpo entero, sino en añicos de espejos rotos, un mundo de vislumbres en cada uno de los cuales ya está la esencia de otra cosa, cortes laterales en una realidad que nos hurta.[32]

One of the collages Sofía creates, 'Gente en un cóctel',[33] contains pasted pieces of foil (taken from a packet of Winston cigarettes), which represent these 'añicos'. Martín Gaite's 'voice', as well as some of her characteristics, minor obsessions and habits, are also reflected in Sofía's writing. Just like the author, she rereads her notes, rewrites them, and makes

---

[28] Martín Gaite, *Nubosidad variable*, p. 33.
[29] Martín Gaite, *Nubosidad variable*, p. 145.
[30] Martín Gaite, *Nubosidad variable*, p. 29.
[31] Martín Gaite, *Nubosidad variable*, p. 9.
[32] Martín Gaite, 'Trascender lo cotidiano', in *Tirando del hilo*, pp. 429–31 (p. 431).
[33] Martín Gaite, *Nubosidad variable*, p. 35.

collages which show her feelings at certain moments.[34] She writes in the Ateneo and even buys her notebooks in one of Martín Gaite's favourite stationers, Muñagorri: 'Me fueron a buscar al Ateneo. Yo estaba describiendo, en el cuaderno comprado en Muñagorri, la fiesta de Gregorio Termes. Ahora he empezado otro'.[35] As Jurado Morales indicates when discussing the author's work: 'El lector recibe no sólo una historia más o menos atractiva sino también, y por encima de todo, la voz subjetiva y sincera de una escritora empeñada en trasmitir su particular visión del mundo.'[36]

The use of the diary form makes Sofía's writing more reflective and allows her to think again about her past. Mariana's writing, on the other hand, is more immediate, although she also uses reflective writing to understand some shared episodes of their life which, as she says, will give two sides or versions of the same experience to whoever reads them: 'Ahora que lo pienso, seguro que hablamos de las mismas cosas en más de una ocasión y con un tratamiento diferente'.[37] As Sofía writes her diary she has her friend in mind as the necessary interlocutor to continue with her *pesquisa* through her past. For example, when she rewrites her notes, Sofía thinks about Mariana reading them: '"Mira, te he traído de regalo este cuaderno"; así que me gozo en irlo llenando despacio, esmerándome en la letra. Eso es como estar ya con ella también ahora según lo escribo'.[38] Equally, Mariana has Sofía in mind: 'Menos mal que has aparecido, que puedo imaginar que me escuchas'.[39] As Ruth Perry indicates in *Women, Letters and the Novel*, 'addressing others on paper

---

[34] As already mentioned, Martín Gaite's love for drawing and collages is well known, and she used one of these collages in the first edition of *Nubosidad variable*. For a study of this collage and others produced by the author, see Kathleen M. Glenn, 'Collage, textile and palimpsest: Carmen Martín Gaite's *Nubosidad variable*', *Romance Languages Annual*, 5 (1993), 408–13.

[35] Martín Gaite, *Nubosidad variable*, p. 156.

[36] José Jurado Morales, 'La narrativa de Carmen Martín Gaite, la esencia misma del ensayo', in *Actas del VIII Simposio Internacional sobre Narrativa Hispánica Contemporánea: Novela y Ensayo* (El Puerto de Santa María: Fundación Luis Goytisolo, 2000), pp. 95–108 (p. 102). Antonio Torres Torres also comments on the similarities between Sofía and the author: 'Sofía ... es quien encarna un mayor número de características autobiográficas de Martín Gaite': 'La perspectiva narrativa en *Nubosidad variable* de Carmen Martín Gaite', *Anuario de Estudios Filológicos*, 18 (1995), 499–506 (p. 504).

[37] Martín Gaite, *Nubosidad variable*, p. 339.

[38] Martín Gaite, *Nubosidad variable*, p. 76.

[39] Martín Gaite, *Nubosidad variable*, p. 70.

evokes their palpable presence.'[40] Perry goes on to say, 'Letters allow a person to keep a relationship going in the imagination.'[41] In the case of *Nubosidad variable*, Sofía is going through a time in her life when she lacks an interlocutor who can listen. Her children are grown up and she lives with a husband with whom she hardly communicates. Consequently, her encounter with Mariana and with her own writing opens new ways of communication.

In her marriage, Sofía finds herself in a similar situation to the protagonist of Esther Tusquets's novel, *El mismo mar de todos los veranos* (1978).[42] They both feel complete indifference towards their husbands, who are more interested in money, success and redecorating their homes (to be one step ahead of others) than in saving marriages that have long stopped functioning. In these two novels, both protagonists see their husbands as if they were strangers with whom they share a bed. As Carmen Alborch comments: 'La soledad aparece cuando eres consciente de la distancia que separa tu propia alma de la persona que está sentada en la butaca de al lado.'[43] In *Nubosidad variable*, the character of the husband (a character both in Martín Gaite's novel and in Sofía's narrative), although present, is not fundamental to the account. As Sofía writes: 'Era un personaje que se había metido equivocadamente en la escena. ¿Salir a comer con él? No, no, qué cosa más aburrida. Menos mal que ya hace mucho que no me lo propone'.[44] Every time she writes about him it is either to show a lack of understanding, 'Me parecía un extraño',[45] or to explain their problems: 'Yo con Eduardo me casé sin estar enamorada y de ahí viene todo'.[46] Later, she explains the reason for their union: 'Me casé embarazada de tres meses'.[47]

This type of male character occurs in other Martín Gaite novels, and seems to represent a stereotype of the 1980s Spanish middle-class man. María del Mar López Cabrales indicates how: 'En estas novelas los

---

[40] Ruth Perry, *Women, Letters and the Novel* (New York: AMS Press, 1980), p. 104.
[41] Perry, p. 114.
[42] For a comparative study of *Nubosidad variable* and *El mismo mar*, see Estrella Cibreiro, '*El mismo mar de todos los veranos* y *Nubosidad variable*: hacia la consolidación de una identidad femenina propia y discursiva', *Letras Peninsulares*, 13 (2000), 581–607.
[43] Carmen Alborch, *Solas: Gozos y sombras de una manera de vivir* (Madrid: Temas de Hoy, 2006), p. 120.
[44] Martín Gaite, *Nubosidad variable*, p. 118.
[45] Martín Gaite, *Nubosidad variable*, p. 15.
[46] Martín Gaite, *Nubosidad variable*, p. 169.
[47] Martín Gaite, *Nubosidad variable*, p. 201.

personajes masculinos que aparecen sirven de contraste con los femeninos que, normalmente, son más fuertes y son el eje de la novela en su totalidad.'[48] The indifference Sofía feels towards her husband allows her to leave her home after listening to a conversation which confirms that he is involved with another woman. For his part, her husband reproaches her for having remained stuck in the past, for not being interested in new ways of life, for not recognizing some of the most influential people in the society he tells her about,[49] and for reading (again) *Wuthering Heights*: '¿No comprendes – dijo Eduardo – que seguir leyendo *Cumbres borrascosas* es quedarse enquistada?'[50] Indeed, both Sofía and Mariana constantly refer to books, films, and the music of their youth or of their present, filling the novel with intertextual remarks which go from *Wuthering Heights* to *Nada*, from Garcilaso and Manuel Machado to Katherine Mansfield and Simone de Beauvoir. Also, there are references to Anna Karenina, Greta Garbo, James Dean, Michael Jackson, the Beatles or Presuntos Implicados, as well as to characters from children's stories, such as *Sleeping Beauty*, *Peter Pan* or *Celia*. All these references provide a tour through the cultural baggage of a generation.[51]

Emily Brontë's novel, though, was fundamental in the development of both friends and appears again and again throughout the narration as a parallel or contrast with situations they have lived through. In fact, Martín Gaite translated *Wuthering Heights* in 1978 and she also wrote prologues to the novel.[52] References in *Nubosidad variable* to this novel also take us closer to the author's preferences, as well as showing the influence of the books she was reading at the time on the novels she was writing. For example, Martín Gaite was reading *Wuthering Heights* during her journey from Dublin to Cork on 23 February 1983: 'Me siento desligada de todo, libre y perdida al mismo tiempo. Me pongo a leer *Cumbres borrascosas*.

---

[48] María del Mar López Cabrales, *Palabras de mujeres: Escritoras españolas contemporáneas* (Madrid: Narcea, 2000), p. 38. It is also worth adding, with reference to Martín Gaite's novels, an observation Martín Gaite used in her critique of Rosa Montero's *Crónica del desamor* (1979): 'no hay en toda la narración un hombre que salga bien parado' (*Tirando del hilo*, p. 275).

[49] Martín Gaite, *Nubosidad variable*, p. 17.

[50] Martín Gaite, *Nubosidad variable*, p. 17.

[51] For a detailed account of the intertextual allusions in the novel, see Carmen Servén, 'La amistad entre mujeres en la narrativa femenina: Carmen Martín Gaite (1992) y Marina Mayoral (1994)', *DICENDA: Cuadernos de Filología Hispánica*, 16 (1998), 233–43 (pp. 235–7).

[52] See, for example, Martín Gaite, *Agua pasada*, pp. 113–21.

De repente tengo veinte años'.[53] Her reaction to reading a novel she had read in her youth is the same that Sofía seems to experience in *Nubosidad variable*.

Sofía prefers to live in a world of literature and imagination, as she confesses: 'Reconozco que no me gusta la realidad, que nunca me ha gustado'.[54] For her, writing is necessary to feel alive. When she was younger she showed her enthusiasm for writing: 'De lo que más me acuerdo es de que escribía muchísimo. Poemas, comienzos de novela, diario'.[55] In the same way Martín Gaite comments on her own love for writing and how she began at an early age: 'yo llevo escribiendo, creo, desde que tenía doce años y que mi primera novela no la publiqué hasta los veintinueve. Lo cual te indica que no tenía prisa.'[56] But when Sofía marries, she stops writing, and when she does occasionally resume (for example when she begins writing a diary after her mother's death),[57] she never feels motivated to continue. However, when she starts writing after her encounter with Mariana, she recovers the feelings of her youth and is able to begin a new stage in her life. That is the reason why other characters see her as a new person; she has been able to get out of the hole she fell into: 'no hay mejor tabla de salvación que la pluma. Gracias, Mariana, por habérmelo vuelto a recordar'.[58]

Writing allows Sofía to realize that she is no longer attached to her home and her husband, and so feels free to leave them. She has her children to support and encourage her need for independence. 'El refugio para tortugas'[59] or 'refu', the name given to her mother's house, where her two older children live now, is, as its name reflects, the refuge Sofía chooses for her escape. In this refuge the wish to write is rediscovered and she chooses the kitchen (after tidying up and cleaning it, like a 'good' housewife) as the place to write:

[53] Carmen Martín Gaite, *Cuadernos de todo*, ed. and intro. Maria Vittoria Calvi (Barcelona: Areté, 2002), p. 545.
[54] Martín Gaite, *Nubosidad variable*, p. 111.
[55] Martín Gaite, *Nubosidad variable*, p. 167.
[56] See Marie-Lise Gazarian Gautier, 'Conversación con Carmen Martín Gaite en Nueva York', in *From Fiction to Metafiction: Essays in Honor of Carmen Martín Gaite*, ed. Mirella Servodidio and Marcia L. Welles (Lincoln, NE: Society of Spanish and Spanish-American Studies, 1983), pp. 25–33 (p. 29).
[57] As was discussed in Chapter 2, Martín Gaite also started a project in diary form after her parents' death, titled 'Cuenta pendiente'.
[58] Martín Gaite, *Nubosidad variable*, p. 210.
[59] Martín Gaite, *Nubosidad variable*, p. 42.

> Termino de recoger también la mesa y le paso una bayeta húmeda por el mármol. Esto ya parece otra cosa. Creo que voy a buscar una lámpara de flexo, en el salón tiene que haber alguna, y me voy a venir aquí a escribir, porque es que ya no me caben en la cabeza las cosas que se me ocurren para apuntar.[60]

The kitchen was also for earlier generations, such as Sofía's mother, their 'kingdom', even though, as Sofía's mother says: 'tal vez porque entre todos fomentaron en mí esa convicción'.[61]

The first move from the marital home to the parents' house does not seem to be a very liberating action; but it is thanks to this first step that Sofía is able to have a dream where she 'becomes' her mother:[62] 'pensaba con sus frases y revivían sus recuerdos'.[63] In this way, she is able to see how her mother actually understood her. Her dream is enough for her to feel liberated from the pressure her mother always exerted on her, and to forgive her. Adalgisa Giorgio explains, in the introduction to the collection *Writing Mothers and Daughters*, how in recent decades there has been a significant shift in the way relationships between mothers and daughters have been represented in European literature: 'It is possible to identify a broad shift from rejection of or indifference to the maternal to a desire on the daughter's part to examine her bond with the mother.'[64] In *Nubosidad variable* we see this shift in the case of Sofía, who moves from feelings of guilt, due to the hatred she felt towards the mother who always wanted to control her life,[65] to a wish to know her mother better

---

[60] Martín Gaite, *Nubosidad variable*, p. 376.

[61] Martín Gaite, *Nubosidad variable*, p. 348.

[62] Leonardo of *La Reina de las Nieves* talks to his grandmother and his mother in his dreams, allowing the reader to hear their voices through him. However, just like Sofía the night she spends at her mother's house, Leonardo smokes hashish, which may be the cause of what could have been a simple hallucination. Sofía's older daughter, Encarna, explains that this kind of *desdoblamiento* which her mother has suffered could be produced by smoking hashish, a substance which also helped her the night before to write her ideas more clearly.

[63] Martín Gaite, *Nubosidad variable*, p. 381. This type of dream can be related to what Freud called 'wish fulfilment', in which we reproduce through the dream a wish not realized in our lives. Thanks to her dream, Sofía will understand her mother and forgive her, just as will occur in Leonardo's dreams in *La Reina* and Águeda's in *Lo raro es vivir*. See Sigmund Freud, *La interpretación de los sueños* (Barcelona: Planeta Agostini, 1985), pp. 16–21 and 587–606.

[64] Adalgisa Giorgio, 'Mothers and Daughters in Western Europe: Mapping the Territory', in *Writing Mothers and Daughters*, pp. 1–9 (p. 5).

[65] 'A mi madre empecé a odiarla desde que supe que me leía las cartas de Guillermo. Hace diez años, cuando murió, me di cuenta de que todavía no había sido capaz de

so as to understand her and forgive her. On this issue, Chodorow explains the need for women to shake off their feelings of guilt in their relationships with their mothers: 'Guilt and sadness about the mother are particularly prevalent female preoccupations, which are as likely to limit female autonomy, pleasure, and achievement as any cultural mandate.'[66] And in fact, the real liberation for Sofía will come after confronting and understanding her feelings towards her mother.

Sofía's dream has also revealed another relationship, the one between grandmother and granddaughter. Encarna (who, like her mother, writes stories and takes her name from her grandmother) was her grandmother's best interlocutor: 'Jamás me ha dado nadie tan buena conversación, con aquella voz dulce, persuasiva y sincera que me llegaba directamente al alma, y mira que es difícil a mí llegarme al alma'.[67] The grandmother–grandchild relationship can be liberating, as can be seen in *Caperucita en Manhattan* or in *La Reina de las Nieves*, in which the grandmothers serve as a refuge for the grandchildren. The three generations of women represented in this novel are important for understanding the position of a woman such as Sofía who, although she followed the traditional route by marrying and having children, is always challenging the reasons for re-enacting certain conventions. Reflecting on her life, she writes:

> Aprobado en hija de familia. Aprobado en noviazgo. Aprobado en economía doméstica. Aprobado en trato conyugal y en deberes para con la parentela política. Aprobado en partos. Aprobado en suavizar asperezas, en buscar un sitio para cada cosa y en poner a mal tiempo buena cara. Aprobado en maternidad activa, aunque esta asignatura, por ser la más difícil, está sometida a continua revisión.[68]

Sofía does not follow the rules of behaviour that a middle-class housewife is expected to follow. She is also close to her children, having with them, as grownups, a good relationship: 'A lo largo de una serie de años, que ahora se pierden en la niebla, mi equilibrio mental estuvo supeditado al

---

perdonarle aquello' (p. 39). Sofía writes this sentence after having repressed the wish to hear her daughter, Amalia's, telephone conversation.

[66] Nancy J. Chodorow, *The Power of Feelings: Personal Meaning in Psychoanalysis, Gender and Culture* (New Haven, CT: Yale University Press, 1999), p. 89.
[67] Martín Gaite, *Nubosidad variable*, p. 349.
[68] Martín Gaite, *Nubosidad variable*, p. 116.

logro de recetas de cocina apetitosas y de un comentario aprobatorio por parte de los duendecillos reflejados en mi espejo'.[69]

As was seen in Chapter 2, Martín Gaite does not understand women who have children and then leave them to be looked after by others. Neither does she understand the difficulty some mothers have in communicating with and caring for their children. In the same way as the author, Sofía's relationship with her children is one of friendship, and Sofía's children also encourage her to continue with her writing:

> nos ponemos [Sofía y Encarna] a hablar de problemas de elaboración literaria, de coincidencias, metáforas, principios y finales, con un entusiasmo propio de quien tiene sed atrasada de algo, quitándonos la palabra una a otra. Parece como si no hubiéramos hablado de otra cosa en toda la vida.[70]

Theories on the importance of the mother in the baby's development were discussed at length during the 1950s and 1960s and are still an important component of most psychoanalytical theories. As Chodorow indicates: 'The experience of satisfactory feeding and holding enables the child to develop a sense of loved self in relation to a loving and caring mother.'[71] And Sofía seems to understand that a child needs 'un cariño incondicional'.[72] This is one of the reasons she defends her children in front of their father, something she feels her mother never did for her.

However, there is not only the need of the child for the mother: the mother also feels pleasure in this relationship. Discussing her relationship with Encarna, Sofía says that she was 'mi mayor fuente de luz y energía'.[73] Indeed, as Chodorow indicates:

> Women get gratification from caring for an infant, analysts generally suggest, because they experience it as an extension of themselves. The basis for 'good-enough'[74] early mothering is 'maternal empathy' with her infant, coming from total identification with it rather than

---

[69] Martín Gaite, *Nubosidad variable*, p. 41.
[70] Martín Gaite, *Nubosidad variable*, p. 383.
[71] Nancy J. Chodorow, *The Reproduction of Mothering: Psychoanalysis and the Sociology of Gender* (Berkeley: University California Press, 1999), p. 78.
[72] Martín Gaite, *Nubosidad variable*, p. 287.
[73] Martín Gaite, *Nubosidad variable*, p. 294.
[74] The idea of the 'good-enough' mother developed by Donald W. Winnicott will be further examined in Chapter 4.

(more intellectual) 'understanding of what is or could be verbally expressed' about infantile needs.[75]

In fact, in Chapter XV ('El trastero de Encarna'), Sofía narrates the first moment of complete understanding between her and her eldest daughter: her poor relationship with her husband and her tiredness after having had another baby collide with the jealousy of her eldest daughter, who needs her mother even more. Yet Sofía finds at that moment that her communication with her daughter is easier than before: 'Me dio un vuelco el corazón y nos miramos en silencio, tanteando la posible certeza de estar compartiendo una emoción rara y preciosa'.[76] The episode narrated by Martín Gaite in *El cuento de nunca acabar*, 'Ruptura de relaciones',[77] about a holiday spent with her daughter, is a reminder of this type of understanding between mother and daughter.

In contrast to a mother's need to protect her children is the idea that the children need independence and have other relationships apart from the maternal. As Chodorow indicates, the preoccupation with excessive protection for children started in the United States:

> Beginning in the 1940s, studies began to claim that mothers in American society were 'overprotecting' their children and not allowing them to separate. ... These mothers were rearing children when the new psychology was emphasizing maternal responsibilities for children's development, when women were putting more time into childcare even as there were fewer children to care for, when family mobility and the beginning of suburbanisation were removing women from daily contact with female kin.[78]

When she was a small child, Encarna witnessed the isolation her mother was feeling and understood her need to be rescued, which is why the child offered her a place to escape from the adults surrounding her:

> – ¿Sabes para lo que tengo ganas de ser mayor? – me preguntó.
> – No sé. Siempre dices que no quieres ser mayor.

---

[75] Chodorow, *The Reproduction of Mothering*, p. 87.
[76] Martín Gaite, *Nubosidad variable*, p. 289.
[77] Carmen Martín Gaite, *El cuento de nunca acabar* [1983] (Barcelona: Anagrama, 1988), pp. 222–7.
[78] Chodorow, *The Reproduction of Mothering*, p. 212.

— Para tener una casa y llevarte a vivir conmigo. Una casa pequeña, con balcones, y delante el mar. Y tú no tendrías que hacer nada, sólo contar cuentos.[79]

Sofía's 'diary' reveals the isolation she still experiences, as she has lost her own friends and feels a stranger amongst her husband's friends. Also present are the accusations she receives not only from her husband, but also from Daría, the maid, and from the psychiatrist she visited after her children left home: 'Que Encarna y Lorenzo no aceptan la realidad tal como es, que no quieren parecerse a su padre en nada. Y que yo tengo la culpa. De eso hablaba con el psiquiatra. Los comprendo, no les doy alas pero los comprendo'.[80] Except for the youngest one, Amelia, who still lives at home but has a job, Sofía's children have not been able to 'leave the womb', living in their grandmother's house and even having the services of the maid her mother sends to clean the house. However, at the same time we see how, when Sofía needs help, the first person she thinks of is her eldest daughter:

La necesidad de ver a Encarna inmediatamente coincidía con el deseo fogoso y repentino de escapar de casa, de rebelarme contra la mentira, de romper amarras. 'Tengo que hablar con Encarna, contarle todo lo que me pasa y lo que siento ahora, no puedo demorarlo ni un minuto más; de las personas que tengo cerca ella es la única que me entiende.' Y el refu se me presentó de repente como aquella casita con balcones al mar que su imaginación infantil edificara para brindarme asilo.[81]

The 'refuge' ('el refu') helps Sofía to find not only her daughter but also her mother. As mentioned previously, Sofía has her dream in what was her parents' house and where her mother died. The encounter with her daughter the morning after the dream is crucial in her decision to

---

[79] Martín Gaite, *Nubosidad variable*, p. 296. Telling stories was always one of Martín Gaite's passions and influenced her decision to take up writing, as stated in the introduction to *El castillo de las tres murallas*: 'lo que más le gustaba era que le contaran cuentos o contarlos ella. ... Lo malo es que no siempre que quería contar un cuento encontraba alguien dispuesto a oírlo ... Se dio cuenta de lo necesario que es escribir los cuentos que no se pueden contar': *El castillo de las tres murallas*, illus. Juan Carlos Eguillor [1981] (Barcelona: Lumen, 1991), pp. 5–6.
[80] Martín Gaite, *Nubosidad variable*, p. 124.
[81] Martín Gaite, *Nubosidad variable*, p. 304.

leave everything and go to find the only person she really wants to be with, her friend Mariana:

> Le hablo [a Encarna] con la mayor superficialidad posible de la pelirroja [la amante de su marido] y de mi decisión de desaparecer de casa por unos días. Sin embargo, al final se me quiebra la voz.
> – ¡Pero qué unos días, mamá! Si lo que tienes que hacer es irte para siempre. Ya hace siglos que no pintas nada ahí, nada en absoluto. ¡Venga, por favor, no te pongas a llorar ahora! Pues sólo faltaba. Que se la coma con patatas a esa cursi. Olvídalos.[82]

Sofía needs to leave both homes to find herself, and it is thanks to her encounter with Mariana and her rediscovery of the pleasure of writing that makes it possible – as Sofía writes to Mariana: 'Desde que me he puesto a escribir, mi vida ha dado un giro copernicano'.[83] Later, she observes: 'escribir me sacaba del infierno'.[84] Eventually, Sofía starts thinking of her writings as part of a novel: 'De pronto me da por pensar en que el comienzo de esta novela debía coincidir con el análisis de aquellos cinco meses y pico en que la hoy doctora León se convirtió para mí en una desconocida'.[85] This episode marks the traumatic beginning of the friends' separation. Writing is Sofía's way of recovering the repressed memories which come back to her after meeting Mariana again. This is the main theme Sofía deals with in her writing.

Mariana's Letters: From Projection to Introspection through Writing

With her opening letter Mariana quickly puts Sofía in the picture by giving what looks like stage directions: 'es de día, en primer término sofá, por el lateral derecha puerta que da al jardín'.[86] She gives the date and the time, describes the room where she is, the location of different objects in the room, the lighting, where she is writing and the paper she

---

[82] Martín Gaite, *Nubosidad variable*, p. 386.
[83] Martín Gaite, *Nubosidad variable*, p. 71.
[84] Martín Gaite, *Nubosidad variable*, p. 125. Adrián M. García, in his study of 'The Silent Interlocutor' in *Nubosidad variable*, dedicates a section of the chapter to 'Writing as Therapy', in *Silence in the Novels of Carmen Martín Gaite* (New York: Peter Lang, 2000), pp. 85–100.
[85] Martín Gaite, *Nubosidad variable*, p. 158.
[86] Martín Gaite, *Nubosidad variable*, p. 20.

is using to write, which was bought in New York.[87] The emotions Mariana feels while sitting looking at the room are also expressed in the letter:

> Del pasillo se entra directamente a la parte del mirador, que llamo para mis adentros 'la boca del lobo'. O sea, que ese espacio, por bonito que te lo pinte, me angustia un poco, para qué te lo voy a negar, a veces casi como una película de miedo. Es donde paso consulta.[88]

Just as Sofía has narrated the encounter between the two friends, Mariana indicates her present state, her place of work, her fears and solitude. From early on she indicates the difficulties she has with her work, even though she is a famous psychiatrist who has achieved success in her career.

It appears that Mariana's occupation, listening to people with problems, makes the need to communicate to Sofía more pressing: 'Yo estoy necesitando de un psiquiatra más que todos mis pacientes juntos. ... Menos mal que has aparecido, que puedo imaginar que me escuchas'.[89] Mariana, who never felt she had any literary inclinations (she comments on more than one occasion on the excellence of Sofía's writing and compares it to her own), uses a form of writing more used in everyday life. Nevertheless, in the second paragraph of her first letter, Mariana describes the new-found pleasure writing this kind of letter has brought her: 'Si supieras el milagro que es para mí volver a tener ganas de escribir una carta no de negocios, no de reproches, no para resolver nada. Una carta porque sí, sin tener de antemano el borrador en la cabeza, porque te sale del alma, porque te apetece muchísimo'.[90] This is a form of writing which Martín Gaite defends as being entirely spontaneous.[91] As was seen in Chapter 1, the formula she describes in *El cuento de nunca acabar* for starting a letter, 'Porque, claro, en una carta no se tiene por desdoro empezar describiendo la habitación de la fonda desde la cual elaboramos el mensaje',[92] is precisely, as noted earlier, that used by Mariana. For Mariana, writing also serves as a 'tabla de salvación',[93] and in the same way that the reading of Sofía's 'primeros deberes' serves Mariana as

---

[87] Martín Gaite, *Nubosidad variable*, p. 21.
[88] Martín Gaite, *Nubosidad variable*, p. 22.
[89] Martín Gaite, *Nubosidad variable*, p. 70.
[90] Martín Gaite, *Nubosidad variable*, p. 20.
[91] See Martín Gaite, *El cuento de nunca acabar*, p. 33.
[92] Martín Gaite, *El cuento de nunca acabar*, p. 33.
[93] Martín Gaite, *Nubosidad variable*, p. 56.

'abono'[94] for her life, the letters written to Sofía but not sent also serve as 'fertilizantes' for her own thoughts: 'Una [de las cartas] – la del tren – metida incluso en un sobre grande con tus señas escritas, la otra ni siquiera. Son fertilizantes para mí. Releerlas me ayuda a coger el hilo del tiempo reciente y estimula no sólo mi recuperación anímica sino también la evolución de mi trabajo'.[95]

As a psychiatrist Mariana knows how to listen and give advice to her patients. As well as using Sofía as her own 'psychiatrist' to whom she can tell what she has never told anyone before, through her letters she is also going to give Sofía a number of guidelines to follow. In the first letter to Sofía, she reiterates the need to continue with the 'homework', as if she were her psychiatrist: 'Te pedí que por favor te pusieras a escribir sobre lo que te diera la gana, pero enseguida, esa misma noche al llegar a casa. ... a muchos de mis pacientes les pido eso mismo'.[96] She also gives her friend advice on how to continue with her writing as if she were referring to the creation of a novel: 'Para próximos capítulos: el personaje de Eduardo no interesa al lector. ¿No podía ser desplazado un poco de la acción, darle menos papel?'[97] The process of writing forms an integral part of the account.

There are, of course, other novels in which psychiatrists encourage their patients to write so as to understand their own problems. A good example is Simone de Beauvoir's *La Femme rompie* (1968), where the protagonist, Monique, writes in response to her analyst's recommendation. In this case, though, instead of understanding her problems and getting better, Monique gets deeper and deeper into a fictional life, and this drives her to complete desperation. In Carme Riera's novel *La mitad del alma* (2004), the protagonist also confesses that it was her psychoanalyst who encouraged her to investigate her mother's past and write her diary-letter about her findings. In the case of *Nubosidad*, Sofía tells her husband that she is writing under psychiatric prescription:

> Pareció alterarse ligeramente y me preguntó que si había vuelto al psiquiatra. Yo bajé los ojos hacia la mesa y mi caligrafía me hacia guiños amistosos desde el cuaderno y los papeles sueltos, como la luz de un faro. Sonreí. Me sentí totalmente dueña de la situación.

---

[94] Martín Gaite, *Nubosidad variable*, p. 144.
[95] Martín Gaite, *Nubosidad variable*, p. 128.
[96] Martín Gaite, *Nubosidad variable*, p. 32.
[97] Martín Gaite, *Nubosidad variable*, p. 34.

– No, hombre, no te preocupes. Es que tengo un alter ego que me manda escribir.[98]

The character of Mariana as a fashionable psychiatrist/psychoanalyst has certain negative aspects. Thus, one of her patients whom Sofía meets describes her as a cold and distant woman: 'Siempre inalterable, siempre por encima de todo, fría como un témpano, no sabía lo que era la pasión'.[99] In her letters to Sofía, Mariana explains the reason for her distant manner and reflects on her past behaviour and how she feels currently. After reminding Sofía of the fact that she left university in her second year to get married, Mariana observes: 'Yo no tiré la toalla, me agarré a ella en una reacción incluso demasiado compulsiva, ésa es la verdad. Y sin embargo, mi trayectoria profesional, valga lo que valga, arranca de aquel enfrentamiento primero con la calamidad'.[100] Subsequently, when she reflects on her fear of solitude, she writes about her life in Madrid and how her busy working life never allows her to be alone:

> Lo único bastante seguro es que sonaría mucho el teléfono, que no pararía de mirar la agenda y que no tendría tiempo de quedarme a solas conmigo misma[101] ni de preguntarme por qué no me aguanto. Me dedicaría a darles recetas sobre cómo aguantarse a sí mismos a los enfermos que vienen a mi consulta aquejados de esa incapacidad.[102]

Mariana's relationships with some of her patients are totally outside the boundaries of psychoanalytical practice, often continuing outside the consulting room (especially when Raimundo becomes her lover), as Mariana informs Sofía: 'Te diré que la relación con gran parte de las personas que trato actualmente me viene por la vía del diván, lo cual a la larga resulta empobrecedor y fatigoso'.[103] The transference[104] in the consulting room between Raimundo (a manic depressive whom

---

[98] Martín Gaite, *Nubosidad variable*, p. 197.
[99] Martín Gaite, *Nubosidad variable*, p. 84. Alborch comments how: 'Hay mujeres que se imponen como disciplina ser frías e inaccesibles para transmitir una imagen de poder' (p. 186).
[100] Martín Gaite, *Nubosidad variable*, p. 26.
[101] Words which remind us of those written by Martín Gaite in America (see Chapter 2).
[102] Martín Gaite, *Nubosidad variable*, pp. 87–8.
[103] Martín Gaite, *Nubosidad variable*, p. 52.
[104] 'Projection (sometimes called externalization) and introjection (sometimes called internalization), as these express unconscious fantasy, are the major modes of transference. In projection and projective identification, we put feelings, beliefs, or parts of our self into an other' (Chodorow, *The Power of Feelings*, p. 15).

she herself diagnosed as 'ciclotímico'[105]) and Mariana is not portrayed positively, for the psychoanalyst allows herself to be led by her feelings towards her patient, trying to cure him of his homosexuality not only on the chaise longue but also in bed.[106] She sees Raimundo as the man who needs her help, but not as his psychiatrist, instead as his 'woman': 'Me sorprendí imaginándome con un mandil y un escobón, abriendo las ventanas y entonando coplas alegres, mientras de la cocina venía un olor a guiso casero, y yo me acercaba a la mesa grande, casi con devoción, a poner en orden los papeles de Raimundo'.[107] Mariana admits being aware of the problems she has with Raimundo although she does not seem to have the power or the will to rebel against them: '[Raimundo] está pasando por una crisis infernal y no se alivia hasta que me la trasfiere a mí'.[108] This countertransference[109] experienced with her former patient leads her to believe that she is the only person who understands him, therefore the only one he needs.

Another of Mariana's patients, with whom she breaks all professional rules, is Silvia, a friend of Raimundo and with whom she has been in love since she was young. She writes to Sofía:

> Para que lo entiendas mejor, te diré que en un trabajo como el mío se requiere un raro equilibrio entre la curiosidad y la pasividad. ... Yo siempre he estado ansiosa frente a Silvia, desde el primer día, y cada vez más. La perturbación que me producen sus informes sobre Raimundo ... es un estorbo para hacerme cargo de sus propias perturbaciones.[110]

And even though she knows that she is not the correct person to treat

---

[105] Martín Gaite, *Nubosidad variable*, p. 55.

[106] Martín Gaite, *Nubosidad variable*, p. 23. In Freud's time homosexuality was studied as a problem which needed to be cured. Freud refers to it as 'inversion', others, such Jean Laplanche and Jean-Bertrand Lefèvre Pontalis, refer to it as 'perversion'. One of the explanations Freud gave for the 'problem' was: 'homosexuality in the male derived from the boy's refusal to relinquish his first love-object, the mother, his subsequent unconscious IDENTIFICATION with her and his consequent search for love-objects that resembled himself': cited in Elizabeth Wright (ed.), *Feminism and Psychoanalysis: A Critical Dictionary* (Oxford: Blackwell, 1996), p. 158.

[107] Martín Gaite, *Nubosidad variable*, p. 63.

[108] Martín Gaite, *Nubosidad variable*, p. 30.

[109] 'Countertransference is broadly defined as the "whole of the analyst's unconscious reactions to the individual analysand – especially to the analysand's own transference"' (Wright, *Feminism and Psychoanalysis*, p. 431).

[110] Martín Gaite, *Nubosidad variable*, p. 99.

Silvia, Mariana not only sees her as a patient, she also lets her believe that they are good friends and uses Silvia's house as a refuge to escape from Raimundo.

For Mariana, taking refuge in Silvia's house will not, though, serve as an escape route and it is not until she decides to leave the house and hide in a hotel, completely alone, that she is able to decide what to do to resolve her situation. Carmen Alborch comments: 'El miedo a la soledad es peor que la soledad misma, sobre todo si nos obliga a soportar relaciones asfixiantes'.[111] And, indeed, the fear of solitude is central to the relationship Mariana has with the world around her. In fact, Martín Gaite comments in her *Cuadernos de todo*: 'El amor dificulta la soledad por las ataduras que cría. Es el mayor escape conocido, el mayor espejuelo de compañía. La gente cuanto más miedo tiene a la soledad física, más se ampara en el amor'.[112]

It is in her role as a psychiatrist that Mariana manages to sustain the longest emotional relationship, the one with Raimundo. The fact that he has never committed totally to their relationship may be because of his homosexuality (or bisexuality). However, she will never feel trapped in this relationship as Raimundo's bipolar disorder makes him desire and reject her continuously. Chodorow proposes that 'The capacities that enable us to create personal meaning – capacities for transference, projection, introjection, and unconscious fantasy – are innate human capacities that develop and unfold virtually from birth, in a context of interaction with others.'[113] These capacities have been developed by Mariana in such a way that she does not seem to be able to relate to others in any other capacity than through her own projection or as different from herself. When people do not conform to her projected image, Mariana feels the need to separate from them so as not to disappear as a person. Mariana's envy of Sofía's capacity to isolate herself in her own interior world, a world Mariana was not able to penetrate, made her react by separating. As Cruz-Cámara observes:

> El análisis de las relaciones amorosas de Mariana pondrán en evidencia las contradicciones del personaje, quien se mueve entre una mirada distanciada e irónica (que desprecia la novela rosa y descubre lucidamente sus trampas) y un inconsciente que, por el

---

[111] Martín Gaite, *Nubosidad variable*, p. 128.
[112] Martín Gaite, *Nubosidad variable*, p. 128.
[113] Chodorow, *The Power of Feelings*, 14.

contrario, ha articulado sus expectativas amorosas en torno a este paradigma literario.[114]

While reflecting on these relationships, Mariana realizes in her letters that what she needs is 'pactar con la soledad', or as Martín Gaite wrote in her *Cuadernos de todo*, 'comerme el mundo desde mi soledad, convertir la soledad en faro'.[115] Accordingly, Mariana writes: 'Por más vueltas que le demos, todo es soledad. Y dejar constancia de ello, quebrar las barreras que me impedían decirlo abiertamente, me permite avanzar con más holgura por un territorio que defino al elegirlo ... Porque ese territorio se revela y toma cuerpo en la escritura'.[116] From this point in the narrative, writing becomes an important part of her life. She wants to follow in her friend's footsteps and starts playing with the idea of writing a novel. Indeed, Mariana changes the way she writes: 'Lo que quizá tendría que hacer es atreverme con un texto poético donde diera rienda suelta a todas estas contradicciones con una novela quizá, y dejarme de tanto psicoanálisis'.[117] She considers different ideas about the path her writing should take: 'Podría ser una especie de diario desordenado, sin un antes y un después demasiado precisos, escrito a partir de sensaciones de extrañeza'[118] and, after days in solitude, she spends her time 'inventando comienzos para un novela epistolar dirigida a un destinatario del que también se ignora casi todo'.[119] In the end, she arrives at the idea of turning her letters and Sofía's 'deberes' into a novel: 'Y me pongo a pensar que igual entre lo que traigas tú y lo que tengo yo salía una novela estupenda a poco que la ordenáramos, o incluso sin ordenar'.[120] Mariana has come to see herself reflected in Sofía, and views Sofía as the person who can encourage her on her new adventure, as her role model: 'Ya llevo varias horas escribiendo en plan "ejercicio de redacción", lo mismo que te receté a ti'.[121]

In her letters, Mariana begins to divide into two characters: the psychiatrist, Dr León, who tries to give advice to the person inside her, the

---

[114] Nuria Cruz-Cámara, *El laberinto intertextual de Carmen Martín Gaite: Un estudio de sus novelas de los noventa* (Newark, DE: Juan de la Cuesta, 2008), p. 46.
[115] Martín Gaite, *Cuadernos*, p. 479.
[116] Martín Gaite, *Nubosidad variable*, p. 130.
[117] Martín Gaite, *Nubosidad variable*, p. 193.
[118] Martín Gaite, *Nubosidad variable*, p. 228.
[119] Martín Gaite, *Nubosidad variable*, p. 323.
[120] Martín Gaite, *Nubosidad variable*, p. 339.
[121] Martín Gaite, *Nubosidad variable*, p. 314.

woman, Mariana: 'Y tú, doctora, me impedías gritar y me mandabas contestar con mesura a las intrincadas sinrazones de mi paciente'.[122] Some episodes show a dialogue between the two characters, such as when she decides to leave her friend Silvia's house and reflects on the decision. Subsequently, Mariana confesses to Sofía at the end of Chapter VIII that her relationship with her superego is deteriorating: 'Porque tú, doctora, no me permites ser grosera ni dejar a un paciente en la estacada, por mucho que lo esté deseando. Y esa simbiosis contigo es mi condena'.[123] The psychiatrist's rationality is, as Mariana realizes, what has stopped her from being a 'real' or 'complete' woman, in the same way that Sofía's marriage was what shattered her dreams. As Mariana informs Sofía: 'Igual dejamos yo la psiquiatría y tú a tu marido'.[124] Thus, they are both going to cut their ties.

Conclusion

Nubosidad variable was the first novel Carmen Martín Gaite published after her daughter's death. Through their writing both protagonists come to understand their past and the reason why they find themselves in the state they are in at the beginning of the novel, when they meet again after years of separation. Once they have acknowledged the reason for their drifting apart, they begin to rid themselves of what stops them from changing their lives. For Mariana it is the fear of solitude, and for Sofía it is her image of being a mere reflection of others: 'yo era un espejo de cuerpo entero que los reflejaba a ellos al mirarlos, al devolverles la imagen que necesitaban para seguir existiendo',[125] a mirror which is not needed any more.

So, Sofía leaves her husband, her marital home and, later on, her maternal home, shedding the guilt she felt for not having been able to

---

[122] Martín Gaite, *Nubosidad variable*, p. 133.
[123] Martín Gaite, *Nubosidad variable*, p. 135. Cruz-Cámara comments that Martín Gaite's rejection of psychoanalysis is reflected in the fact that the character of the psychoanalyst gives a very negative portrait of this career. The critic observes: 'El signo más evidente del desprecio por el psicoanálisis se halla en el hecho de que, al final de la novela, Mariana abandone su profesión, para la cual, además, confiesa no tener vocación ni creer en su capacidad curativa' (*El laberinto intertextual*, p. 64). Nonetheless, as has been seen in this chapter, Martín Gaite has a good knowledge of the practice of psychoanalysis and knows how to apply its fundamental terms, which seems to belie any 'disdain' she may have felt towards it.
[124] Martín Gaite, *Nubosidad variable*, p. 340.
[125] Martín Gaite, *Nubosidad variable*, pp. 40–41.

forgive her mother. For her part, Mariana escapes from a relationship she created and breaks the bonds which keep her tied to Raimundo when she leaves Silvia's house: '¡He conseguido escapar! Fue como una bombilla encendida en mi mente. Porque además, el gozo de comprenderlo arrastró la decisión de una nueva escapatoria'.[126] Having taken these steps one by one, with the constant help of their writing and with the idea of the interlocutor in their minds, both women find the necessary strength to start again. The two characters gradually merge into one which is close to Martín Gaite the writer, culminating in the last occasion when they meet again and put together their writing with the intention of creating a novel with the title *Nubosidad variable*:

> Cuando te enseñe mis cartas sin enviar ... verás que la primera es fruto del insomnio en ese mismo tren [en el que se encuentra Sofía en ese momento]. Forman un montón considerable, más de cien folios. Me doy cuenta de que no he hecho otra cosa desde que salí de Madrid más que escribirte, que gracias a eso me he mantenido en vida y no puedo dar por perdido un viaje tan absurdo. Pero mi mayor alegría en este momento es saber que tú tampoco has abandonado tus 'deberes' y que me traes el regalo de varios cuadernos. ... Y me pongo a pensar que igual entre lo que traigas tú y lo que tengo yo salía una novela estupenda. ... Y fíjate si estaré loca, hasta me he puesto a acordarme de que cuando vivía en Barcelona conocí a alguno de los editores que ahora están pegando, por ejemplo Jorge Herralde,[127] que tiene fama de descubrir a gente nueva y atreverse a lanzarla.[128]

Through her letters, Sofía served Mariana as the ideal interlocutor, so as to be able to order her own thoughts, revealing desires and frustration she had never before disclosed: 'Yo esta noche te estoy contando cosas que no he contado nunca, que ni a mí misma me había contado así, tan despiadadamente'.[129] In effect, Sofía has been her psychoanalyst, the one to whom the patient can relay their most intimate feelings. As Chodorow notes: 'Psychoanalysis enables us to see how patterns from the past affect,

---

[126] Martín Gaite, *Nubosidad variable*, p. 134.
[127] Jorge Herralde is in real life a writer, editor and the owner of Editorial Anagrama, who first published *Nubosidad variable*.
[128] Martín Gaite, *Nubosidad variable*, pp. 339–40.
[129] Martín Gaite, *Nubosidad variable*, p. 97.

shape, and give meaning to the present and enables the present to reshape memory and the past.'[130]

In *Nubosidad variable*, Sofía needed that first push from Mariana to start writing again and she writes with the idea of showing her writing to Mariana. Writing has served both of them as a cure and Martín Gaite has presented in her protagonists two middle-aged women who were experiencing a mid-life crisis and who helped each other, as interlocutors and mirrors, to confront themselves and be born again, as 'el conocimiento de sí mismo [que] se adquiere a través de la exposición que destina a su interlocutor'.[131] As Alborch comments: 'Aprendimos que la amistad entre mujeres podía ser un buen antídoto contra el asunto principal de este libro, el desamor y la soledad.'[132] And these two states are what both friends conquer, through their writings and the possible publication of their memoir – which will allow them to regain their freedom.

---

[130] Chodorow, *The Power of Feelings*, p. 249.
[131] Iñaki Torre Fica, 'Discurso femenino de autodescubrimiento en *Nubosidad variable*', *Espéculo: Revista de estudios literarios* (Madrid: Universidad Complutense, 2000), available at: <http://www.ucm.es/info/especulo/cmgaite/ina_torre.html>.
[132] Alborch, p. 12.

4

La Reina de las Nieves: a Personal Search through Diaries and Letters

La Reina de las Nieves was published in 1994 although, as Martín Gaite indicates in her 'nota preliminar', it started as a project at the end of the 1970s. Although she sets the narration in the 1970s, many of the problems referring to Spanish youth became more acute in the following decade, and the length of time and the difficulties that Martín Gaite encountered during the years of preparation for this novel make it a complex piece of work.[1] The four chapters which constitute the first part of the novel are structured in a way which makes it difficult for the reader to instantly understand the relationship between the main characters. In fact, the two main characters do not meet until page 320, and their relationship is not clear until page 299. However, the author gives hints throughout that first part that suggest their paths will cross sometime in the future.

The novel is divided into three parts. The first and third parts consist of four chapters each and are recounted by an extradiegetic narrator. The second part, written in diary form, is 'taken' from the 'cuadernos de Leonardo', the work's protagonist. Leonardo starts writing these notebooks after his parents' death, a time when he feels he needs to make sense of his past to understand his present circumstances. Leonardo describes his thoughts and feelings, as well as the steps he needs to take in order to search through his past and make sense of his present. He seems to have lost all memory of his past after spending some time in prison and starts rediscovering it through his writing; as he admits, 'gracias a la escritura, la estoy empezando a recuperar'.[2] The writing of the notebooks will also allow him to see himself reflected in them, enabling him to study his situation from an objective perspective. As in *Nubosidad variable* the

---

[1] See Chapter 2 for a study of the development of this novel in the *Cuadernos de todo*.
[2] Carmen Martín Gaite, *La Reina de las Nieves* [1994] (Barcelona: Anagrama, 2002), p. 161.

process of writing is central to the narrative, making Leonardo's writing a self-conscious text.

The novel is closely related to Hans Christian Andersen's story, *The Snow Queen*. This fairy tale was one of Marta's favourites and Martín Gaite comments in the novel's 'nota preliminar' that she had great difficulties continuing with the story (after Marta's illness and death): 'a partir de enero de 1985, y por razones que atañen a mi biografía personal, solamente de pensar en *La Reina de las Nieves* se me helaba el corazón, y enterré aquellos cuadernos bajo siete estadios de tierra, creyendo que jamás tendría ganas de resucitarlos'.[3] In the 1980s Martín Gaite published two children's books, *El castillo de las tres murallas* and *El pastel del diablo*, and worked on another, *Caperucita en Manhattan*. These stories, together with the translations she did of other fairy tales and children's stories, amongst them Cott's anthology *Cuentos de hadas victorianos* (1993) and MacDonald's classic *La princesa y los trasgos* (1995), all influenced *La Reina de las Nieves*. The author seems to have escaped into children's literature to forget her traumatic losses.

There are other literary works which also throw light on the presentation of the two main characters, Leonardo and Casilda. They are both clearly reflections of the characters in Andersen's tale and, in addition, Leonardo is compared to the protagonist of *L'Étranger* (1942) by Albert Camus, while Casilda is seen as a projection of the protagonist of Henrik Ibsen's *The Lady From the Sea* (1888). In these two works the protagonists are presented as different, independent and nonconforming to social norms, in a similar way to the two main characters of *La Reina de las Nieves*. This way of looking at Casilda and Leonardo as essentially nonconforming types is principally the view of Eugenio, Leonardo's father. In the letter Casilda reads in Chapter 3, Eugenio compares her and Leonardo with himself: 'también sé que me desprecias. Como Leonardo. ... Pertenecéis a una raza distinta. A ese grupo de seres privilegiados y superiores para quienes la soledad supone liberación y no condena'.[4] The use of the words 'solitude' and 'freedom' indicates the main themes in the novel, which were dealt with extensively by Martín Gaite in her previous works, especially in *Cuadernos de todo* and *Nubosidad variable*. In *Cuadernos*, Martín Gaite wrote: 'no podemos pensar, carecemos de soledad y libertad para ello',[5] suggesting the importance which both states have in moments

---

[3] Martín Gaite, *La Reina de las Nieves*, p. 11.
[4] Martín Gaite, *La Reina de las Nieves*, p. 47.
[5] Carmen Martín Gaite, *Cuadernos de todo*, ed. and intro. Maria Vittoria Calvi

of reflection. While in *Nubosidad variable* the protagonists try to achieve solitude to attain freedom, in *La Reina* the main characters are on their own from the beginning, having rejected company and social conventions. As seen in Chapter 2, the idea of solitude was part of the novel's story from the beginning when Martín Gaite started writing it in the 1970s.

Letters are also an important part of the narrative. Leonardo discovers a number of letters and other documents hidden in his father's safe. These put him in contact with his father's past, a past which Leonardo knew little about. The characters of Casilda and Eugenio (as well as the grandmother) develop through the letters which are merged in Leonardo's notebooks. In the third part of the novel, Casilda also gives the reader a number of clues which will clarify some of the circumstances Leonardo has been investigating.

Suspense is one of the characteristics of the diary-novel, as H. Porter Abbott explains in *Diary Fiction: Writing as Action*.[6] And in *La Reina de las Nieves*, Martín Gaite has indeed applied this literary technique to give the narrative authenticity. Discovering his past is a slow process for the protagonist. First of all, Leonardo must discover the identity of the mysterious woman known only in his father's documents as S. For the reader, the development of the story is as slow and full of suspense as the process of discovery the protagonist must go through as he reads the documents in his father's study and writes up his discoveries afterwards.[7]

Leonardo's Notebooks: Writing (oneself)/Discovering (oneself)

H. Porter Abbott distinguishes three different functions in what he calls 'diary fiction as a field'. In his section 'Thematic Functions: Isolation and Self-Reflection', Abbott considers the solitude the writer requires in order to write. Another characteristic of the diary-novel is that the text is a mirror (reflection) for the diary-writer who will reread it: 'We are restricted to a document that emanates from *inside* the story. We sit at and read what the diarist describes himself as sitting at, writing, and often, as we are, reading himself.'[8] A third aspect is discussed in his section

---

(Barcelona: Areté, 2002), p. 56.

[6] H. Porter Abbott, *Diary Fiction: Writing as Action* (Ithaca, NY: Cornell University Press, 1984), p. 27.

[7] Catherine O'Leary and Alison Ribeiro de Menezes see this technique as typical of the 'classic detective novel': *A Companion to Carmen Martín Gaite* (Woodbridge: Tamesis Books, 2009), p. 147.

[8] Abbott, p. 24.

'Temporal Functions: Immediacy, Suspense, and Timelessness.'[9] Here he considers the way the writer lives in the present and how the future forms the diary that is written, since the diary gives form to past, present and possibly the future. A sense of suspense is created by the fact that both the diary-writer in a narrative and the reader are unaware of what will happen; they will discover this together. Apart from those functions, Abbott proposes that it is the plot itself that is closely connected to diary-writing: 'It is a reflexive text – not simply in the sense of a self-reflecting or self-conscious text, but in the sense that the text exerts an effective influence on its writer.'[10]

The title of the second part of *La Reina de las Nieves* makes it clear that the reader is dealing with Leonardo's notebooks: 'Segunda parte. (De los cuadernos de Leonardo)'.[11] At the same time, Leonardo immediately acknowledges that he is in the process of writing: 'igual que ahora sé que tengo la pluma en la mano'.[12] He starts writing the 'story' of his life, just like Mariana and Sofía of *Nubosidad variable*. In Chapter II of the second part, Leonardo starts the story from the beginning, from the moment he arrives back home, as, he comments, is done in 'good' novels: 'Empezaré contando cómo fue la llegada. Las buenas novelas, él [su padre] lo decía siempre, suelen empezar con una llegada'.[13]

Leonardo's writing of the notebooks normally takes place in his late father's study. This room is important not only as the place where he is writing his diary, but also as a place of origin for Leonardo, where he will discover his beginnings. Opening his father's safe, having found the code, allows him into a world which his father, in life, could not let him explore, but for which he had offered clues. Opening the safe also opens a dialogue between father and son, something that was not possible during their life together. Inside the safe there are documents which, in the novel, alternate with Leonardo's own writing, and which reveal to the reader past times, before the protagonist's birth. These documents describe the father's youth in Galicia. In addition there are letters written to the father, signed with the initial 'S', indicating an unknown relationship. Together with those the grandmother wrote to her son, S's letters gradually complete the puzzle which constitutes the life of Leonardo until, at the end, the reader

---

[9] Abbott, p. 27.
[10] Abbott, p. 38.
[11] Martín Gaite, *La Reina de las Nieves*, p. 67.
[12] Martín Gaite, *La Reina de las Nieves*, p. 69.
[13] Martín Gaite, *La Reina de las Nieves*, p. 73.

is able to understand his mysterious and strange character, as well as his isolation from his family.

Leonardo gives many details of what is happening in his life from the moment he arrives in his father's study and decides to start writing. He even notes the conversations he has with people, dead or alive, who cross his path. These conversations and documents from the past (letters, manuscripts and other material found in his father's safe) help Leonardo unravel a past he never understood. He narrates the methodology he adopts when writing these notebooks:

> A ratos atiendo a los argumentos plasmados en los papeles que don Ernesto me dejó, otras veces a los que se esconden detrás del faro [donde se encuentra la caja fuerte]. Y de esta mezcla de pasado y presente surge un nuevo surco intemporal: el de mi escritura.[14]

The dialogues reproduced in Leonardo's notebooks, such as the one when his father appears in the study, help the reader to understand certain details. For example, this dialogue with his father refers to past conversations and the relationship which existed between them. His father is also presented as an ideal interlocutor, someone who can listen all night long. The differences and difficulties which they had when his father was alive are erased after his death and now Leonardo is free to talk to him as his equal: 'Y entonces nos miramos. ... Sencillamente nos estábamos mirando por primera vez en la vida con equivalente fijeza, estableciendo una especie de complicidad'.[15] Just as with his father, Leonardo converses with his mother (Gertrud) and his grandmother. These conversations are guided by Leonardo; he finds it easier to 'talk' to them now, especially with his mother, as he can decide what to talk about and when to finish the conversation:

> Casi siempre es después de apagar la luz y extender el cuerpo buscando un acomodo para convocar el sueño, cuando me habla mi madre de problemas domésticos. Nunca le contesto. ... No me gusta humillar a los muertos. Y además, aunque la convenciera de algo, que lo dudo, ya no tiene remedio.[16]

Leonardo does not have friends to return to when he leaves prison.

---

[14] Martín Gaite, *La Reina de las Nieves*, p. 119.
[15] Martín Gaite, *La Reina de las Nieves*, p. 70.
[16] Martín Gaite, *La Reina de las Nieves*, pp. 221–2.

Formerly friends, who involved him in the situation which took him to prison, belong to a past he cannot remember. It is as if he had to forget everything that happened before going to prison in order to be able to start anew. His hallucinations and dreams at the beginning of the novel are produced by hashish; in prison, that substance helps him relax and forget his situation. Then, when he leaves prison and is still in a catatonic state, he uses hashish to be able to think. Arriving at his parents' house he describes his state in the following way:

> '¿Para qué he venido', me preguntaba. '¿Para qué?' Incapaz de detener mis pasos o de retroceder, ... luchaba entre dos fuerzas encontradas ...: una que me urgía a seguir avanzando en nombre de una inercia olvidada, otra que me avisaba del peligro y me aconsejaba escapar de nuevo a la falsa aventura, a buscar un remedo de refugio en viviendas y voces más o menos recordadas, en locales ruidosos donde corren la droga y el dinero ... Obedecí por fin al mandato primero, pero sin convicción, pensando: '¡Qué más da, también esto es un sueño!'[17]

The lack of an available interlocutor (especially after his father's former chauffeur/secretary, Mauricio Brito, leaves the house) and the need to understand the fog of his past, makes Leonardo take up a pen and start writing his notebooks. As Martín Gaite notes many times, there is a close relationship between the lack of an interlocutor and the need to write.[18]

Thanks to the importance he has always given to his notebooks he can reread them, thus providing the reader with information on his whereabouts before prison:

> Me incluyen, a pesar mío, en escenas como de cine mudo ocurridas en Tánger, en Ámsterdam, en Verona, en una cárcel, en el Boulevard Saint-Germain. ... Me veo dentro de sueños sucesivos, gesticulando junto a seres borrosos, diciendo palabras que no oigo, fingiendo pasiones que no siento.[19]

Leonardo's notebooks have similarities with Martín Gaite's *Cuadernos de todo*. He writes, 'antes las estuve releyendo y copiando en limpio con algunas rectificaciones en el mismo cuaderno que estoy usando ahora,

---

[17] Martín Gaite, *La Reina de las Nieves*, p. 74.
[18] See Chapter 1 for Martín Gaite's ideas on the search for an interlocutor.
[19] Martín Gaite, *La Reina de las Nieves*, p. 72.

amarillo con argollas, tamaño folio',[20] while she notes in her *Cuadernos de todo*:

> Hoy, en la tarde del 27 de octubre de 1974, voy a tratar de pasar a limpio, en este cuaderno tan agradable que me regaló Torán, algunas de las notas que salgan a relucir en mis cuadernos viejos y que tengan que ver con el asunto de la narración.
> Procuraré no limitarme a copiarlas sino ampliarlas a la luz de ese nuevo propósito ...
> [R]evisar cuadernos viejos, llevo mucho tiempo sabiendo que es esto lo primero que tengo que hacer, volver al origen, partir de mis primeros cuadernos de todo, pero no me atrevía. Es como bajar a la bodega a explorar los cimientos de la casa y es duro de pelar.[21]

In fact, this note was written by Martín Gaite at a time when she was working on *La Reina de las Nieves*, although then the novel still did not have its title. But with these words it is possible to see that the way the author writes in her notebooks influences her protagonist. Another characteristic which both author and protagonist share is the writing of their dreams where they both 'meet' their dead parents and talk to them. As was seen in Chapter 2, Martín Gaite started her own *pesquisa* in *Cuenta pendiente*. The worlds of the writer and her fictional character are constantly interlaced.

Reading old notebooks, however chaotic they may be, also helps Leonardo, in the same way that they helped Martín Gaite, to understand the need to start again. Leonardo writes:

> Hoy he revisado cuadernos de los últimos años, y me ha parecido pasar la mano por las cicatrices de mi conflicto frente a la escritura. En todos ellos se alternan los más inconsistentes desvaríos y las notas más caóticas con algún espacio en blanco, a partir del cual la caligrafía se recompone y, durante unas líneas, que progresivamente se van desintegrando, se mantiene un propósito de orden: la promesa de un auténtico comienzo.[22]

But that beginning will not happen until he starts in the place where he lived and where his parents' spirits are still alive. Leonardo finds it

---

[20] Martín Gaite, *La Reina de las Nieves*, p. 78.
[21] Martín Gaite, *Cuadernos*, p. 301.
[22] Martín Gaite, *La Reina de las Nieves*, p. 71.

difficult to confront the person he has become in the last few years, years when he decided to escape from his family, from a mother he never loved, from his wealth, and from a life he saw as inauthentic.

After his grandmother's death (the only member of the family whom he feels gave him love), Leonardo decides to escape. But after his parents' death he is able to return home and start again: '¡Sí, he vuelto! ... Ahora voy a empezar. ... he cerrado todos mis cuadernos y los he guardado en el macuto. ... Tengo que emprender la pesquisa solo'.[23] As has been seen, solitude and isolation are fundamental to reflect on and write about those reflections. Consequently, the writing of the diary, and the writing of a novel, start merging in Leonardo's head. Is he writing for his readers or for himself? At the same time, his own writing is muddled up with his father's frustrated desire to be a novelist: 'de joven había querido ser escritor'.[24] Ultimately, he follows his father's rules of writing.

Leonardo relates where and how he writes, what made him start writing at such and such a moment, as well as his thoughts or the circumstances which led him to write his thoughts:

> Hice un alto en la labor para sacar de mi macuto, que había dejado contra la pared, una libreta con tapas de hule que estrené en la enfermería de la cárcel y apuntar este paralelo entre la reconstrucción de los sueños y la de la cama, tema bien sugerente. Las sugerencias luego se fueron ampliando y me senté en el suelo para escribir más cómodo. Llené varias páginas.[25]

The above detailed account makes his narration a statement to be read by others and also one which is written with an imaginary interlocutor in mind.

Leonardo's diary writing also reveals a double perspective. He is both the narrator and protagonist of his story; he is living it and writing it: 'Mi vida era aquella marea de palabras, pero al mismo tiempo la

---

[23] Martín Gaite, *La Reina de las Nieves*, p. 73.
[24] Martín Gaite, *La Reina de las Nieves*, p. 114. Many of Martín Gaite's characters are frustrated writers who keep folders with beginnings for novels which, for one reason or another, never reach an end, similar to her daughter, who never finished anything as the author stated in *Cuaderno 35* (*Cuadernos*, p. 613). There are, for example, folders like the one C. keeps in *El cuarto de atrás*, full of newspaper and magazine cuttings and ideas for books and articles. Eugenio also has another similarity with the author, his love for the eighteenth century. This is developed by Águeda in *Lo raro es vivir*.
[25] Martín Gaite, *La Reina de las Nieves*, p. 77.

contemplaba desde lo alto, impávido, con ojos de gaviota'.[26] As Abbott observes: 'In diary fiction of any psychological pretension, the diarist is usually concerned, with greater or less intensity, to see himself through the agency of his diary. It can be a task roughly equivalent to levitation, involving as it does the difficulty of the subject being its own object.'[27] In his diaries, Leonardo emerges as different people: the one who wrote in his notebooks (and the 'character' he was writing about), different from the 'I' in the present moment. This 'I' also divides itself into the narrator and the protagonist, as well as the reader of the diaries: 'Pero mis cuadernos, además, me atrapan con tentáculos mucho más peligrosos, al sugerirme la identificación con las andanzas y mudanzas de la persona que los escribía'.[28] This split even leads him to talk to himself: 'Pero no escribas más, mírame y dime. ¿Has vuelto de verdad?, ¿te has atrevido?, ¿no será, como siempre, retazos de tu sueño?'[29] In the same way that in *Nubosidad variable* Mariana separates into the woman and the psychiatrist, Dr León, Leonardo also compares himself with Dr Jekyll when he sees himself in the mirror. Gérard Genette explains the different layers that form this type of narrative:

> The journal and the epistolary confidence constantly combine what in broadcasting language is called the live and the prerecorded account, the quasi-interior monologue and the account after the event. Here, the narrator is at one and the same still the hero and already someone else. The events of the day are already in the past, and the 'point of view' may have been modified since then; the feelings of the evening or the next day are fully of the present, and here focalization through the narrator is at the same time focalization through the hero.[30]

Leonardo is afraid of not noting down everything that happens to him. When he leaves the house, he despairs about not having a piece of paper on which he can write down as soon as possible what has just happened to him and the thoughts which develop after these experiences:

---

[26] Martín Gaite, *La Reina de las Nieves*, p. 71.
[27] Abbott, p. 25.
[28] Martín Gaite, *La Reina de las Nieves*, p. 72.
[29] Martín Gaite, *La Reina de las Nieves*, p. 72.
[30] Gérard Genette, *Narrative Discourse*, trans. Jane E. Lewin (Oxford: Basil Blackwell, 1980), p. 218.

> 'Necesito otro lector agregado, eso es lo que pasa, ni más ni menos, una persona que me leyera', pensé en un rapto de iluminación repentina. Y me pareció tan importante el hallazgo que lo apunté en una servilleta de papel, medio a escondidas.[31]

Indeed, writing his diary becomes the most important thing for him: 'Soñaba con un cuaderno sin estrenar a la luz tamizada de la lámpara verde'.[32] In fact, there are moments of despair when he finds himself without a notebook. So, when he has to leave his father's study to visit the family accountant to clear up some points about his situation, this makes him lose his way. His steps take him to the bars where he used to go with his old friends,[33] although, just like Sofía when she wakes up in 'el refugio', Leonardo cannot remember how he got there. He realizes his personality has changed but he is still unable to go against his impulse:

> Y es que los deseos de huir chocaban con algo que me resistía a registrar por las buenas como ganas de acostarme con la primera mujer que se me había puesto a tiro. ... Por otra parte, la ginebra y el hash incrementaban mi fatiga, tanto para hacer el esfuerzo de levantarme como para interpretar síntomas de motivación compleja.[34]

The meeting in the bar with old friends makes him reflect on his tendency to run away: in this case what he wants to run away from are drugs and also the inertia which does not allow him to think. He needs to continue writing down every question which comes into his head and, to this end, he borrows pen and paper from the girl in the cloakroom. Thanks to his inertia, though, the other girl he meets in the bar drives him to her home, where he meets another character of the novel and this gives him the last clues he needs to get to Casilda Iriarte. Mónica, the room-mate of the girl from the bar, puts Leonardo in contact with some 'old friends', literary works which will bring him memories of his early youth and of his former interests: Erich Fromm's *El miedo a la libertad*,[35] Mircea Eliade's *Lo sagrado y lo profano*,[36] Adelbert von Chamisso's *El hombre*

---

[31] Martín Gaite, *La Reina de las Nieves*, p. 179.
[32] Martín Gaite, *La Reina de las Nieves*, p. 201.
[33] This episode, narrated over two chapters XI and XII, shows a group of young people in a bar in Madrid exposed to the influences of drugs, alcohol, music and free love.
[34] Martín Gaite, *La Reina de las Nieves*, p. 180.
[35] Martín Gaite, *La Reina de las Nieves*, p. 208.
[36] Martín Gaite, *La Reina de las Nieves*, p. 210.

que perdió su sombra[37] and Casilda Iriarte's *Ensayos sobre el vértigo*.[38] This last work, mentioned in the context of real literary works, becomes part of the reader's reality. The image on the cover of Casilda's book, 'Caminante sobre un mar de niebla' by the German Romantic painter, Caspar David Friedrich, an artist whom Leonardo mentions in other moments of the novel, gives Casilda's book yet another level of artistic reality.

As was seen in Chapter 3, what Martín Gaite reads becomes part of what her protagonists read. For instance, there is a comment on Erich Fromm's *Psicoanálisis de la sociedad contemporánea* in *Cuaderno 2* of *Cuadernos de todo*[39] where the author writes about solitude and intimacy. Furthermore, in an article published in 1990, Martín Gaite mentions Mircea Eliade's book in the context of young people's need for solitude: 'En las aficiones de la juventud actual se ha instalado el terror al aburrimiento y la necesidad de conjurarlo como sea, de no dejar espacio sin imágenes ni ruidos por donde pueda colarse el aprendizaje de la soledad'.[40] This idea links with the novel's themes of solitude and Leonardo (and Mónica) as different to others.

The encounter with Mónica suggests another recurrent theme in Martín Gaite's work, destiny. The meeting between Leonardo and Mónica not only happens in a physical way: it also works through literature, opening the possibility of dialogue between man and woman, crossing gender barriers and revealing common intellectual interests. This situation recalls the conversation between aunt and nephew in *Retahílas* or between C. and the man in black in *El cuarto de atrás*. Furthermore, the conversation between Mónica and Leonardo, and the books they discuss, also gives indications of their characters. Mónica identifies her situation with Chamisso's protagonist, the man who lost his shadow (her shadow being her mother), then links the lack of shadow (mother) with the feeling of vertigo, the theme of Casilda Iriarte's book. And this book connects in the novel with the fear of freedom, or the vertigo felt in moments of freedom. The symbiosis between reality and fiction, or the 'amalgama vida-literatura',[41] as much in Leonardo as in Mónica, serves as a reminder

---

[37] Martín Gaite, *La Reina de las Nieves*, p. 217.
[38] Martín Gaite, *La Reina de las Nieves*, p. 219.
[39] Martín Gaite, *Cuadernos*, pp. 79–82.
[40] Carmen Martín Gaite, 'La lectura amenazada', in *Tirando del hilo (Artículos 1949–2000)*, ed. and intro. José Teruel (Madrid: Siruela, 2006), pp. 437–9 (p. 438).
[41] Martín Gaite, *La Reina de las Nieves*, p. 126.

of the difficulty Sofía in *Nubosidad variable* has in separating life from what she reads.[42]

Meeting Mónica and the consequent reading of Casilda's book gives Leonardo courage to make his final decision. At the beginning of the novel, he is presented as not responsible for some of his actions. Indeed, it is not until the development he goes through as he writes his diaries that he is able to make the decision to meet Casilda, with all its consequences. From that moment onwards, the diary disappears from the novel, having lost its main function of serving as a guide for the future.[43] Leonardo's decision to visit Casilda Iriarte changes his life forever.

The Letters: Searching for the Mother

The letters can be seen as 'secondary characters' of the narrative as reading them helps Leonardo (and the reader) to understand the past, and to hear the voices of those who wrote them. The first letter in the novel is that written by Leonardo's father, Eugenio, and sent to Casilda, also being the final letter Eugenio wrote before his death. As Leonardo discovers, Casilda and Eugenio maintained an epistolary relationship for most of their lives: 'mi padre, aunque posiblemente ya hubiera conocido a Gertrud Scribner, seguía manteniendo relaciones epistolares con la nieta del farero'.[44]

The letters Leonardo finds in the safe, the fragments of which are merged in his narrative, come from two women, the initials of whose first names, together with that of Leonardo, make the code which opens the safe. These are the initials of what his father termed 'personas queridas'.[45] This is the first mystery Leonardo has to solve: the name of a flower, which read the other way is the name of a river, gives him 'Lis'/'Sil'.

---

[42] There are other characteristics which link Sofía and Leonardo, such as their love for George Moustaki's music (Martín Gaite, *La Reina de las Nieves*, p. 178; *Nubosidad variable* [1992] (Barcelona: Anagrama, 2002), p. 40); the need to write what is happening in order to be able to assimilate what is going on in their lives, 'demasiados datos de una vez' (*La Reina de las Nieves*, p. 126); or the inertia which dictated their lives until the moment they started writing themselves.

[43] Leonardo takes all his notebooks with him to Galicia. Thinking about the possibility of losing them he reflects: 'comprendía que perderla [la maleta en donde se encuentran los cuadernos] habría significado perder el rastro de los últimos meses y de todo el tiempo que dormita en el lago helado de la memoria' (p. 322), which resembles the moment when, arriving at Kennedy Airport, Martín Gaite herself feared she was going to lose the suitcases with all her notebooks (*Cuadernos de todo*, pp. 613–16).

[44] Martín Gaite, *La Reina de las Nieves*, p. 238.

[45] Martín Gaite, *La Reina de las Nieves*, p. 116.

Although he knows the subjects of two of the initials, I for Inés, his grandmother, and L for Leonardo (his mother's initial G, is, of course, not one of them), S is a mystery to him. This initial comes to reveal not one but three women: Sila, his father's girlfriend; Silveria, the young girl who travels to England to meet her father and who writes the story and becomes the protagonist of the novel *El periplo*; and Casilda, the woman who bought La Quinta Blanca, and who is also the author of the book on vertigo that Leonardo found in Mónica's house.

Each one of these women develops through the letters, books and other documents that Leonardo reads, until the moment the protagonist discovers that they are all one person:

> Después de un repaso febril a los papeles de Sila, donde ya tanto sale a relucir el vértigo, padecí un espejismo. Las vi fundirse a la una con la otra dentro de un hexágono que contiene todo el zumo rosado y gris de los atardeceres precipitados desde que el mundo sobre la isla de las gaviotas, la C abrazándose a la S, los ojos de la niña que mira al mar y sueña con viajes imposibles desembocando en los de la mujer que retorna de esos viajes, los mismos ojos que se sustituyen y confunden, la misma cosecha de mirada, la misma mujer, el mismo faro.[46]

In the third part of *La Reina*, the character of Casilda comes to the fore. As a writer herself the process of writing, and the need to write, is brought into play. Similar to the protagonists in *Nubosidad variable*, Casilda uses writing as a refuge and, like Martín Gaite herself, her need to write and the pleasure she gets out of it can be clearly seen in her face: 'y cuando te metes en tu cuarto y empieza a sonar el tecleo de la máquina, ... te sienta tan bien. Se te nota en la cara'.[47] In this third part Casilda talks about old letters and documents and their use when writing a story. She also confesses to Mauricio that, since she talked to Leonardo, she now uses him as her interlocutor: 'escribiendo para él, soñando con él'.[48] Sila's old letters also seem to be addressing Leonardo, who responds as if they were a real person talking to him: 'Tienes razón – le digo –, para eso está

---

[46] Martín Gaite, *La Reina de las Nieves*, p. 236.
[47] Martín Gaite, *La Reina de las Nieves*, pp. 292–3. In 'Retahíla con nieve en Nueva York', Martín Gaite recounts how her mother could see in her face the moment when she had a new project in mind: *Agua pasada* (Barcelona: Anagrama, 1993), pp. 26–32 (p. 31).
[48] Martín Gaite, *La Reina de las Nieves*, p. 307.

el arte'.[49] He then begins to sense that the person who writes the letters is closer to himself, giving him the feeling, once he starts reading Casilda's *Ensayos sobre el vértigo*, that he is the one who is writing it: 'lo escribo al leerlo'.[50]

Written to different parts of the world, the letters not only make the person who wrote them present, but also show the trajectory of the addressee. Through the addresses written on the envelopes, 'Mi padre está en Santiago estudiando Derecho, mi padre está en Madrid, mi padre está en América del Norte, estado de Illinois, lo veo por los sobres, que algunos se conservan',[51] and through the observations that the letter writers make of what he had written to them, more of Eugenio's personality emerges:

> Después de besarnos, sé que estamos llenos de deseos que nos separan. ... Dices: 'te estás evaporando', y suena a reproche. ... Por ejemplo, cuando no te hago caso y me quedo mirando el mar. De nada te sirve entonces preguntarme rabioso '¿qué piensas?', forzándome a que atienda y quite los ojos del mar. No me zarandees, déjame, no sé explicar lo que pienso.[52]

The fragments of the letters written by the grandmother also reveal some of Eugenio's feelings: '«Te crees que no sé lo que te pasa», le dice en una carta, «pero cuanto más me hablas de dinero, de negocios y de la gente tan importante que estás conociendo, más atisbo lo que escondes a tu madre»'.[53]

Eugenio's letters to his son, although infrequent in the narrative, give an idea of their relationship. Although Leonardo maintained a 'relación epistolar'[54] with his father for a long time after leaving home, this was abandoned when his mother's signature started appearing on Eugenio's letters, causing Leonardo to resent her interference in the genuinely spontaneous relationship between father and son:

> En la esquina superior del texto se había colado ahora una apostilla oblicua y siempre idéntica: «Besos, mamá», decía. ... La incursión de su firma no sólo mediatizaba y teñía de convencionalismo las

---

49 Martín Gaite, *La Reina de las Nieves*, p. 123.
50 Martín Gaite, *La Reina de las Nieves*, p. 224.
51 Martín Gaite, *La Reina de las Nieves*, p. 122.
52 Martín Gaite, *La Reina de las Nieves*, p. 124.
53 Martín Gaite, *La Reina de las Nieves*, p. 129.
54 Martín Gaite, *La Reina de las Nieves*, p. 145.

palabras de mi padre, sino que entorpecía, por añadidura, la espontaneidad de mi respuesta.[55]

These letters are documents from the father's past but, by copying parts of them in his notebooks, Leonardo is giving them a new temporality, forming part of the text which in the present helps form his future. The protagonist/diary-writer thus becomes the editor of the letters which he transcribes.[56] One of the facts that Leonardo comes to understand better is the difficult relationship he had with his mother. In effect, the difficulties in their relationship hindered the development of the child Leonardo. As Winnicott observes:

> Only if there is a good-enough mother does the infant start on a process of development that is personal and real. If the mothering is not good enough then the infant becomes a collection of reactions to impingement, and the true self of the infant fails to form or becomes hidden behind a false self.[57]

The idea of the 'good-enough mother' developed by Winnicott, discusses the needs the baby has from the moment it is born and how the mother is the facilitator of those needs: 'The good-enough mother ... starts off with an almost complete adaptation to her infant's needs, and as time proceeds she adapts less and less completely.'[58] The mother must be the one who facilitates the child's adaptation to the environment. For normal development to take place, the child needs a 'facilitating environment': 'The facilitating environment is first absolutely and then relatively important, and the course of development can be described in terms of absolute dependence, relative dependence, and towards independence.'[59] In Leonardo's case, the narrative reveals the rejection his mother felt for him, a mother who denies him an adequate environment in which to

---

[55] Martín Gaite, *La Reina de las Nieves*, p. 145.
[56] A similar example of this type of writing is found in Carme Riera's novel, *La mitad del alma* (Madrid: Alfaguara, 2004), where the writer/protagonist/narrator writes the novel with the hope of finding the mystery man who gave her a number of letters written by her mother to a lover the protagonist knew nothing about. The narrator/protagonist's choice of passages from the mother's letters is made, in her words, with regard to the need to find the mystery man.
[57] Donald W. Winnicott, *The Family and Individual Development* (London: Tavistock/Routledge, 1989), p. 17.
[58] Donald W. Winnicott, 'Transitional Objects and Transitional Phenomena', *International Journal of Psycho-Analysis*, 34 (1953), 89–97, p. 94.
[59] Winnicott, *The Family*, p. 19.

develop. The father, who could have given the boy the emotional support to mature, was too weak to confront even his own mother. Eugenio found that the only way out was separation from a strong mother (and also from the woman he loved). In the United States, he finds another woman who, although physically weak, knows how to keep him close to her.

Casilda, Leonardo's blood mother, is the only character in the novel who is not afraid of freedom. When she leaves her Galician village, she is not escaping but confronting her past, travelling to meet her father. Although in love with Eugenio, Casilda knows that the difference in social class will never let them continue with their relationship.[60] She also needs a freedom he would never have been able to give her, while Eugenio needs to leave the country to find success, to show the world (and his mother) how much he is worth. As Fromm notes: 'The self-confidence, the "feeling of self", is merely an indication of what others think of the person. It is not *he* who is convinced of his value regardless of popularity and his success on the market.'[61] Of course, Casilda never really abandoned Eugenio, and even showed her love after his marriage by giving him the son his wife could not.

Other than the letters found in Eugenio's study, important letters in the novel include those written to be read only after a death. For example, the letter from Inés that his mother gave him does not give Leonardo the confession he was expecting. His grandmother asks him to keep La Quinta Blanca, which she gave him as an inheritance. However Leonardo, rebelling against the person who loved him most, decides to get rid of the property as soon as possible and escape. On the other hand, the letter given by the priest to Casilda on the death of Antonio Moura (the former schoolteacher and an old friend of her grandfather) brings great, although sad, memories from the past, showing how Moura had recognized Casilda upon her return to the village as the granddaughter of the lighthouse keeper, even though he never told her.

Casilda's character is presented mainly through her letters, and is developed in the first part of the novel by the narrator and in the third part through her own confession. Chapter III of the third part is titled 'Confidencias' and shows two characters, a man and a woman, who during one night converse about their past, serving as another reminder of Martín Gaite's other two novels where that type of interlocution is central. In these confessions, or *confidencias*, Casilda talks about her life,

---

[60] A theme which will come up again in *Irse de casa*.
[61] Erich Fromm, *The Fear of Freedom* (London: Routledge, 1961), p. 103.

but her interlocutor, Mauricio, thinks that she should write her memoirs, 'la novela de su vida',[62] instead of recounting it to him. Eugenio had also asked her to write and publish her autobiography, for he needs her memoirs to understand what happened to his life: 'Lo que me estaba encargando era que hablara por escrito de nuestros amores'.[63]

For Casilda it is difficult to talk about her past since the most difficult chapter of her life was her son Leonardo's birth, the son she gave to Eugenio and his wife to be raised as their own: '¿Cuándo mete tijera la censura? ¿Cuándo nos enteramos de que tu bella esposa es estéril o un poquito más tarde?'[64] Casilda also has documents, given with Moura's package, which help her remember her story: letters, photographs, and the diary she wrote in her youth, and in which she described the first time she talked to Eugenio. The photograph of Casilda that Leonardo found in the safe links with a copy of the photograph Casilda finds amongst the other documents, connecting the two protagonists once again. As occurs in *Nubosidad variable*, Leonardo catches the night train to meet Casilda, taking with him his notebooks. Thus the union of the two stories will come to constitute the novel.

The Fairy Tale: A Psychoanalytic Perspective

As seen, the influence of fairy tales is very important in the development of *La Reina de las Nieves* and this is shown in the use of Andersen's story *The Snow Queen* as intertext.[65] Martín Gaite interpolates and reworks parts of the fairy tale in her novel, so that certain characters in Andersen's story are reflected in Leonardo. Like Kay, the protagonist of *The Snow Queen*, Leonardo has to put together the pieces of mirror which compose his life, achieving this through the writing of his notebooks.[66] Some of Kay's characteristics, especially the coldness he feels in the presence of

---

[62] Martín Gaite, *La Reina de las Nieves*, p. 296.
[63] Martín Gaite, *La Reina de las Nieves*, p. 299.
[64] Martín Gaite, *La Reina de las Nieves*, p. 299.
[65] As this novel has such a close relation to Andersen's story it has often been studied as part of Martín Gaite's children's stories. Mercedes Carbayo Abengózar includes it under the subtitle 'Los cuentos de hadas' in *Buscando un lugar entre mujeres: Buceo en la España de Carmen Martín Gaite* (Malaga: Servicio de Publicaciones de la Universidad, 1998), p. 130, and Lissette Rolón Collazo under 'Representación y re-escritura del cuento de hadas', in *Figuraciones: Mujeres en Carmen Martín Gaite, revistas femeninas y ¡Hola!* (Madrid: Iberoamericana, 2002), p. 154.
[66] The pieces of mirror are a further reminder of Natalia Ginzburg's words that serve as an epigraph to *Nubosidad variable*, as described in Chapter 3.

the Snow Queen, are also experienced by Leonardo in the presence of his mother, who is portrayed as a woman with a heart of ice. In addition, Leonardo is seen writing his notebooks to save his future, in the same way that Kay assembles the pieces of glass in order to escape the Snow Queen's castle. Furthermore, Leonardo's resolution to continue with his search is also a reminder of Gerda's determination to find Kay. On one occasion, he thinks of Gerda and follows her example after deciding to go and meet Casilda: 'Se acordó de Gerda y fue como quitarse una venda de los ojos. ¿Había tenido ella en cuenta los cambios de temperatura para seguir adelante en el complicado periplo que había de llevarla … a devolverle la memoria a Kay?'[67]

Although many critics link the character of Gerda to Casilda, Casilda does not take the necessary steps to rescue Leonardo/Kay from his 'prison'. The only moment when the protagonists are compared is in the encounter at the end of the novel: 'Por fin has venido Gerda, cuánto has tardado en venir',[68] Leonardo says to Casilda. During the second part of the novel Leonardo never stops his quest to understand his past and save himself, in the same way that Gerda never gives up in her search for Kay. Rolón Collazo comments on the fact that Leonardo takes control, but using Casilda's writing as 'enigma que debe desentrañar'.[69] Finally, in Martín Gaite's words, 'Gerda lo llora sin que él se sepa llorado'.[70]

The novel contains another two works as intertext, and even though they are not as obvious as Andersen's story, they do serve to illustrate some of the characteristics of the protagonists. Meursault, the main character in Albert Camus's *L'Étranger*, is mentioned by Leonardo as someone his father used to compare him to:

> El papel del extranjero me vino adjudicado el día en que mi padre me comparó con el protagonista de la novela de Camus, cuando se la di a leer. Yo, por mi cuenta, ya me había identificado con ese personaje de ficción. Pero el espaldarazo definitivo me lo dio él cuando me dijo, al devolverme el libro, que no le extrañaba que me hubiera gustado tanto porque el protagonista era igual que yo.[71]

This link between Camus's character and Leonardo helps to reinforce

---

[67] Martín Gaite, *La Reina de las Nieves*, p. 310.
[68] Martín Gaite, *La Reina de las Nieves*, p. 331.
[69] Rolón Collazo, pp. 163–4.
[70] Martín Gaite, *Cuadernos*, p. 288.
[71] Martín Gaite, *La Reina de las Nieves*, pp. 138–9.

the connection with Andersen's protagonist for, like Kay and Leonardo, Meursault cannot cry:

> In our society any man who doesn't cry at his mother's funeral is liable to be condemned because he doesn't play the game. In this sense, he is an outsider to the society in which he lives, wandering on the fringe, on the outskirts of life, solitary and sensual.[72]

These words of Camus, found in his epilogue to *L'Étranger*, are a reminder of Leonardo's impassivity at certain moments, which makes him seem detached and different. Leonardo's attitude when in prison is reminiscent of Meursault when he finds himself incarcerated. Furthermore, Leonardo does not seem to feel any emotion when told that he is going to be a father, while the news of his parents' death, even though it makes him react and leave the car when he finds out, does not seem to alter his catatonic state. Finally, Leonardo associates the reading of Camus's novel with the period of his grandmother's death and when he decided to separate from his parents: 'Creo que el libro de Camus lo leí el mismo otoño en que murió la abuela de repente y que más o menos por ese tiempo di por cancelada la obligación de bajar a sentarme con ellos a la mesa de caoba del comedor'.[73]

The second work which encapsulates some of the characteristics of the other main character of Martín Gaite's *La Reina de las Nieves* is Henrik Ibsen's *The Lady from the Sea*. In this case, Casilda is compared to Ibsen's Elida. Moura is the first person to do this, but Eugenio also compares them in a letter and, subsequently, Leonardo links both characters. Elida is easily compared to Casilda: they are both descended from a lighthouse keeper, and both love the sea and feel as free as the sea:

> Haven't you noticed that the people who live out there by the open sea are a different race? It's almost as though they lived the same life as the sea does. Their way of thinking, feeling – they're like the tide, they ebb and flow. And they can never uproot themselves and settle anywhere else.[74]

---

[72] Albert Camus, *The Outsider*, trans. Joseph Laredo (London: Penguin, 2000), p. 118.
[73] Martín Gaite, *La Reina de las Nieves*, p. 147.
[74] Henrik Ibsen, *The Lady from the Sea*, trans. Michael Meyer (London: Rupert Hart-Davis, 1960), p. 75.

These words spoken by Elida's husband about his wife's character anticipate those written by Casilda in a letter to Eugenio:

> ¿Y qué si soy del mar, si él me trae y me lleva y me conoce y no le tengo miedo? No te fíes de mí, ya te lo aviso, Eugenio, ni me eches la culpa de mis mareas altas ni de mis remolinos o resacas. No tiene explicación (ni se la busques) el oleaje libre de la vida, qué le vamos a hacer, eso no se controla. Si dices tú que la pasión te ha hecho perder la libertad, es porque no conoces la pasión por la libertad misma.[75]

The difficulty Elida has in committing herself to her husband is also, up to a point, reflected in Casilda's reticence to be with Eugenio. Both protagonists need freedom to be able to choose their own course of action.[76]

Looking more closely at the relationship between Andersen's fairy tale and the novel, what emerges is the importance of the figure of the grandmother in Leonardo's life. This is not only because she was the one who looked after him when he was a child, because of the difficulties his mother found in caring for him, but also on account of the great influence the fairy tales she told him had and continue to have on his life, especially Andersen's *The Snow Queen*. Throughout her career, Martín Gaite indicated her belief in the importance of the fairy tale in a child's development, its importance for the child lying not only in the fable as such, but also in the narrator of the story and the mode of narration:

> A través de los cuentos que le dedican a él, el niño recibe dos dones de diferente índole: uno, relacionado con el asunto del cuento mismo; otro, con la actitud y la identidad de la persona que se lo cuenta. ... porque significa una prueba de atención y de amor por parte del narrador físicamente presente, cuya voz oye y cuyos ojos le miran.[77]

Indeed, in *La Reina de las Nieves*, Leonardo asks his grandmother to tell him Andersen's story again and again: 'Había otra particularidad que

---

[75] Martín Gaite, *La Reina de las Nieves*, p. 122.

[76] Although as María Elena Soliño affirms: 'In many respects, Ibsen's Elida is a much weaker character than Sila': *Women and Children First: Spanish Women Writers and the Fairy Tale Tradition* (Potomac, MD: Scripta Humanistica, 2002), p. 152.

[77] Carmen Martín Gaite, *El cuento de nunca acabar* [1983] (Barcelona: Anagrama, 1988), p. 85.

nunca variaba ... Y es que la abuela las leía. O por lo menos fingía leerlas, porque se las debía de saber de memoria, lo mismo que yo'.[78]

The first time Andersen's fairy tale is mentioned is in Chapter II of the first part, in relation to dreams and the unreality of living in prison. With Chapter IV of the second part, the story starts being intercalated in Leonardo's narrative. The opening four lines of the fairy tale beginning with, '*Principiaba el estío*',[79] introduce the chapter titled 'El rapto de Kay'. This chapter contains one of the most dramatic references to the tale, the moment when Kay is taken and kissed by the Snow Queen. The last chapter of the novel, Chapter IV of the third part, 'El cristalito de hielo', also reworks and refers to the end of Andersen's story.

Throughout Martín Gaite's novel, Leonardo sees himself constantly reflected in the fairy tale's protagonists: 'Yo había dibujado muchas veces en mis cuadernos aquellos dos protagonistas infantiles de Andersen, con los cuales compartía, desde mi solitaria condición de niño rico y enfermizo, la alegría por la llegada del verano'.[80] This identification helps him to escape his own self, to see himself from the outside, writing about himself as if he were a different person. Sometimes the tale seems as real as the circumstances he is going through. Thus he links the passage about Kay and Gerda's last journey in the sledge with the journey to the cemetery after his grandmother's death, and the tears for her death, with the last time he was able to cry. He relates the answer his grandmother gave him, having asked her when he would get the splinter of ice in his eye, 'Tardará, tardará, ya me habré muerto yo',[81] with the moment when he reads the letter she had written for him to read after her death: 'mi madre se fue por fin del cuarto, tras darme un beso en la mejilla, apenas rasgado el sobre y recorridas las primeras líneas del texto, sospeché que el cristalino de hielo se me estaba metiendo por un ojo'.[82] At the same time he associates his mother with the Snow Queen: 'Tu carta póstuma me la trajo en persona la Reina de las Nieves'.[83]

In his notebooks, Leonardo had already referred to his mother as the Snow Queen when he narrated the dream of the first night that he spent back in his parents' house. This dream recalls Sofía's in *Nubosidad*, the night she goes back to her mother's house. Leonardo starts his dream:

[78] Martín Gaite, *La Reina de las Nieves*, p. 105.
[79] Martín Gaite, *La Reina de las Nieves*, p. 97.
[80] Martín Gaite, *La Reina de las Nieves*, p. 97.
[81] Martín Gaite, *La Reina de las Nieves*, p. 103.
[82] Martín Gaite, *La Reina de las Nieves*, p. 158.
[83] Martín Gaite, *La Reina de las Nieves*, p. 160.

'Me quedé dormido y me transformé en mi madre'.[84] This is a dream which he had experienced many times before, in fact since childhood. In the dream he is Kay and the statue in La Quinta Blanca's garden is the Snow Queen, who transforms herself into his mother: 'También era, al mismo tiempo, el pequeño Kay siguiendo a la Reina de las Nieves y sabía ... que, para salvarme del peligro, tenía que recordar el cuento y contárselo a alguien'.[85] And that is what Leonardo is doing in his notebooks, remembering, telling and retelling to himself and the reader his story and Andersen's fairy tale.

Bruno Bettelheim's theories suggest a child needs fairy tales to be able to make sense of their own reality: 'Los cuentos de hadas suelen plantear, de un modo breve y conciso, un problema existencial. Esto permite al niño atacar los problemas en su forma esencial ... El cuento de hadas simplifica cualquier situación.'[86] As Leonardo writes his narrative, he evokes the image of himself as a child, listening to his grandmother telling the story of *The Snow Queen*, and this makes him think about his own origins: 'Yo tampoco sabía por dónde había llegado hasta el jardín de las estatuas'.[87] Leonardo uses the tale from his childhood, through the meaning that story had for him, to reach a conclusion about his feelings and the circumstances which have taken him to the present moment. Telling the tale makes him understand his fears. As O'Leary and Ribeiro de Menezes indicate: 'The Snow Queen is thus associated with memory and a desire to rediscover childhood roots, leading to a fuller sense of self-understanding.'[88] The child Leonardo, not having fully understood or accepted the fairy tale, needs to go back to it to decipher it, and it is then that he starts linking his own life to the character from *The Snow Queen*, his mother, and the distance between them. From that moment on he is able to liberate himself from his obsession and grow up.

The end of Martín Gaite's novel links the end of the Andersen fairy tale with the end of a period of Leonardo's life, and the beginning of a new phase with his real mother, Casilda:

> Casilda se incorporó, adelantó el cuerpo y empezó a besarle despacio en la frente, en las mejillas, en los párpados. Luego, cuando vio que

---

[84] Martín Gaite, *La Reina de las Nieves*, p. 84.
[85] Martín Gaite, *La Reina de las Nieves*, p. 85.
[86] Bruno Bettelheim, *Psicoanálisis de los cuentos de hadas* (Barcelona: Editorial Crítica, 1977), p. 16.
[87] Martín Gaite, *La Reina de las Nieves*, p. 109.
[88] O'Leary and Ribeiro de Menezes, p. 151.

llegaba el momento, juntó las manos y las colocó bajo la barbilla de Leonardo, a modo de cuenco, para recoger aquel llanto que, desbordando los ojos incapaces de contenerlo, ya le resbalaba manso por la cara.

Notó que, dentro de la primera lágrima, relucía una especie de aguja de vidrio que vino a pincharse, al caer, en la palma de su mano izquierda. La cogió con dos dedos de la otra y la miró al trasluz. Era el cristalito de hielo.[89]

Conclusion

At the beginning of the novel Leonardo was in a cataleptic state, living his reality as if he were part of a fairy tale. Andersen's story obsessed him in such a way that he completely identified with its protagonist, and his stay in prison made him bury his previous life and the memories from that time in his unconsciousness.[90] These memories would have to be recovered. From his prison cell Leonardo was able to reach the Snow Queen's castle, induced by hashish. The narrative reveals how the protagonist needs to escape from that condition through connecting with the fairy tale in order to be able to grow up and also to belong. As Bettelheim explains:

> El psicoanálisis se creó para que el hombre fuera capaz de aceptar la naturaleza problemática de la vida sin ser vencido por ella o sin ceder a la evasión. ... Este es precisamente el mensaje que los cuentos de hadas transmiten a los niños, de diversas maneras: que la lucha contra las serias dificultades de la vida es inevitable, es parte intrínseca de la existencia humana; pero si uno no huye, sino que se enfrenta a las privaciones inesperadas y a menudo injustas, llega a dominar todos los obstáculos.[91]

But instead of confronting his family problems, Leonardo had previously chosen to escape. Instead of confronting his grandmother's death which left him 'extraviado y sin protección alguna',[92] he decides to destroy what he loves most and blots out his memories of her. It is only

---

[89] Martín Gaite, *La Reina de las Nieves*, p. 331.
[90] Bettelheim comments: 'Si se reprime el inconsciente y se niega la entrada de su contenido al nivel de consciencia, la mente consciente de la persona queda parcialmente oprimida por los derivados de estos elementos inconscientes o se ve obligada a mantener un control tan rígido y compulsivo sobre ellos que su personalidad puede resultar seriamente dañada' (p. 14).
[91] Bettelheim, p. 15.
[92] Martín Gaite, *La Reina de las Nieves*, p. 150.

when he decides to go back to his origins and make sense of his past that Leonardo can start the cure, confronting his past even though he still feels he is in a dream. In the second part of *La Reina de las Nieves*, Leonardo's notebooks and the process of writing are foregrounded. The reader follows, together with Leonardo, the steps he needs to take to discover his past, following his thinking process as he writes his notebooks. The writing is central to the narrative and, at the same time, through the reading of his father's letters, Leonardo discovers a time in the past he knew little about. The natural development from childhood to maturity is going to evolve, in Leonardo's case, through the writing of his notebooks over a period of three months. It is a process that takes place from the moment he returns to his father's study to the moment he is seen to be born again after meeting his real mother for the first time and being accepted by her.

This novel shows a way of using psychoanalytic techniques to recover the past: Leonardo needs to go back to his childhood, to his life even before he was born, to understand his past in order to be able to continue with his life; the beginning of his 'therapy' coincides with his parents' death and his release from prison. Through his writing, Leonardo is going to find his real mother. The fairy tale helps, in this case, as a place for Leonardo to escape to while he is trying to understand the world around him. In *La Reina de las Nieves*, Martín Gaite once again gives the protagonist the tools to search for his past, make sense of his present and take charge of his future, and, in this novel, he is also helped by a mature woman, a writer, who chose isolation in order to be creative and find freedom. In this way at the end of the novel the 'happy ending' is achieved, just as in Andersen's fairy tale.

5

Lo raro es vivir: Personal Reflections from Historical Research

Lo raro es vivir is the only novel of the 1990s in which Martín Gaite gives the leading role to a woman much younger than herself,[1] and so bestows this novel a special place in her *oeuvre*. It is written from the point of view of a generation of women born in the late 1950s, and repeats many of the themes discussed in Martín Gaite's other novels of the 1990s – the relationship between parents and children, divorce, Madrid nightlife, alcohol, drugs and lack of motivation amongst young people. Águeda, the protagonist of the novel, closes a chapter of her life involving the apathy and indifference that followed the first years of the *movida*,[2] and moves into another chapter where she is able to take decisions for herself, continue with her career and create a family, all of which give her purpose in life. In this novel there is an underlying belief in hope for the future.

Águeda does, however, have certain characteristics in common with Martín Gaite and some of her earlier characters. She is a researcher who works in archives, which links her with Martín Gaite's own work as a cultural and historical researcher. And like other characters of the 1990s novels, Águeda goes on a series of quests, not only to find out about her research subject but also about her own life. She tries to give sense to her life and her relationship with her mother, writing, by the end of the novel, about her life and the changes brought about by her (re)search.

The idea of death and the purpose of existence is developed as a theme

---

[1] The same age as Martín Gaite's daughter when she died and a similar age to Leonardo in *La Reina*.

[2] *La movida* was an artistic and socio-cultural movement in Madrid during the 1970s and 1980s, which represented a backlash against the repression of Franco's final years of dictatorship. In the words of Marta Moriarty (a gallery owner at the time), the *movida* signified 'la muerte de los ideales, la muerte de la familia, la muerte de la sociedad, aquello que rompe estructuras': cited in Nuria Cruz-Cámara, *El laberinto intertextual de Carmen Martín Gaite: Un estudio de sus novelas de los noventa* (Newark, DE: Juan de la Cuesta, 2008), pp. 77–8. For a study of the *movida* in *Lo raro es vivir*, see *El laberinto intertextual*, pp. 91–113.

from the beginning of the novel and pursued throughout the narration. As José Jurado Morales comments: 'Desde un principio la autora ha ideado la novela y su protagonista bajo una perspectiva existencialista. La concepción de la muerte como fin último de la existencia humana.'[3] The chapter titled 'Cuatro gotas de existencialismo' suggests the principal idea of the novel as 'la extrañeza ante el vivir'.[4] The notion of anguish or nausea is explained to Águeda by Moisés (the owner of the bar that Águeda uses as a refuge from her insomnia): 'La angustia nace de la conciencia de mortalidad'.[5] This notion provides the focal concept of the novel. The idea of life, the passing of time and the death of loved ones is central to Martín Gaite's trajectory, in her notebooks as well as in her fiction. Also, the possibility of communicating with the dead is an important part of her work, as seen in *Nubosidad* and *La Reina de las Nieves*.[6] As suggested, in these two novels and in *Lo raro es vivir*, the dead talk to us in our dreams, although as Águeda comments: 'porque hablan, claro, pero se olvida'.[7]

At the beginning of the narrative, Águeda's mother has just died (eight weeks before the first visit to her grandfather). Her mother's death is fundamental to the protagonist's development as a woman, as at the end of the story Águeda narrates her own pregnancy and motherhood. For the study of this novel, Nancy Chodorow's ideas will once again be brought into play, and her *Feminism and Psychoanalytic Theory* (1989) will shed light on some of the points of development in the life of the protagonist, especially the independence that Águeda must gain through a better understanding of her mother in order to become her own self.

---

[3] José Jurado Morales, *La trayectoria narrativa de Carmen Martín Gaite (1925–2000)* (Madrid: Gredos, 2003), p. 338.

[4] Carmen Martín Gaite, *Lo raro es vivir* [1996] (Barcelona: Anagrama, 1999), p. 75.

[5] Martín Gaite, *Lo raro es vivir*, p. 76. It is interesting to observe the similarities, granted the many differences, between Águeda and Antoine Roquentin, the protagonist of Sartre's *La Nausée*, a novel which Águeda discusses with Moisés in Chapter VII (pp. 77–8). Both Águeda and Antoine are researching into the eighteenth century and spending many hours of their days in the library surrounded by manuscripts.

[6] Martín Gaite also relates moments of communication with her dead parents, especially through dreams, as seen in Chapter 2 in relation to 'Cuenta pendiente'. Other times she comments on the positive influence people can have from 'the other world': 'Era "la primera vez que una persona desde el otro mundo me mandaba sus bendiciones"', the author commented on her grandmother after receiving the Premio Nadal for her first novel, *Entre visillos*, which she presented under her grandmother's name, Sofía Veloso: cited in Teruel's introduction to Carmen Martín Gaite, *Obras completas*, I, ed. and intro. José Teruel (Barcelona: Galaxia Gutenburg/Círculo de Lectores, 2008), pp. 9–54 (p. 13).

[7] Martín Gaite, *Lo raro es vivir*, p. 76.

Also in this chapter, ideas about the mother/daughter relationship, which were developed in earlier chapters, will be revisited using texts such as Chodorow's *The Reproduction of Mothering* (1999) and also the concept of the 'Good-enough mother' developed by Winnicott, thereby pursuing again a psychoanalytic perspective in the study of Martín Gaite's presentation of her protagonist's feelings and development.

Historical Research: Waking Up to Life by Diving into a World of Lies

From the beginning of the novel the reader is made aware that what is to come is a retrospective story. The epilogue is the only part of the novel written in the present, the moment when the protagonist is writing her story. Águeda reveals that the events of which she is writing occurred two years earlier, starting on the 'treinta de junio' at 'las siete de la tarde más o menos'.[8] These events immediately make her aware of her own existence, taking her out of her routine, of a life she lived without thinking. She starts reflecting on life, and later in the narrative these reflections expose the idea which is central to the novel:

> Lo raro es vivir. Que estemos aquí sentados, que hablemos y se nos oiga, poner una frase detrás de otra sin mirar ningún libro, que no nos duela nada, que lo que bebemos entre por el camino que es y sepa cuándo tiene que torcer, que nos alimente el aire y a otros ya no, que según el antojo de las vísceras nos den ganas de hacer una cosa o la contraria y que de esas ganas dependa a lo mejor el destino, es mucho a la vez, tú, no se abarca, y lo más raro es que lo encontramos normal.[9]

These ideas are a reminder of something Martín Gaite revealed in her *Cuadernos de todo* after a friend's death:

> Uno tiene su tiempo en esta vida, no tiene otra cosa. Y yo desde el día en que murió mi amigo he sentido más acuciante y alta que nunca la llamada de las cosas que él ya no veía para que mirara yo, de las gentes para que las atendiera. ... Y con mayor deseo que nunca de ponerme a escribir. Pocas veces me ha sido más difícil.[10]

---

[8] Martín Gaite, *Lo raro es vivir*, p. 11.
[9] Martín Gaite, *Lo raro es vivir*, p. 73.
[10] Carmen Martín Gaite, *Cuadernos de todo*, ed. and intro. Maria Vittoria Calvi

In *La Reina*, death was seen to provoke reflections on life and this will also be the case in *Irse de casa*, just as it was in those pages of *Cuadernos de todo* that Martín Gaite wrote after her friend's death. The difficulty she felt when sitting down to write is also found in Águeda, who needs to put her life in order before she can continue with her writing. The immediacy of the diary and letter-writing of the first novels in some ways disappears in *Lo raro es vivir*, even though, as will be seen, the freshness of the events that Águeda recounts, and which changed her life, is not completely lost.

Chapter I describes Águeda's visit to her grandfather in a residential home. Her conversation with the director of the home reveals the circumstances which provoked such a visit, with the reader made aware of the mother's sudden death and of the similarities between mother and daughter: 'Estoy asombrado de cómo se parece usted a su madre. ... Supongo que se lo habrán dicho infinidad de veces,'[11] says the director to Águeda as soon as he sees her. It is also indicated that mother and daughter did not have a very good relationship, as Águeda tells the director: 'Vamos a dejarlo en un trato distante'.[12]

Consequently, the director feels that Águeda could impersonate her mother for a few hours, in order to say goodbye to the grandfather as he is not aware of his daughter's death. Such a strange proposition arouses feelings in Águeda about her relationship with her parents and her life in general, which she had tried to forget. Águeda reflects especially on her emotional situation, looking back at the changes she has gone through since she met her partner, Tomás. In fact, Tomás is one of the few male characters in Martín Gaite's 1990s novels who is given a positive role. He is presented as a man who understands a woman's need for space, encouraging Águeda in her research and questioning her about her relationship with her mother and the way she presents it.[13]

The idea of becoming another person gives free rein to Águeda's imagination which, for a few days, is involved in a world of fantasy where lies overtake any kind of reality. As María Castrejón Sánchez points out, some of the chapter titles serve as metaphors for aspects of the protagonist's life: 'Podemos comprender el carácter que quiere imprimir a la

(Barcelona: Areté, 2002), p. 140.
[11] Martín Gaite, *Lo raro es vivir*, p. 16.
[12] Martín Gaite, *Lo raro es vivir*, p. 16.
[13] It transpires that Tomás never met Águeda's mother as she feared her mother's powers of seduction would take him away from her.

obra: la vida es para Águeda un compendio de metáforas personales.'[14] And indeed, the titles of these also take the reader into a world of fantasy – 'El planeta de cristal', 'Bajada al bosque', 'La estatua viviente' and 'Las escaleras del diablo' – and are a reminder of some of Martín Gaite's stories for children.

Águeda used her imagination by writing song lyrics before she qualified as an archivist. This artistic gift seems to have been taken from Sofía in *Nubosidad* who, although she had a great ability to compose songs and poems,[15] never explored her potential in the financial way that Consuelo, her maid's daughter, encouraged her to do. Another characteristic which Águeda seems to have inherited, in this case directly from Martín Gaite, is her interest in eighteenth-century history. Her research on Luis Vidal y Villalba (a project that Martín Gaite wrote about in her notebooks but never pursued)[16] comes from an idea which, Águeda explains, was taken from a French academic at the Sorbonne.

The need to go into the archives to escape from reality is a theme of this novel and Martín Gaite had indeed commented on the addictive nature of this activity: 'Meterse en archivos es un opio, si das dos chupadas vuelves.'[17] Research practice helps Águeda to escape her own life; 'beber olvido'[18] is how she refers to her research into other people's lives. This is the researcher's escapism: 'si yo me seguía metiendo en averiguaciones sobre un aventurero del siglo XVIII y sus mentiras, ¿no era para escurrir el bulto de otra pesquisa pendiente y mucho más sinuosa, que interfería aquella?'[19] Or, as she admitted earlier in the novel: 'Hurgar en el pasado remoto puede ser un lenitivo. El cercano hace más daño'.[20] Yet the historical research is going to turn into personal research in her own life in the present: 'En lo que me equivoqué fue en creer que entregarme

---

[14] María Castrejón Sánchez, '*Lo raro es vivir*', in *Carmen Martín Gaite*, ed. Alicia Redondo Goicoechea (Madrid: Ediciones del Orto, 2004), pp. 185–97 (p. 195).

[15] Martín Gaite's love for poetry and song-writing is well known. She published books on poetry and also used to read her poems or sing songs in La Manuela (a bar in the centre of Madrid), together with her brother-in-law, Chicho Sánchez Ferlosio. Martín Gaite even performed with Amancio Prada, a recital which was made into a record, *Caravel de caraveles*. See Alicia Ramos, 'Conversación con Carmen Martín Gaite', *Hispanic Journal*, 1 (1980), 117–24 (p. 118).

[16] See Martín Gaite, *Cuadernos*, pp. 287, 367, 401.

[17] See Federico Campbell, 'Carmen Martín Gaite: La búsqueda de interlocutor', in *Conversaciones con escritores* (Mexico D.F.: CONACULTA, Dirección General de Publicaciones, 2004), pp. 231–40 (p. 240).

[18] Martín Gaite, *Lo raro es vivir*, p. 42.

[19] Martín Gaite, *Lo raro es vivir*, p. 97.

[20] Martín Gaite, *Lo raro es vivir*, p. 50.

de lleno a mi trabajo ... significaba tomar una vía que me apartaba de aquella tupida maraña'.[21] As María Luisa Guardiola Tey indicates: 'La joven investigadora participa en un juego de espejos dirigidos uno hacia otro y descubre cómo es ella misma al identificarse con el personaje dieciochesco.'[22] This is similar to Martín Gaite's own research, as Elide Pittarello observes: 'Su busca del tiempo perdido fue siempre doble, porque dar con partes olvidadas de la vida ajena era también sacar a la luz partes remotas de su propia vida.'[23]

The results of Águeda's research on Vidal y Villalba, which is interspersed with the developments during her week of self-discovery, seem to have been provided by the author so as not to be completely lost. Thus she finds a fictional context in which to situate her historical research. Chapters IV, VII, IX, and X contain many details of the life of Vidal y Villalba and José Gabriel Tupac Amaru, a historical character who, as Águeda confesses, is someone who 'verdaderamente me enamoró'.[24] The confusion Águeda has to confront is how to connect all the threads her research presents, and how to shape them into a publishable study. This raises questions concerning how researchers should present their findings and these reflections are a reminder of those Martín Gaite committed to her notebooks on 7 January 1977:

> Acabamos de pasar Galapagar, antes de llegar a Villalba. De repente he revivido la escena del piquete que Floridablanca mandó a esperar al extraño prisionero Luis Vidal y Villalba, que venía de Londres. La exploración de su equipaje. Tengo la suerte de recordar esta historia como si fuera verdadera y actual, como si me hubiera pasado a mí. Historia abierta, enigmática. ¿Por qué no la escribo así, en plan historia fantástica, enigmática y abierta, explicando el proceso que me ha traído a recordarla? No necesitaría casi ni tener que volver a los archivos. Sería un ejercicio literario divertido y apasionante para mis ratos de desaliento. Inventar el montaje original que le podía dar. Explicar mis reflexiones posteriores a Macanaz, las diferencias y concomitancias entre la historia y la novela. A pegotitos sueltos.

---

[21] Martín Gaite, *Lo raro es vivir*, p. 29.

[22] María Luisa Guardiola Tey, '*Lo raro es vivir*: Propuesta vitalista de Carmen Martín Gaite a finales del siglo XX', in *Género y géneros II: Escritura y escritoras iberoamericanas*, ed. Ángeles Encinar, Eva Löfquist and Carmen Valcárcel (Madrid: Servicio de Publicaciones de la UAM, 2006), pp. 133–42 (p. 137).

[23] Elide Pittarello, 'Artesanías autógrafas de Carmen Martín Gaite', *Journal of Interdisciplinary Literary Studies*, 5 (1993), 101–18 (p. 102).

[24] Martín Gaite, *Lo raro es vivir*, p. 51.

Sin pretender cerrar ni redondear. Tal como se conserva en mi memoria.[25]

Martín Gaite, indeed, wrote parts of that story through Águeda. In a similar way, although Águeda has set out to write a thesis titled 'Un aventurero del siglo XVIII y su criado',[26] the novel shows how the facts she discovers are so interesting, and in some cases so incredible, that they could be out of the pages of a mystery novel. But should a researcher use the facts she has discovered as if they were fiction? Tomás recommends that Águeda write them as she tells them: 'Parece una novela – decía Tomas –. Es una pena que no puedas escribirlo en forma de novela',[27] to which she answers: 'Hombre, qué cosas tienes. Eso no sería una tesis doctoral'.[28] Nevertheless, she feels that the best way to tell the story would be as if it were a tale:

> Hasta que me di cuenta de que era con él [su gato] con quien necesitaba hablar antes de ponerme escribir nada, que se había subido allí para escucharme y que si le contaba la historia de Tupac Amaru como a un gato de cuento de hadas, no sólo lo entendería sino que tal vez me ayudase a entenderlo a mí.[29]

This is what Águeda does every time she relays her discoveries and this is what her interlocutors encourage her to write.

To be able to represent the role of her mother, Águeda needs to investigate her life in a similar way to how she studies her historical characters; she needs to find photographs and old papers to remember her mother as she really was: 'mi infancia yacía mutilada sobre la moqueta, habría que hacerle la respiración artificial o tal vez la autopsia, buscar fotos, papeles, recordar cómo se vestía, el gesto tras el cual ocultaba sus enfados, prepararme, en una palabra'.[30] Thus her personal research becomes tangled up with historical research. Going through such difficult times, Águeda finds it impossible to separate her life from sus estudios, behaving in many cases like the subject of her investigations: '¿Será posible? – me dije –.

---

[25] Martín Gaite, *Cuadernos*, p. 401.
[26] Martín Gaite, *Lo raro es vivir*, p. 44.
[27] Martín Gaite, *Lo raro es vivir*, p. 45.
[28] Martín Gaite, *Lo raro es vivir*, p. 45.
[29] Martín Gaite, *Lo raro es vivir*, p. 85.
[30] Martín Gaite, *Lo raro es vivir*, p. 54.

Estoy tan loca como él, todo se contagia. ¡Voy a acabar como Vidal y Villalba!'[31]

Although the letters and other documents used in her research are not present in the novel, Águeda is constantly referring to them. On occasions it even seems that she believes herself to be the only interlocutor Vidal y Villalba has. He talks to her through his letters, letters which, in some cases, had not been read for centuries. 'Vidal y Villalba ... llevaba más de cuatro años pegándome voces por dentro a ver si lo sacaba de los papeles polvorientos y me hacía cargo en serio de su historia'.[32] This recalls how Martín Gaite felt Macanaz was talking to her: 'En una de aquellas cartas ... Macanaz, una mañana, me habló por primera vez directamente. ... fue cuando me dijo que acaso aquello que venía escribiendo con tanta urgencia no lo iba a recoger nunca nadie. ... me lo decía como para que se lo desmintiera'.[33]

Although the author considers herself, like Águeda, the direct interlocutor of a character from the past, at times Martín Gaite doubts the author's and researcher's rights to publish letters and diaries without the expressed consent of the author:

> Los archivos están plagados de cartas, que nos ayudan a componer, fragmentariamente, el rompecabezas de la historia. Sin el estímulo de un interlocutor concreto a quien dirigir esas quejas, peticiones, confidencias o declaraciones, muchos personajes del pasado no habrían dejado noticia de su vida ni de su alma. Pero, ¿es lícito hacer pasar por producto literario lo que nunca pretendió serlo y, precisamente por eso, nació con tan genuina frescura?[34]

Here, again, the theme of the need for an interlocutor surfaces. In the chapter 'Un gato que escucha', Águeda tells her cat the story of Vidal y Villalba, a story which, as seen earlier, other people had suggested to her that she relate as fiction. The night – an important moment for confessions – when Águeda talks to her cat, Gerundio, helps her to reflect on her historical research and she starts writing it:

---

[31] Martín Gaite, *Lo raro es vivir*, p. 81.
[32] Martín Gaite, *Lo raro es vivir*, p. 201.
[33] Carmen Martín Gaite, *La búsqueda de interlocutor y otras búsquedas* [1973] (Barcelona: Destinolibro, 1982), pp. 58–9.
[34] Carmen Martín Gaite, *El cuento de nunca acabar* [1983] (Barcelona: Anagrama, 1988), pp. 247–8.

Pero lo más importante de aquella vigilia es que el relato oral dirigido a Gerundio me había abierto cauce a la palabra escrita. Le perdí el respeto al cuaderno de Tomás y fue como desatrancar un desagüe, lo empecé decidida, sin miedo a las tachaduras ni a las repeticiones.[35]

Personal Written Reflections

Although Águeda's narration is written with hindsight, reconstructing past events, the immediacy of the changes developed in the protagonist is not lost. As Jurado Morales observes:

> En *Lo raro es vivir* resulta imposible imaginar a Águeda en compañía. Esa ajetreada y decisiva semana de su vida es sólo realizable desde la reflexión. El presente se explica desde el pasado gracias al recurso de la escritura y la autobiografía, método habitual en la novela existencial para reconstruir la trayectoria vital del personaje por lo que tiene de lenitivo.[36]

As discussed, a writer needs isolation to be able to reflect and not just act, finding in that solitude her independent self, an idea expounded in Virginia Woolf's *A Room of One's Own*. In the 1960s Martín Gaite also wrote her ideas on the need for solitude:

> Lo malo de la relación con los seres humanos es la capacidad de concentración que nos roba. Si se pudieran mantener despiertas y en forma nuestras disposiciones mentales tanto en presencia de los otros seres como en la soledad, claro que el fruto de ese ejercicio sería más rico y más interesante, que las mismas alteraciones que la interferencia de los demás produciría en el campo de nuestro interés, caso de poder ser correctamente registradas, lo abonarían y ampliarían mucho. Pero, por el contrario, nos comen y hacen desaparecer del campo.[37]

Although the writing in *Lo raro* describes past events, the reader has access to the character's meditations and how they change her personal history. In Águeda's case, writing her past makes her understand what happened after her mother's death and how her life changed forever.

In *Lo raro es vivir*, Águeda reflects constantly on her relationship with

---

[35] Martín Gaite, *Lo raro es vivir*, p. 90.
[36] Jurado Morales, *La trayectoria narrativa*, p. 348.
[37] Martín Gaite, *Cuadernos*, p. 132.

other people, both in her present life and her past, not from a position of isolation as a unique and solitary person, but in relation to those who were part of her past. Águeda meets some of the characters she knew in her first years as a young independent woman. She finds old night-life companions, 'comparsas de mi alborotada juventud',[38] people she calls 'rizofita',[39] for whom the idea of settling down and finding a proper job is only something that a psychiatrist would suggest.[40] Moriarty comments on the years of the *movida*: 'El compromiso era una mala palabra ... En los 80 estaba muy mal tomarse en serio cualquier cosa. Incluso profesionalizarse, porque era meterse en la rueda.'[41] Águeda now sees the friends she had in her early youth as characters belonging to another life, in a similar way to Leonardo. These casual meetings make her think about her life and value her relationship with Tomás.

Reflecting on the past makes her relive a dream she used to have when she was younger, between the ages of thirteen and eighteen, and links the man in her dream to her present partner: 'Estaba emocionada porque acababa de hacer un descubrimiento asombroso: Tomás se parecía al chico de mis sueños de adolescente más que nadie. Había estado ciega. Era él.'[42] Furthermore, writing and reflecting about oneself, as seen in the other novels studied, makes the protagonist split into different characters. In Águeda's case, thinking about her present circumstances led her to try to see herself before she arrived in Tomás's life: 'De pronto se produjo una especie de desdoblamiento, como si hubiera perdido mi identidad como pareja de Tomás, sin dejar por eso de moverme con soltura por aquella casa que conocía y de la que tenía llave'.[43] This split induces a dialogue with herself: '¡Largo, basta de encerrona! La calle abre otra perspectiva, ¿no lo sabes ya?'[44]

Although the account is narrated two years after the events described, the moments in the novel when Águeda is writing are apparent. She, like the author, always carries a notebook with her: 'lo apunté en una agenda

---

[38] Martín Gaite, *Lo raro es vivir*, p. 37.
[39] Martín Gaite, *Lo raro es vivir*, p. 37.
[40] The word *rizofita* occurs in *Cuadernos*, p. 231. Águeda, just like Sofía and Mariana in *Nubosidad*, Sara in *Caperucita en Manhattan* and Martín Gaite herself, makes up words to express ideas or feelings which only their closest companions understand. As was seen in *Nubosidad variable*, this is the 'léxico familiar', to use Natalia Ginzburg's term. Águeda's mother, she informs us, also used to make up words.
[41] Cited in Cruz-Cámara, *El laberinto intertextual*, pp. 94–5.
[42] Martín Gaite, *Lo raro es vivir*, p. 152.
[43] Martín Gaite, *Lo raro es vivir*, p. 66.
[44] Martín Gaite, *Lo raro es vivir*, p. 66.

que saqué de la maleta del prestidigitador, en una zona que titulo «EXCRE-CENCIAS»'.[45] In many cases, her writing is linked to discoveries in her historical research, in others, though, she transcribes thoughts, poems or her dreams in order to be able to analyse them later: 'Me desperté y busqué a tientas mi agenda para apuntar el sueño'.[46] This, again, will be written in the section titled '«EXCRECENCIAS»'.[47] This noting down of dreams was seen in *Cuadernos de todo* and, as mentioned, is also practised by many of Martín Gaite's other characters. In fact one of Águeda's dreams, as will be seen, helps her to develop an understanding of her mother and is the trigger which makes her decide to visit her grandfather, posing as her mother.

In her writing, Águeda reveals her relationship with her mother and the similarities between them, similarities from which for many years she had escaped but which, in the present, are going to help her understand better not only her mother, but also herself. Indeed, she will discover her mother through her father's eyes, when he looks at Águeda as if she were her mother: 'Sigo oyendo su voz al oírte a ti. Y viéndola al mirarte',[48] her father confesses. This confession allows her to see herself in a different way and decide to take on the role of her mother: 'Ahora mismo soy ella,'[49] she admits to herself. After writing up the dream, she starts looking at the mirror and talking as if she were addressing her mother: 'Me acerqué al espejo y puse los labios sobre mi imagen. Eran las paces que habían quedado pendientes en el sueño'.[50] Similar to Sofía, Águeda is able to forgive her mother after making sense of the dream.

There is another aspect to Águeda's story. As she writes, Águeda narrates the way she discovers and makes sense of some of the events in her past: 'Tomás que odia las tinieblas, me había sacado de la luz, porque despide luz. ... Estaba emocionada porque acababa de hacer un descubrimiento asombroso'.[51] Thus she needs to tell her story to understand it: 'cuando te pones a atar cabos, cada uno tenemos nuestra propia novela enquistada por ahí dentro. Hasta que no la cuentas a otro no lo sabes'.[52] And the discoveries she makes in writing and relating her life will change

---

[45] Martín Gaite, *Lo raro es vivir*, p. 107.
[46] Martín Gaite, *Lo raro es vivir*, p. 118.
[47] Martín Gaite, *Lo raro es vivir*, p. 120.
[48] Martín Gaite, *Lo raro es vivir*, p. 111.
[49] Martín Gaite, *Lo raro es vivir*, p. 111.
[50] Martín Gaite, *Lo raro es vivir*, pp. 121–2.
[51] Martín Gaite, *Lo raro es vivir*, pp. 151–2.
[52] Martín Gaite, *Lo raro es vivir*, p. 208.

her forever. As the director of the residential home informs her: 'No parece usted la misma que hace una semana ... [M]e encuentro ante alguien que no se esconde, que va de bulto de las cosas, ante una persona de verdad'.[53]

Mother/Daughter Relationship: The Future, Maternity

Águeda's mother, Águeda Luengo, is a famous artist, a strong and independent woman – in this respect she reminds us of Casilda in *La Reina*, Mariana in *Nubosidad* and Amparo in *Irse de casa* – who divorced her husband and went to live in a duplex which she designed in order to house her daughter in an independent apartment. This situation, though, was not accepted by Águeda, who moved to an attic apartment in the old centre of Madrid. Yet although Águeda does not want to live with her mother, she finds her another companion, Rosario, a woman a few years older than herself, to serve as a surrogate daughter. Rosario was also the individual who introduced Águeda to the theme of her quest for the purpose of existence: 'Desde que el mundo es mundo, vivir y morir vienen siendo la cara y la cruz de una misma moneda echada al aire. ... Para mí, si quieren que les diga la verdad, lo raro es vivir'.[54]

The relationship between the mother and Rosario is not entirely clear and at times one could suspect that there might be a romantic relationship: 'Yo no era don Blas de Hinojosa, ni se trataba de interrogarla sobre el tipo de relaciones que hubiera podido mantener con mi madre, ni de echar cuentas o sacar trapos sucios del pasado'.[55] Águeda has these thoughts the day she decides to visit Rosario (at her mother's duplex) to collect some of her mother's clothes, and after she has decided to impersonate her mother. The problem with Águeda's mother seems to be her independence. As Chodorow indicates:

> For the infant, the mother is not someone with her own life, wants, needs, history, other social relationships, work. She is known only in her capacity as mother. Growing up means learning that she, like other people in one's life, has and wants a life of her own, and that loving her means recognizing her subjectivity and appreciating her separateness.[56]

---

[53] Martín Gaite, *Lo raro es vivir*, p. 216.
[54] Martín Gaite, *Lo raro es vivir*, p. 184.
[55] Martín Gaite, *Lo raro es vivir*, p. 203.
[56] Nancy J. Chodorow, *Feminism and Psychoanalytic Theory* (New Haven, CT: Yale University Press, 1989), p. 90.

Although the mother wants to be a good mother, giving her daughter a place to live, Águeda feels that her mother's life, which is full of engagements, does not leave space for her: 'Me gustaba presumir ante mis amigos de madre no empachosa ni fiscalizadora, pero nada ansiaba tanto como sus preguntas y el gozo maligno de dejarlas sin contestar. La verdad es que ella había llegado a hacerme cada vez menos'.[57] This feeling of not being of interest to her mother is repeated throughout the novel. Chodorow notes: 'Idealization and blaming of the mother are two sides of the same belief in the all-powerful mother.'[58] And when Águeda decides to leave her mother's home, the best way she finds to express her feelings is by letter, although she never dares to send it:

> Querida madre:
> Cuando te dije ayer que me marcho de casa, no me pediste explicaciones. Eso es lo que más me duele de ti, ... hubiera preferido que dieras un portazo y que se tambaleara alguna de las paredes de ese dúplex reciente y suntuoso que detesto.[59]

In the letter she is also able to confess the link between her parents' separation and her escape from her mother's house, and presents herself as a little girl who wants her mother's attention. However, in general, she writes letters more for herself than to send to others, noting: 'muchas cartas las escribo y no las mando nunca. Viven un tiempo dentro de mí, repito su texto y llego a olvidar que no las he mandado'.[60] She used to send letters to her mother when she was younger, although they were letters which her mother never answered, and which Águeda believes she must have destroyed as she was not 'amiga de conservar papeles viejos'.[61]

Águeda's need for her mother is visible in the narrative, as well as the pride which prevented her from getting close enough to express that need. On the other hand, with her father she feels freer to express her feelings, since she also feels more protective towards him. She writes: 'Mis esperanzas, ya bastante problemáticas, de encontrar consuelo y apoyo en aquel señor se volatilizaron. ... yo seguía siendo una especie de coraza para él, desde niña supe que era más débil que mamá'.[62] Furthermore, Águeda

---

[57] Martín Gaite, *Lo raro es vivir*, p. 162.
[58] Chodorow, *Feminism and Psychoanalytic Theory*, p. 90.
[59] Martín Gaite, *Lo raro es vivir*, pp. 185–6.
[60] Martín Gaite, *Lo raro es vivir*, p. 148.
[61] Martín Gaite, *Lo raro es vivir*, p. 148.
[62] Martín Gaite, *Lo raro es vivir*, p. 108. Once again we see a weak man dragged

can confess to him her need for her mother after her death: 'Ahora daría lo que no tengo por oírla. Me conformaba con cinco minutos, aunque fuera para echarme una bronca. Que además, por desgracia, no me las echaba nunca'.[63] Mother and daughter are very similar; they look alike and have the same voice and similar writing. These characteristics, which might at other times have irritated Águeda, will help her pay the last debt her mother left unpaid, the last goodbye to her father. Consequently, Águeda writes and delivers a letter to the director of the residence and to her grandfather in the role of her mother when she decides to impersonate her, informing the reader of her decision: 'Creo que empiezo a considerarme preparada para el juego'.[64]

Some of the most important and dramatic moments of the novel occur when Águeda decides to dress up as her mother to visit her grandfather. This point marks a radical change in the protagonist's attitude to life. Before taking the decision she needed to discover many sides of her relationship with her mother: 'No me estaba preparando en absoluto para suplantar a mamá, no me atrevía con ese papel. No me atrevía con ella, ... nunca me había atrevido a derribarla de su pedestal'.[65] As Chodorow explains, one of the most important actions needed to change the mother/daughter relationship is to take the mother down from the pedestal of the perfect mother: 'To begin to transform the relations of parenting and the relations of gender, to begin to transform women's lives, we must move beyond the myths and misconceptions embodied in the fantasy of the perfect mother.'[66]

Águeda, as she noted at the beginning of the novel, had a distant relationship with her mother. In her writing Águeda reflects on the moments she spent with her mother and the kind of association they had. She starts remembering and writing stories about moments when they were both close, moments of happiness which erase her resentment over the lack of love she felt from her mother. Moments such as the last

---

into a life of consumerism by a new, young and attractive wife, more concerned with her house and new furniture than with her husband's intellectual needs. The character of Águeda's father is similar to that of Leonardo's father in *La Reina* or to Sofía's husband in *Nubosidad*. Tomás, however, serves as contrast. He is a young man who has a different attitude towards women, and is what Castrejón Sánchez calls 'un modelo masculino nuevo' (p. 193).

63 Martín Gaite, *Lo raro es vivir*, p. 111.
64 Martín Gaite, *Lo raro es vivir*, p. 112.
65 Martín Gaite, *Lo raro es vivir*, p. 57.
66 Chodorow, *Feminism and Psychoanalytic Theory*, p. 96.

day they spent together, which she admits was 'una verdadera fiesta'.[67] Also, she remembers their trip to Tangier, when her mother had a miscarriage.[68] This particular episode shows her how at times her mother needed her daughter close to her: 'Sabía que no podía apartarme de allí porque la estaba protegiendo, que mi sitio era ese, nunca en mi vida he vuelto a saber con tanta certeza que estoy donde tengo que estar como aquel atardecer en Tánger'.[69]

During the time she reflects on her life, Águeda dreams of her mother: not as a strong and powerful woman, but as a weak woman living in poverty and abused by her partner, a woman who needs her daughter's help. But this help will not be received: 'Supe que todo se arreglaría si nos abrazábamos ella y yo, pero no era capaz de acercarme ni de decirle una frase cariñosa, aunque lo deseaba mucho'.[70] This type of dream could be categorized as 'wish fulfilment' for, as a result, Águeda sees herself for the first time in her life as stronger than her mother, in control of both her mother's life and her own. She manages, thanks to the dream, to dismantle the pedestal onto which she had put her mother. This kind of reflection helps her to change her relationship with her mother (although the change happens after the mother's death). From the moment of the dream, Águeda realizes that it was not her mother who was the cause for their distancing. As Castrejón Sánchez suggests: 'no queda a nadie a quien echarle las culpas. Quizá esto sea crecer.'[71] Taking responsibility for her actions instead of blaming others is Águeda's way of growing up.

After the dream, Águeda experiences a split in her personality which prepares her for the visit to her grandfather. He will be the one to reveal her mother's opinion of her, which is similar to how she regards her mother: 'Dices que es despegada, que no le dan tus cosas ni frío ni calor, pero puedes equivocarte, seguramente te necesita más de lo que pensamos'.[72] The idea of motherhood, dealt with in many of Martín Gaite's novels, will have a point of inflection in *Lo raro es vivir*. While in novels such as *Retahílas* or *Nubosidad variable* the decision to be or not to be a mother varied amongst the different female characters (Sofía is a mother, Mariana is not; Lucía is a mother, Eulalia is not), in *Lo raro es vivir* the reader is

---

[67] Martín Gaite, *Lo raro es vivir*, p. 200.
[68] Martín Gaite travelled with her daughter to Tangier in July 1972. There is a drawing by the author of a local street scene in *Cuadernos*, p. 167.
[69] Martín Gaite, *Lo raro es vivir*, p. 169.
[70] Martín Gaite, *Lo raro es vivir*, p. 118.
[71] Castrejón Sánchez, p. 197.
[72] Martín Gaite, *Lo raro es vivir*, pp. 221–2.

presented with Águeda's change of attitude towards the idea of maternity. From the first decisive dismissal, '¿Embarazada yo? – protesté –. De ninguna manera, ¡Dios me libre! No quiero hijos nunca, nunca. ¡Jamás en mi vida!',[73] to the conclusion of the novel, 'Aquella misma noche me quedé embarazada',[74] Águeda has gone from the complete rejection of motherhood to embracing it, and with all its consequences.[75] This change of attitude in the protagonist parallels the changes experienced amongst the different generations of feminists during last century. As Chodorow observes:

> In the late 1960's and early 1970's, feminists raised initial questions and developed a consensus of sorts about mothering. ... These consensual positions among feminists all centred on the argument that women's lives should not be totally constrained by child-care or childbearing. Women should be free to choose not to bear children; should have easy access to safe contraception and abortion; should be able to continue their other work if mothers; and should have available to them good day-care. In contrast, recent feminist writing on motherhood focuses more on the experience of mothering: if a mother wants to be a mother, what is or should be her experience? ... Feminist writing now recognizes that many women, including many feminists, want to have children and experience mothering as a rich and complex endeavor.[76]

In *Cuadernos de todo*, as seen in Chapter 2, Martín Gaite exposed her ideas on motherhood, including the possibility of reconciling being a mother with a professional career:

> A un niño hay que vestirlo, lavarlo, darle de comer. Y en esta reata de acontecimientos a que la mayoría de las mujeres dedican un esfuerzo casi siempre de inútil derroche, van dejando su piel y sus ilusiones con amargura. Creen que ya no les queda tiempo 'para lo otro'.

---

[73] Martín Gaite, *Lo raro es vivir*, pp. 19–20.
[74] Martín Gaite, *Lo raro es vivir*, p. 226.
[75] Kimberly Chisholm makes an interesting comment on Águeda's 'overly ardent protestation' of maternity as a disguise for 'a desire for maternal-filial connection', in 'Maternal-Filial Mirroring and Subjectivity in Carmen Martín Gaite's *Lo raro es vivir*', in *Carmen Martín Gaite: Cuento de nunca acabar/Never-ending Story*, ed. Kathleen M. Glenn and Lissette Rolón Collazo (Boulder, CO: Society of Spanish and Spanish-American Studies, 2003), pp. 109–27 (p. 114).
[76] Chodorow, *Feminism and Psychoanalytic Theory*, p. 79.

> Separan lo uno de lo otro. Intuyen que hay otra cosa ¡Pero si todo está mezclado! Claro que hay otra cosa que no son las papillas, pero esa cosa se puede encontrar y descubrir también mientras se hacen las papillas.[77]

These reflections, written in the 1960s, are a pointer towards the protagonist's attitude to maternity at the end of *Lo raro es vivir*. Águeda will be able to look after her daughter and continue writing her thesis, and will combine both responsibilities with pleasure. In fact, it is interesting to see how, during the 1960s, Martín Gaite criticized the attitude women had on maternity and work in her *cuadernos* when she was herself researching on Macanaz and the cultural history of the eighteenth century, demonstrating by her example the possibility of working and also caring for her daughter, just as Águeda will come to do. As the author stated in an interview: 'Nunca he pensado que la condición de ser mujer o ser madre, pueda robar tiempo a una escritora.'[78]

For Águeda, maternity is not synonymous with a lack of independence. Together with her partner, who encourages her in her work, Águeda is able to combine maternity and writing:

> Cierro el gas, porque el café ya está. Me lo sirvo y me lo traigo en una bandeja a un rincón con escritorio que se ha puesto en un recodo de la cocina. Fue idea de Tomás. Quiere que si me visita la inspiración cuando estoy guisando o dando de comer a Cecilia tenga a mano un lugar donde apoyar mis libros y cuadernos sin que se pringuen de yogur.[79]
>
> Hace una semana que he vuelto a ponerme con la historia de Vidal y Villalba y me gusta repasarla por las mañanas. Es como hacer memoria.[80]

Going back to her research, which she interrupted in order to make sense of her life, is what has allowed Águeda to relive those events of the past. Instead of using it as escapism, her research has helped her to review and give shape to her own life.

---

[77] Martín Gaite, *Cuadernos*, p. 81.
[78] Ramos, p. 119.
[79] The kitchen is again shown as a place where it is possible to find independence.
[80] Martín Gaite, *Lo raro es vivir*, pp. 227–8.

Conclusion

Throughout *Lo raro es vivir* there are many parallels which can be drawn between Martín Gaite's interests and preoccupations of the 1960s, as she researched her biography of Macanaz and was preparing her thesis, and those of Águeda. The protagonist of the novel, though, belongs to a later generation and brings with her a message of hope for the future, thanks to the independence and freedom women of her generation experience and their ability to create their own families without losing that freedom.

At the beginning of the novel Águeda was researching the life of the historical character Luis Vidal y Villalba, and through that work enters another investigation, that of her own life catalysed by her mother's death and the idea of impersonating and 'becoming' her mother for a few hours. Her study of both her mother and Vidal y Villalba becomes entwined in her narration. Trying to play the role of her mother well, she reflects on her own life, and also meets acquaintances from the past. They allow her to see herself reflected in others, and this enables her to discover other sides of her life and personality that she had tried to erase. Even though Águeda spends much of her time on her own, she needs those secondary characters in order to understand her past. She starts writing her findings, both about her life and about the historical character of her research, and through the analysis of her dreams, which she records in her notebook, she is able to take the decision which is going to change her life, to 'become' her mother. Before she adopts this role, Águeda has to understand their relationship and be able to forgive her mother through writing about the moments of happiness they experienced together.

The catalyst for Águeda to research her own life is her mother's death; and even though the type of writing she produces in *Lo raro es vivir* is not as immediate as in the novels studied earlier, her research into her mother's life and her own past will change the course of her future. The death of the mother, as one of the characters tells Águeda, is the moment when maturity really starts: 'a partir de ahí es cuando empiezas a envejecer'.[81] In *Lo raro es vivir*, the real catalyst for life-writing, though, is going to be the birth of her own daughter. Águeda does not seem to need writing as *tabla de salvación*, as was seen in the other protagonists, despite using a metaphor that likens the moment she starts writing to 'desatascar un desagüe'.[82] Indeed, the search into her past changes

---

[81] Martín Gaite, *Lo raro es vivir*, p. 148.
[82] Martín Gaite, *Lo raro es vivir*, p. 90.

her attitudes, especially towards motherhood. While in *La Reina de las Nieves* the novel ended at the moment the protagonist finds the mother, in *Lo raro es vivir* the narrative goes beyond this point and the reader is able to see into the protagonist's future. Martín Gaite seems to have crossed a barrier with this novel and reached a point in the future where writing is just part of life and not a way to be able to live.

6

Irse de casa: Life through the Cinematographic Lens, Writing One's Own Life-Script

Irse de casa (1998) is the last of Martín Gaite's novels to be published in her lifetime. It shares some of the structure and themes of her other novels of the 1990s, but at the same time reveals a parallel with the author's first novel, *Entre visillos* (1958), especially in the number of characters present and voices heard. The novel is narrated in the third person singular with an omniscient narrator, allowing the reader to be witness to the lives of the novel's various characters at different times in their histories. As Jurado Morales notes: 'necesita de un narrador externo que logre hilvanar con verosimilitud esos fragmentos y encauzar el argumento hacia su final sin quedar nada suelto.'[1] The epigraphs of the novel, from Aldous Huxley and Clarice Lispector, in fact, refer to the idea of a history formed by many stories, and one of the characters of the novel, Florita, comments: 'Gente ... lo que hay que añadir a ese argumento es gente. ... Gente que vaya contando también sus historias, ... un choque de historias.'[2] The third-person narration and the way the narrative is presented from not just one perspective takes away some of the intimate atmosphere of the earlier novels discussed here.

In *Irse de casa*, Amparo Miranda, a sixty-three-year-old woman resident in the United States, returns to her Spanish home town after forty years of absence. The reason for her journey, the reader learns, is the film script her son Jeremy has written, *La calle del olvido*, which will be the catalyst for her life-writing. After a few days wandering aimlessly, a series of encounters makes Amparo decide to take charge of her own story and start taking notes about her experiences in her home town in order to contribute to and modify her son's script. As in Martín Gaite's other novels of the 1990s, where protagonists take charge of their present

---

[1] José Jurado Morales, *La trayectoria narrativa de Carmen Martín Gaite (1925–2000)* (Madrid: Gredos, 2003), p. 399.
[2] Carmen Martín Gaite, *Irse de casa* (Barcelona: Anagrama, 1998), p. 34.

situation in order to change their fate, Amparo adopts a series of decisions concerning her life after having 're-encountered' her past. Although Amparo is the protagonist of the novel, she only appears in some chapters of the work (fewer than half), and this gives a greater prominence to the many secondary characters who populate the pages.

This final novel by Carmen Martín Gaite bears what Gérard Genette would term a 'thematic title',[3] in that it signals the principal theme of the narrative whereby a number of characters are seen to have left either the parental or marital home – usually on account of difficult or failed personal relationships or conflicts of one kind or another. 'Leaving Home' was also a game that Amparo used to play as a child to escape the sad reality of her dark and unhappy home. Her son Jeremy wanted to play that game with her too, as he could see that his mother also felt trapped amongst her husband's family despite knowing that 'A veces escaparse es peligroso'.[4] However, coming back 'home' for Amparo is the catalyst that enables her to confront her memories and free herself from a repressive past which she always tried to forget. Indeed, Amparo talks about New York as a place for forgetting one's feelings: 'En estos días he pensado mucho en mis defectos especialmente. Tengo agujetas de tanto pensar, te lo juro, había perdido la costumbre. En América se piensa poco'.[5]

Certainly one of the key points in *Irse de casa* is the need to confront and remember the past, and the difficulty this causes. This is addressed in the book which Valeria gave her aunt, Manuela, to read after her separation, 'un ensayo sobre la memoria':[6]

> Exigir a la memoria que se enfrente con lo desagradable ayuda a esclarecer qué decisiones se tomaron libremente y cuales bajo esclavitud, sin olvidar que esa esclavitud puede fomentarla la protagonista misma que hace memoria por culpa de la habitual sumisión femenina a las medias verdades.[7]

The need to confront the past, and the decisions taken in the past, is the common theme in Martín Gaite's novels of the 1990s: analysing oneself in order to start anew and thereby seek a better future.

---

[3] See Gérard Genette, *Paratexts: Thresholds of Interpretation*, trans. Jane E. Lewin (Cambridge: Cambridge University Press, 1997), pp. 81–5.
[4] Martín Gaite, *Irse de casa*, p. 303.
[5] Martín Gaite, *Irse de casa*, p. 324.
[6] Martín Gaite, *Irse de casa*, p. 93.
[7] Martín Gaite, *Irse de casa*, p. 93.

In addition to themes found in Martín Gaite's novels of the 1990s, such as parent–child relationships and youth and drugs, this novel alludes to *Entre visillos*, reminding the reader about the social and cultural repression of the Franco era and the differences with present-day Spain.[8] It is also possible to see in this novel the influence of the film scripts Martín Gaite wrote in the 1980s. Discussion of the device of the draft of a film script as the vehicle for life-writing in *Irse de casa* will be central to the assessment of this chapter.

Mother/Daughter Relationship: Letters of Love and Friendship

The novel opens with a prologue titled 'Pórtico con rascacielos', which has the reader witness a scene between two young people, Jeremy and Florita, in a restaurant on Third Avenue in New York. They are discussing the possible shooting of a film. Jeremy's idea is to relate the story of his mother, Amparo, using episodes from her past in Spain, but also looking at the present, represented by another rootless woman in the city, with his mother's 'voz en *off*',[9] just as she uses when she talks to herself. This first idea for the structure of the film does not make sense to Florita, the actress who may perform the role of the other woman. Even though Amparo will take her son's script with her to Spain, she has not given him much hope that she will finance the project. Jeremy says of his mother: 'No me ha querido financiar la película, pero la está copiando'.[10] Everything changes, however, after Amparo confronts her past in Spain and also observes the transformations that her home town has gone through while she was living away. She will become both the script-writer and the protagonist of her own story, as well as the producer of the film.

Amparo is the daughter of a single mother, a circumstance which was viewed unsympathetically in postwar Spain. Her mother, Ramona Miranda, took refuge in a small city after giving birth to her illegitimate daughter and, late in the novel, the narrator remembers the time when Amparo was told of her father's existence: 'Tardó en saber que era hija de soltera. ... Cuando murió ese padre nunca visto fue la primera vez

---

[8] For a study of the parallels between *Entre visillos* and *Irse de casa* as *quest-romance* and autobiography, together with *El cuarto de atrás*, see Nuria Cruz-Cámara, *El laberinto intertextual de Carmen Martín Gaite: Un estudio de sus novelas de los noventa* (Newark, DE: Juan de la Cuesta, 2008), pp. 182–96.
[9] Martín Gaite, *Irse de casa*, p. 15.
[10] Martín Gaite, *Irse de casa*, p. 31.

que Amparo tuvo noticia de él ... tendría ella once años'.[11] This secrecy concerning her origins contrasts with the situation of Amparo's own daughter, María, who has a child with a Greek artist and is pregnant again by him, even though he is living with another woman. As Amparo comments towards the end of the novel: 'Hoy día ser hija de madre soltera tiene poco de folletín'.[12]

Overprotectiveness and resentment towards other people formed an integral part of the upbringing that Ramona gave her daughter, whom she encouraged to work hard at school and to be proud and ambitious: 'A la señora Ramona le gustaba poco que aceptara favores o regalos de "esa gente"; pueden creer que somos unas muertas de hambre, tú te estás costeando todos los estudios por ti misma'.[13] The dressmaker Ramona was jealous of anybody who had a close relationship with her daughter, such as Olimpia Moret, the rich girl who was one of the few friends Amparo made in the town. In Chodorow's opinion, the relationship between a single mother and her child can be damaging: 'My view is that exclusive single parenting is bad for mother and child alike. ... mothers in such settings are liable to overinvest in and overwhelm the relationships.'[14]

The feeling of being different, and the repressive conditions that her mother imposed on her, made Amparo careful about her friends, and Olimpia and Abel Bores were the only people who related to her before she left to go abroad with her mother and work in Geneva as an interpreter.[15] However, Amparo's relationship with these two is complicated by class difference,[16] as both were from the best families in the town and both were in love with her.

Late in the narrative, during a conversation with Agustín, her doctor and confidant, Olimpia confesses her first loves: 'yo de niña me enamoré de un chófer de mi padre, y luego de una amiga a la que idealicé durante años porque era pobre y guapa, lo contrario que yo'.[17] Agustín also confesses: 'su gran pasión de juventud había sido un compañero del instituto que

---

[11] Martín Gaite, *Irse de casa*, p. 189.
[12] Martín Gaite, *Irse de casa*, p. 325.
[13] Martín Gaite, *Irse de casa*, p. 191.
[14] Nancy J. Chodorow, *The Reproduction of Mothering: Psychoanalysis and the Sociology of Gender* (Berkeley: University of California Press, 1999), p. 217.
[15] In fact, the author's sister, Ana María, worked in Geneva during the 1980s. See Carmen Martín Gaite, *A Fondo*, interview 1981, available at: <http://video.google.com/videoplay?docid=8932946931150749996>.
[16] The women of the Greek chorus at the beginning of Chapter Two are the first characters to discuss the class difference between Amparo and Olimpia and Abel.
[17] Martín Gaite, *Irse de casa*, p. 274.

escribía versos y que luego murió de tuberculosis'.[18] This confession is answered by Olimpia: 'somos homosexuales vergonzantes'.[19]

Olimpia, after Amparo left the town, wrote a love letter to her friend. Amparo, though, wished Abel Bores (who never wrote to her) had been the writer of Olimpia's letter, which she kept for a number of years: 'se estremecía de placer imaginando que hubiera podido recibir de Abel Bores una carta parecida y por eso la guardó, en vez de romperla inmediatamente'.[20]

Amparo never answered Olimpia's letter, nor did she give anybody her address in New York since she chose to cut the threads that linked her to her past. Another important epistolary aspect of the novel is Ramona's correspondence with Társila del Olmo, her only friend in Spain (even though in the narrative only one of the letters is reproduced). Amparo's mother was never able to break completely with her past, even though she had to suffer the rejection of conservative Spanish society. Their exchange of letters, 'su último enlace secreto con la ciudad',[21] did not end until Ramona's death.

These letters, which Amparo never saw, were intercepted by her son, Jeremy, after his grandmother's death. He decided to burn her letters, erasing the evidence of a woman who always felt rootless in a society where she never learned the language. In fact, the burning of the letters is treated as a ritual similar to the scene in *Retahílas*, when Germán and his girlfriend burn all their letters in the bonfire on St John's night, or the moment in *El cuarto de atrás* when C. recalls the burning of letters and other documents, which Garlinger terms a 'purification ritual.'[22] In *El cuarto de atrás* the process is described as follows:

> He quemado tantas cosas, cartas, diarios, poesías. A veces me entra la piromanía, me agobian los papeles viejos. Porque de tanto manosearlos, se vacían de contenido, dejan de ser lo que fueron. ... La última gran quema la organicé una tarde de febrero, estaba leyendo a Machado en esta misma habitación y me dio un arrebato.[23]

---

[18] Martín Gaite, *Irse de casa*, p. 275.
[19] Martín Gaite, *Irse de casa*, p. 275.
[20] Martín Gaite, *Irse de casa*, p. 217.
[21] Martín Gaite, *Irse de casa*, p. 185.
[22] Patrick Paul Garlinger, *Confessions of the Letter Closet: Epistolary Fiction & Queer Desire in Modern Spain* (Minneapolis: University of Minnesota Press, 2005), p. 43.
[23] Carmen Martín Gaite, *El cuarto de atrás* [1978] (Barcelona: Destino, 1996), p. 45.

In *Irse de casa*, Jeremy chooses the Bronx as the ideal place to burn the letters: 'Eran cartas de una amiga de España y se referían a gente que él no conocía. Se puso en cuclillas y las fue tirando despacio a la hoguera, los niños negros se reían muchísimo. ... La última carta tardó en quemarse'.[24] Through Ramona's last letter to Társila, remembering an afternoon when she was happy, the reader learns of her feelings and regrets concerning her daughter's upbringing: 'Vivo en una casa que tiene de todo, mi yerno me respeta y está enamoradísimo de Amparo, ahora tienen otra niña. ... si sufre nunca te va a pedir ayuda ... Yo la enseñé a ser como es, me moriré con ese remordimiento'.[25]

From an early age Amparo knew that it was better not to tell her mother what she felt, fearing her mother's reproaches for going out with people of her own age, or for the fact that she had fallen in love with a man from a higher social class, as had happened before they left the town: 'dos años antes de abandonar definitivamente la ciudad, cuando conoció a Abel Bores'.[26] Her mother would presumably have worried that her daughter might suffer the same misfortune of being abandoned as she had been by Amparo's father. Even in America her mother did not trust anybody: 'Su madre desconfiaba de todo el mundo y estaba con el alma en un hilo hasta que la oía volver'.[27] The fact that Ramona never learned English always made her dependent on her daughter, although Amparo felt a great distance between them: 'Estoy siempre sola, es mi condición,'[28] Amparo tells her future husband the day she meets him.

Although Amparo's life apparently seems fulfilled after marrying, having children and becoming a successful designer, at the age of sixty-three she still feels she has not made any real decisions in her life, having always done what other people expected of her. Most of Amparo's decisions in life seem to arise from inertia, thinking only about what would be best for her mother. Chance also seems to play a significant part in her life, such as the evening when she met her husband: 'Supo con total certeza que, si quería, se podía casar con él',[29] but she is practical and does not talk about love when considering the outcome. The sentimental relationship with her lawyer after her husband's death is also not explained. He, to her surprise, declared his love to her and she decided

---

[24] Martín Gaite, *Irse de casa*, p. 257.
[25] Martín Gaite, *Irse de casa*, p. 310.
[26] Martín Gaite, *Irse de casa*, p. 310.
[27] Martín Gaite, *Irse de casa*, p. 197.
[28] Martín Gaite, *Irse de casa*, pp. 194–5.
[29] Martín Gaite, *Irse de casa*, p. 197.

to maintain a comfortable and unassuming relationship which lasted until his death. Similar to other characters in Martín Gaite's novels, Amparo does not seem to take any decisions but allows things to happen to her, even during the week she spends in her home town. It is not until the end of the novel that Amparo decides to change her life by taking a decision for herself. The theme of chance in life is also what Abel Bores has been taking notes on the same morning that he meets Amparo: 'el concepto de azar en Bergson'.[30]

In the prologue to the novel the relationship between Amparo and her children is presented from their point of view. Furthermore the actress, with whom Jeremy is talking at the beginning of the novel, tells him before leaving: 'si habla sola será porque tiene secretos, todas las madres los tienen. ... Sabemos muy poco de nuestras madres'.[31] This theme, the lack of communication between parents and children, is recurrent throughout the novel. Everyone in the novel, except Abel Bores and his daughter Rita, seems unable to communicate adequately. Indeed, it is Jeremy's desire to learn more about his mother that has driven him to write the script.

The prologue also contains the first letter of the novel, written by Amparo to her daughter María the day she decides to travel back to Spain: 'por una vez no pienso en los demás, y me voy. Ha sido un impulso súbito'.[32] Jeremy reads the letter in the 'sewing room' of his mother's luxury apartment, which reveals to the reader the only place in the house where Amparo has retained any traces of her past in Spain. Her sewing room in New York serves as a reminder of the small home where she grew up in Spain, a basement flat (of 'cincuenta metros cuadrados y un retrete con ducha'[33]) which served also as a dressmaker's workshop. In her sewing room 'El desorden y la aglomeración del cuartito lo convertían en recodo clandestino de subversión, en escondite y nido'.[34] This sewing room represents for Amparo not only a place of subversion, but also the only link with Spain. This is also the first place she thinks of when, in her home town, she buys a doll from an antique shop situated where her family home had once been. Amparo contemplates the moment she will give the doll to her granddaughter: 'El paquete lo abriría Caroline en el

---

[30] Martín Gaite, *Irse de casa*, p. 319.
[31] Martín Gaite, *Irse de casa*, p. 15.
[32] Martín Gaite, *Irse de casa*, p. 22.
[33] Martín Gaite, *Irse de casa*, p. 42.
[34] Martín Gaite, *Irse de casa*, p. 23.

cuartito de costura de Lexington Avenue. Esperaría a que estuvieran las dos solas'.[35] The shop where she buys the doll for her granddaughter and the place she lived as a child are linked here, and at the same time Amparo makes up a story around the doll, remembering the stories she used to tell herself as a child. The house, repressive at the time she lived in it, was escaped from in her imagination.

Jeremy's psychiatrist is helping him to analyse his relationship with his family: 'Hoy le tocaba contarle cosas de la abuela Ramona ... qué tipo de relaciones mantuvo con la familia Drake y hasta qué punto influyó su condición de madre soltera en la educación que su hija Amparo les dio a ellos'.[36] For Jeremy, Spain is represented through his grandmother. Jeremy seems to understand the relationship between his mother and his grandmother, maybe due to his analysis with different psychiatrists: 'Jeremy dijo que María no había acertado nunca a tratar a la madre, que lo que necesitaba era cariño, había recibido poco cariño de la abuela Ramona, y se había vuelto desconfiada, y un poco rígida'.[37] Amparo also reflects on her own inflexibility towards her children:

> Tú, Jeremy, idealizas a la abuela, porque no la padeciste en la época de miseria.
> Y sin embargo – pensó de pronto, y fue como si el aire se parara – yo también he exigido sacrificio a mis hijos, me he empeñado en que lo consigan todo con esfuerzo y sin ayuda.[38]

Throughout the novel the changes in Amparo's position in relation to her children, after finding her past and understanding the reason for her own attitudes towards them, are apparent. She remembers when her older child was born and her wishes at that moment: 'Y nació Jeremy, y ella pensó que nunca tenga miedo a la libertad, que sepa crecer por sí solo y que se enfrente a mí cuando haga falta'.[39] On her last day in her home city, Amparo imagines the conversation she will have with her son, telling him of her decision to finance his film. And during her dinner with Abel Bores, she inwardly admits the envy she feels towards the relationship between her old friend and his daughter: 'Yo a mi hija nunca supe tratarla'.[40] She

---

[35] Martín Gaite, *Irse de casa*, p. 213.
[36] Martín Gaite, *Irse de casa*, p. 252.
[37] Martín Gaite, *Irse de casa*, p. 251.
[38] Martín Gaite, *Irse de casa*, pp. 288–9.
[39] Martín Gaite, *Irse de casa*, p. 330.
[40] Martín Gaite, *Irse de casa*, p. 324.

recognizes that she has made mistakes but that it is not too late: 'siempre se puede rectificar'.[41] It is possible to see the changes which Amparo goes through as the narrative progresses and as she takes notes for the film script. From Chapter Twenty-three, comments on the film are more common. The film becomes more and more part of the narrative and the romantic evening spent with Abel encourages her to change: 'Ya no teme al futuro porque sabe que siempre podrá recordar esta noche'.[42]

Although *Irse de casa* cannot be classified as an epistolary novel, letters have an important role in the narrative as they serve as links between past and present and give background information on certain characters and situations. As Jurado Morales indicates: 'Las cartas del presente ayudan a avanzar la acción',[43] while the letters of the past reveal moments lost in the memory of those who lived them. The letters written by Amparo inform the reader of her decisions or impulses, initially of leaving New York (the letter written to María) and finally of leaving Spain (that written to Ricardo). The letters written by Ramona and Társila del Olmo link past and present and, even though only one letter is included in the novel, the existence of the correspondence is mentioned at different times in the narrative. The other two letters in the novel also tell of decisions taken by other characters. Thus the note written by Marcelo to Amparo, inviting her to the last performance of his play, as well as the note written by Agustín to Olimpia, are letters which bring a close to different subplots of the narrative.

The final letter in the novel, written by Amparo to the waiter in the Spanish hotel, Ricardo, serves as a continuing link between Amparo's return to New York and the town she has rediscovered in Spain. In this letter, Amparo expresses her desires to keep in contact with Ricardo with the idea of involving him in the writing of the film dialogues. It is clear in the letter that her decision to go back to New York and start working on the film is imminent: 'Mi hijo va a empezar a rodar una película que tiene por escenario una provincia española y necesitamos un persona con buen oído y olfato literario como tú'.[44] Indeed, Amparo specifically asks him to watch the women of the so-called Greek chorus: 'No dejes de estar atento a las señoras del coro griego'.[45]

---

[41] Martín Gaite, *Irse de casa*, p. 324.
[42] Martín Gaite, *Irse de casa*, p. 326.
[43] Jurado Morales, *La trayectoria narrativa*, p. 402.
[44] Martín Gaite, *Irse de casa*, p. 344.
[45] Martín Gaite, *Irse de casa*, p. 344.

The Greek Chorus: Themes and Characters of the Novel

In *Irse de casa*, Amparo is presented to the reader as a mature, beautiful woman, with money and style. Her presence as a rich, attractive woman is constantly endorsed by the narrator's observations: 'Se alisa el vestido frente al espejo de tres cuerpos,[46] sonríe, se mira los zapatos italianos carísimos, la cintura sin michelines, no representa ni cincuenta'.[47] It is also confirmed by the comments of other characters:

> Cuatro señoras que salen de la cafetería se la quedan mirando. ... Se fijan sobre todo en los zapatos, a juego con el bolso y el cinturón.
> – ¡Que mujer más elegante! ¿Habéis visto? Debe de ser extranjera.[48]

At the same time Amparo is portrayed as a mystery to people in her home town. She pretends to be a foreigner, using her husband's surname and even, at times, imitating an American accent, as if playing the role of the foreigner. Only one character seems to have realized who she is: Ricardo, the hotel Excelsior's waiter, is the only one who has linked her with a figure from the past mentioned by the 'Greek chorus'. He also plays the role of 'spying' on the gatherings of the ladies who meet every day at the hotel's café to gossip about everyone in the town.

This 'Greek chorus', as Ricardo calls them, are the first to talk about Amparo's past: 'Son otros tiempos. Yo veo lógico que la gente quiera medrar. Amparo y su madre se adelantaron a su tiempo. Eso es lo que nos escuece'.[49] Chapter Two, where these women first appear, is almost entirely written like a film script in which dialogue takes over narration. In the tradition of the classical Greek theatre, these women serve the reader as a link with other characters of the novel, commenting and giving information about characters who are presented later in the narrative.[50]

---

[46] The mirror is again an important item in the narrative just as it was in *Nubosidad* and *La Reina*. At times, it serves as a witness of the character's moments of solitude and the interlocutor in those moments.
[47] Martín Gaite, *Irse de casa*, p. 59.
[48] Martín Gaite, *Irse de casa*, p. 61.
[49] Martín Gaite, *Irse de casa*, p. 42.
[50] Ignacio Soldevila Durante, in his study of the novel, suggests a parallel between the 'Greek chorus' and the comedies of Jacinto Benavente: 'Este paso de comedia incisivo por el despliegue de la superficialidad de la burguesía provinciana, recuerda el recurso habitual de las comedias benaventinas': '*Irse de casa*, o el haz y el envés de una aventurada emigración americana', in *Carmen Martín Gaite*, ed. Alicia Redondo Goicoechea (Madrid: Ediciones del Orto, 2004), pp. 199–206 (p. 202).

Most of the characters who cross paths in the novel are under their scrutiny. These 'señoras de toda la vida',[51] of a similar age to Amparo, have witnessed many changes in their Spanish provincial society, and each one of them knows someone who is going through one type of crisis or another. Divorces, diets, youth, drugs and anorexia are just some of the themes which these women present to the reader, with a realism typical of Martín Gaite's narratives. But above all, these other characters serve as a contrast to Amparo who, although the same age, has lived through very different circumstances.

The first of these characters are Manuela Roca and Dr Agustín Sánchez del Olmo, whose marriage has ended in divorce. This match between the daughter of one of the 'best' families and the son of a seamstress, Társila del Olmo, generated a great amount of gossip. The ill-fated Manuela (she dies in a car accident when travelling back to her family holiday home) is a character who, although she finds some independence leaving home, will never understand her role in society. She seems to be followed by a camera, as she is mainly presented in cinematic situations, such as reading by the swimming pool or driving her car through the city streets. Like Manuela, Agustín also seems to be followed by a camera, which witnesses different moments of his life. He is seen meeting people, putting the reader in contact with another stock character, the problematic youth who lacks a goal in life. This character type includes Marcelo, a young man from Madrid, who leaves the big city to break with a life 'a la deriva'[52] and with drugs, and also Alicia, a young anorexic who lives with her divorced mother and seems to choose self-destruction as her way of rebelling against social norms.[53]

In a note to the novel found in *Cuadernos de todo*, it emerges that Martín Gaite first intended Amparo to be the one who would put the reader in contact with the social reality of the ordinary people she finds in her home town:

> El desvivir de Amparo a medida que va perdiendo las nociones de tiempo y geografía. Se encuentra (extrañada) hablando con la gente de barrios marginales, preguntándoles por el paro, por precios de

---

[51] Martín Gaite, *Irse de casa*, p. 46.
[52] Martín Gaite, *Irse de casa*, p. 118.
[53] For a study of the young in *Irse de casa*, especially of the characters of Alicia and Valeria, see Cruz-Cámara, *El laberinto intertextual*, pp. 113–28.

alquiler, por la demolición de lo viejo, cuestión okupas, se cree que es una socióloga.[54]

Although in the novel Amparo does not interrogate the people she comes across, she does, indeed, wander the town, but mainly keeping to the new prosperous residential district where the hotel is, or the old centre where she used to live.

The decision to leave social themes (and gossip) to the women of the 'Greek chorus' works better in the novel, allowing the reader to see the attitudes and points of view of insiders, instead of using the 'foreigner' to study the behaviour of the 'natives', as if she were a sociologist or anthropologist. The reactions of the women to change and its repercussions on the everyday life of their society show a more realistic, local (although largely negative) portrait of that society. Amparo, on the other hand, is given the role of the silent witness who, like a camera, shows the scenes that happen in front of her.

Those women who form the 'Greek chorus' in *Irse de casa* recall the young girls in *Entre visillos*, whose banal conversations suggest the reality of the society they live in. Also, the great number of characters in the novel presents what Jurado Morales calls an 'efecto de mosaico a base de fragmentos.'[55] These characters reveal the different types which form the social range.

The presentation of the different characters emphasizes the key theme of the novel which, as the title indicates, is leaving home. The contrast between the different generations and the repressions which some of the characters feel with regard to the paternal home, especially Manuela and Valeria, or Alicia in the case of the maternal one, may well reflect the social and cultural repression suffered in Franco's Spain during Amparo's youth. Although times have changed dramatically, and Spanish society of the 1990s is much more progressive, *Irse de casa* suggests a clear critique of the lack of freedom and limited goals that young people still experience. This is possibly due to the economic pressures that consumerist society exerts. Indeed, in her *Cuadernos de todo*, Martín Gaite develops the theme of women as victims of the consumerist society which

---

[54] Carmen Martín Gaite, *Cuadernos de todo*, ed. and intro. Maria Vittoria Calvi (Barcelona: Areté, 2002), p. 668.
[55] Jurado Morales, *La trayectoria narrativa*, p. 399.

began in the 1960s,[56] and continues on this topic with articles such as the one published in *La Vanguardia* in 1994:

> No es la pérdida de memoria, sino la imposibilidad de adquirirla lo que se extiende como inquietante epidemia en la juventud actual, ansiosa de consumir y devorar por entero el presente en el instante mismo en que es percibido. Incapaces de relacionar cosa con cosa, desvinculados del ayer y del mañana, muchos de nuestros jóvenes viven con el hilo perdido.[57]

The Script: Taking Charge of One's Own Life Through Writing

During the 1980s, Martín Gaite worked on different television scripts, such as the television series *Santa Teresa de Jesús* (1983), *Fragmentos de interior* (1984) and *Celia* (1993). She also produced the script for the documentary 'Salamanca', an episode in the series *Ésta es mi tierra* (1983).[58] The influence of this involvement can be seen in her novels: details on narrative 'sets' or the attitude of a character in a scene, as well as the beginning of chapters which take the reader right to the heart of the action are typical of the film or TV script (or of theatre plays, a genre which Martín Gaite also practised). As Margaret Parker observes: '[*Irse de casa*] features cinematic techniques used in previous novels, such as unmarked transitions, multiple points of view, and accounts of the same event from various perspectives.'[59] Furthermore, this novel is laden with references to film and cinema, and we can also 'hear' the 'soundtracks' which follow the characters in different scenes. For example, 'Strangers in the Night' is the song that Amparo listened to in her future husband's car the night they met; while 'Yesterday' is the one Abel Bores plays to celebrate his re-encounter with his former love.

From the prologue onwards the author seems to be creating film scenes. Comments on script-writing and filming are made throughout the novel, especially in the prologue, where the film script or filming is referred to on nearly every page, as well as towards the end of the novel, from

---

[56] See for example, 'Buscar un ambiente' in *Cuaderno 3* (Martín Gaite, *Cuadernos*, pp. 96–7).

[57] Carmen Martín Gaite, 'Cosa por cosa', in *Tirando del hilo (Artículos 1949–2000)*, ed. and intro. José Teruel (Madrid: Siruela, 2006), pp. 481–3 (p. 483).

[58] See Jurado Morales, *La trayectoria narrativa*, p. 476.

[59] Margaret Parker, 'Revisiting Spain as Liberation from the Past in *Irse de casa* and *A Woman Unknown*: Voices from a Spanish Life', *South Central Review*, 18 (2001), 114–26 (p. 115).

Chapter Twenty-three onwards. One of the many examples is the early scene in Amparo's apartment in Manhattan when her children find their mother's money while looking through her clothes:

> Venga vamos a repartir. Lo importante es que te guste la escena. ¿Verdad que no desentona?
> – En absoluto. Es un *gag* genial.
> – Me alegro que sepas apreciarlo. … En una escena como ésta, si se les hubiera ocurrido, acabaría llegando la policía.[60]

At other times, the sense of a scene being filmed is completely explicit: 'La cámara iba siguiendo sus pasos vacilantes a través de edificios en ruinas'.[61] Thus the dramatic impetus for the novel and its development are provided by Jeremy's project.

With the idea of the film is constantly present in the narrative of *Irse de casa*, the life-writing is produced through the rewriting of the film script. There are a number of circumstances, places and people which stimulate Amparo's consciousness, making her understand the reason for her journey. The first place to remind her of her past in a town she hardly recognizes is the Plaza del Rincón, an encounter that marks the beginning of her writing:

> Llevaba dos mañanas viniendo tempranito a sentarse allí y seguía sin pasar casi nadie, o los que pasaban no la veían, en eso consistía la magia del lugar, la misma que la llevó de adolescente a elegirlo como escondite, tan inconfundible para ella como invisible para los demás; y recuperar esa sensación de privilegio vino a suponer el primer acontecimiento digno de reseña en su travesía del desierto: 'He estado en la plazuela del Rincón y existe', anotó escuetamente por la noche en su agenda.[62]

This square, which she finds by chance, is where she used to take refuge from her mother and her home. These associations again take her back to her childhood experiences.

Tarsi's home is the second place where Amparo confronts her past. Tarsi's mother, Társila del Olmo, had worked for Ramona as a seamstress, and had been gifted items of furniture by her employer before Amparo and

---

[60] Martín Gaite, *Irse de casa*, p. 30.
[61] Martín Gaite, *Irse de casa*, p. 32.
[62] Martín Gaite, *Irse de casa*, p. 142.

Ramona went abroad. Here in Tarsi's apartment, Amparo's unexpected encounter with 'su viejo armario de luna'[63] takes her back to the times when she felt her only friend was the image she could see in the mirror. Talking to herself, or to her reflected image, was one of the games her friend Olimpia taught her, a game which, as the reader sees, she still likes playing. Through the mirror, Amparo recalls the moment she left the town with her mother to move to Geneva. The encounter with her old wardrobe encourages Amparo to continue writing her own story: 'Necesitaba tomar notas de todo aquello, rumiarlo a solas. Ya empezaba a haber argumento'.[64] This encounter also encourages her to reread her son's script: 'Recién concluida la relectura al sexto día de estancia en su ciudad, Amparo supo con certeza no sólo que ese texto había sido el desencadenante del viaje emprendido, sino que se había movido a su dictado desde que llegó'.[65] Writing and reading her own story breaks with the indifference she had assumed since her arrival, and she begins to take charge of her future: 'Me quiero salir del guión de Jeremy – dijo –. Ir de verdad a la calle del Olvido'.[66]

'La calle del Olvido', the title of Jeremy's script and also the name of the street where Amparo grew up, brings her back into contact with a past she wanted to forget. Her old family home has been converted into an antique shop (where Amparo buys the doll for her granddaughter), coincidentally run by Rita Bores, the daughter of Amparo's old love. When Amparo had lived there the house had been full of gloom, with partition walls creating tiny rooms, but now the shop's open-plan design makes the building airy and light and this takes Amparo back to her childhood dreams: 'Soñaba con demoler todos los tabiques y convertirse en habitante de un lugar grande y silencioso para ella sola'.[67] Together with the Plaza del Rincón, this scene suggests the feelings of repression and entrapment Amparo suffered in her home town and which she can still feel now: 'No era capaz de encontrarle sentido a su viaje. Y sin embargo, no se quería ir. No podía. La ciudad la tenía atrapada'.[68] In this way, Martín Gaite evokes the physical and psychological oppression that any citizen of a small Spanish town might feel.

Having stepped out of what once was her home, Amparo crosses the

---

[63] Martín Gaite, *Irse de casa*, p. 182.
[64] Martín Gaite, *Irse de casa*, p. 187.
[65] Martín Gaite, *Irse de casa*, p. 207.
[66] Martín Gaite, *Irse de casa*, p. 207.
[67] Martín Gaite, *Irse de casa*, p. 210.
[68] Martín Gaite, *Irse de casa*, p. 149.

street to look at Olimpia's house. Olimpia is reciting part of Macbeth's address to the witches, which could be seen as a scene within a scene. The person who appears on the balcony looks like an old woman with white hair, and Amparo recognizes her former friend. By contrast, Amparo's cosmetic surgery means that she herself does not feel like an old woman. Her friend's image awakes in her a 'mezcla de remordimiento, piedad y éxtasis'[69] but, most importantly, this scene ends with Amapro anxious to continue her modification of Jeremy's script: 'Tenía hambre y sed, pero sobre todo muchas cosas que apuntar para inyectarle vida al guión de Jeremy'.[70]

As discussed earlier, Amparo adopts the role of a spectator, or witness, who does not interfere with the town's life and the people she meets. She is the camera who looks without being seen: 'Amparo levanta el telón de sus párpados'.[71] In fact, Martín Gaite defined Amparo as 'una especie de ojo que ve todo lo que ocurre a su alrededor y lo que pasa a los demás.'[72] After Manuela Roca's death, and once each of the characters in the novel have taken centre stage, the reader is witness to what could be termed the film's key scene. In Amparo's version of the script, the very first scene could begin with the funeral service for Manuela:

> La película podría empezar ahora, se dijo Amparo Miranda, mientras subía las escaleras de la Catedral. Esa mujer que hemos visto deambular por parajes desiertos e irreales mientras se suceden los títulos de crédito está llegando a un templo donde hay mucha gente, pero nadie la mira ni la reconoce. Ha sobrevolado mares, ciudades y montañas para asistir al entierro de una amiga o tal vez de un pariente cercano, eso mejor que lo decida Jeremy.[73]

Inside the cathedral Amparo, who is completely detached from the funeral service, merely witnessing, reflects on her days in the town and the steps to follow. She has changed her attitude to life and has decided to go back to New York and take advantage of a new opening, a new future: 'este viaje ha sido como cascar una alcancía y que se derrame todo el caudal de

---

[69] Martín Gaite, *Irse de casa*, p. 219.
[70] Martín Gaite, *Irse de casa*, p. 219.
[71] Martín Gaite, *Irse de casa*, p. 193.
[72] Cited in Jurado Morales, *La trayectoria narrativa*, p. 399.
[73] Martín Gaite, *Irse de casa*, p. 286.

pensamiento cautivo, los argumentos del pasado, del presente y del futuro se han echado a rodar como monedas vertiginosas'.[74]

Towards the end, the novel seems to have turned into a film which has already started to be shot. As mentioned earlier, Chapter Twenty-three is littered with commentaries on the script and the filming, as if each of the scenes has a camera present, following the character's movements. At the same time Amparo imagines the instructions to be followed as if she were directing the filming:

> Amparo sigue de pie con la espalda apoyada en la columna y el órgano lleva unos minutos sonando; a ti que no te vean, le dice Amparo a Jeremy, que se oculta con su cámara en el coro, pero sácalo todo. Fíjate bien en los gestos de las señoras, detente en los rostros que se miran con pasmo, cada una puede estar recordando una anécdota de la difunta y entre todas compondrían una historia que tal vez no coincidiera con lo más escondido de su persona.[75]

In a way, the scene in the cathedral could be regarded as ending the novel and beginning the film; an ending similar to those of *El cuarto de atrás* or *Nubosidad variable*, where the novel is revealed to the reader as the pages that have previously been read. In this case it is the script that Amparo has been rewriting and that can now start to be filmed. However, what Amparo had not counted on is an encounter which will add a new scene to the script. This new scene will also be fundamental to her way of looking at the future, and will close unfinished business or an 'asignatura pendiente' from her past. The moment when Amparo sees Abel Bores inside the cathedral changes her plans for the day and the script of the developing film.

This encounter, which Amparo had wished for from the moment she arrived in the town,[76] but which she decided to leave to chance, makes the romantic ending she had actually rejected as 'barato y ventajista'.[77] Abel and Amparo have supper, on her sixty-fourth birthday (a birthday he still

---

[74] Martín Gaite, *Irse de casa*, p. 288.
[75] Martín Gaite, *Irse de casa*, p. 288.
[76] In Chapter Three and after reading in the local newspaper an article about Abel Bores, the narrator comments on Amparo's feelings: 'ha encontrado un motivo fulminante para salir. No a buscarlo, sino a pasear por la misma ciudad donde él aún vive y por la que puede apetecerle salir a pasear ... El viaje de Amparo ha cobrado sentido, se ha convertido en una aventura' (p. 59).
[77] Martín Gaite, *Irse de casa*, p. 287. Marcelo had sent her a 'carta medio de amor' (p. 248) and asked her to meet him at the theatre, which she decides against.

remembers), in a secluded, mountain restaurant while the Beatles song, 'Yesterday', plays in the background. This scene could easily compete with the best *novelas rosas*. The 'restaurante con velitas',[78] which she had pictured with Marcelo, is used in the scene with Abel. Even though this scene is a real cliché of the best sentimental novels or romantic films, Martín Gaite decides not to give her character the classical happy ending reuniting them forever, now that they are both free, but instead leaves an open ending in which their paths may cross again. Amparo suggests that Abel could be part of the film: 'podríamos llamarte para el rodaje'.[79] Yet, Amparo decides not to stay in the town and live the love story which she had dreamed of all her life. Instead, she decides to go back to New York, give up her business, change her profession, and start a new and better relationship with her children. For the first time in her life, she takes a decision on her own. After the death of her mother, her husband and her lover, Ralf, she is alone for the first time, finding with that isolation the freedom to choose her own path.

Conclusion

The prologue to the novel includes the first letter written by Amparo to her daughter María, giving her the news of her departure for Spain. The final chapter, Chapter Twenty-eight, ends with Amparo's letter to Ricardo informing him of news of her departure for New York. These two letters show a different person. The first reveals a woman who had just followed an impulse and who is not sure of her aim; she is just leaving to find 'una bocanada de olvido'.[80] The last letter presents a woman much more sure of herself, who seems to know exactly what she wants: 'se me ha ocurrido a última hora, pero lo veo tan claro'.[81] Instead of finding a 'gust of oblivion', Amparo has confronted her past and has decided to make the film of her life, *La calle del olvido*, so as not to forget it. Her journey has taken her to her past, made her reflect on her present, and taken charge of her future. As with the characters of the other Martín Gaite novels of the 1990s, Amparo has changed her life through reflection and writing. But, of course, the life-writing in this novel is begun through the film script her son, Jeremy, had written to explore his mother's past.

---

[78] Martín Gaite, *Irse de casa*, p. 287.
[79] Martín Gaite, *Irse de casa*, p. 323.
[80] Martín Gaite, *Irse de casa*, p. 22.
[81] Martín Gaite, *Irse de casa*, p. 344.

Jeremy's film script is rewritten by Amparo, who starts rediscovering her past in flashbacks, interposing scenes from the past with scenes from the present she is experiencing. The people and places she encounters inspire her to take notes to add to and develop her son's original idea. In her notebook or diary, she jotted down 'impresiones de la ciudad, muchas de las cuales se entretejían ya con el guión'.[82]

Thematically, the novel also relates back to a repressive past which reminds the reader of the era of *Entre visillos*. This period is presented by Amparo's memories, the letters of Ramona and Társila del Olmo, as well as the comments made by the women of the 'Greek chorus' regarding the transformation their society has gone through. The life in Spain of the 1950s is what Amparo has to confront, the period of her life when the society she lived in with her mother did not allow her to be whatever she wanted, so she ran away from it, trying to forget it. These memories are what Amparo is going to rescue through her writing. These memories are also going to make her realize the importance of her upbringing, her relationship with her mother, in the context of her relationship with her own children, and the way she has repressed their impulses. Reflecting on her past is going to make Amparo realize the need to change, to take decisions in order to have a better relationship with her children and also take control of her life. Even though this novel and its characters are not as close to the personality of the author as her characters from the other 1990s novels, it is still possible to see the influence of Martín Gaite's biography, especially during the periods spent in the United States. And even though Amparo is not the 'writer' of the novel, we can still witness the transformation she goes through while writing the script of her life.

---

[82] Martín Gaite, *Irse de casa*, p. 287.

CONCLUSION

The use of diaries, letters and other types of life-writing in literature has evolved during the centuries, developing a more introspective and metafictional character, as well as presenting a therapeutic side of self-writing. That evolution can also be seen in Carmen Martín Gaite's literary career, as diaries and letters have been part of the author's output from her first novels and short stories. She not only used diaries and letters as a narrative strategy, but she also reflected on this kind of writing in many of her essays and articles.

Looking at the development of letters, diaries and life-writing in literature provided me with parameters for understanding the development of these types of writing and their function in Martín Gaite's work. In literature, this went from narratives which started as mirrors of life, presenting novels, especially epistolary novels, as the simple reproduction of 'real letters' found by the editor, towards a more clear fictional narrative which indeed copied real life. The development of life-writing goes from an objective representation of female characters portrayed by male writers, to a subjectivity of women who take control of their own narratives and present themselves as the creators and protagonists of their own stories. In relation to the different kinds of life-writing, it was seen that there are differences and similarities between letters and diaries even though it is difficult to separate the different types of life-writing, as many of their characteristics overlap. In Foucault's words both types of writing share an aspect of self-examination, and this is writing as a self-reflective act. Studying this in turn took me to life-writing as therapeutic writing, the writing cure, writing after traumatic or difficult times, where the writers (or their fictional characters) are able to see themselves from an objective point of view and, by studying themselves and looking at their past, to understand their problems. This is a writing which also serves as mirror or reflection: as Didier points out, 'miroir, reflect, regard'[1] ['mirror,

---

[1] Beatrice Didier, *Le Journal intime* (Paris: Presses Universitaires de France, 1976), p. 113.

reflect, look'] are terms which often appeared in diaries, life-writing which becomes *desdoblamiento* ('dédoublement' in Didier's words) of the one who writes, or is a kind of 'levitation'[2] in Abbott's terms. As José Teruel expresses it: 'En el momento en que escribo *yo* comienza a nacer mi *otro*',[3] the writers look at themselves from the outside, writing themselves, creating themselves.

In this book I have attempted to show how the foregrounding of various kinds of self-reflective writing in Martín Gaite's work culminated in her 1990s novels, especially *Nubosidad variable* and *La Reina de las Nieves*, which were also the ones most popular with the Spanish reading public. These are novels where the author seems to be in some way projecting herself into her own characters. In Martín Gaite's fiction prior to the 1990s, although several principal characters write diaries and letters (as was seen, for example, with Natalia in *Entre visillos*) this writing does not involve changes in their lives or a quest to understand how they have developed. The diaries and letters these characters produced served as a place in which to note their experiences and preoccupations, but without the self-reflective, self-examining aspect her later novels would reveal. Maturity and personal loss brought about a more reflective type of writing so, in the novels of the 1990s, Martín Gaite's characters use writing as a way to understand their lives, and to make sense of their present after going through difficult or traumatic experiences. As José Teruel indicates:

> A partir de de *Nubosidad variable*, de esos desconcertantes laberintos afectivos y desarraigados empezaron a salir sus protagonistas con desenfado e ironía, con la terapia de la palabra escrita y buenas dosis de representación, que en el fondo fueron las mejores armas de Carmen Martín Gaite.[4]

With the publication of her *Cuadernos de todo* in 2002, Martín Gaite's readers were able to penetrate a personal world which before had mostly been hidden. The *Cuadernos* are, in effect, the author's intimate diaries

---

[2] H. Porter Abbott, *Diary Fiction: Writing as Action* (Ithaca, NY: Cornell University Press, 1984), p. 25.

[3] José Teruel, 'El rescate del tiempo como proyecto narrativo: *El cuarto de atrás* y otras consideraciones sobre Carmen Martín Gaite', in *Mostrar con propiedad un desatino: La novela española contemporánea*, ed. José María Martínez Cachero et al. (Madrid: Eneida, 2004), pp. 191–209 (p. 194).

[4] José Teruel, introduction to Carmen Martín Gaite, *Obras completas*, I, ed. and intro. José Teruel (Barcelona: Galaxia Gutenburg/Círculo de Lectores, 2008), pp. 9–54 (pp. 44–5).

and, even though they can also be regarded as the writer's workshop or *dietarios*, in them the reader is given access to many of the preoccupations Martín Gaite had throughout her life. Starting in the 1960s, her *cuadernos* constituted a new way to approach and develop a more intimate side of writing. Adopting her daughter's suggested title of 'cuadernos de todo', Martín Gaite's notebooks become a place to write everything.

Even though there is little information in the *cuadernos* about the author's private life, these notebooks can be seen as a kind of escape valve where the writer could articulate thoughts which were difficult to express elsewhere. The themes dealt with, especially in the first *cuadernos*, were indeed very close to the author's preoccupations as a woman and a mother. Themes such as the role of women in society, female friendship, relations between men and women, love, motherhood and family relationships are a fundamental part of the first pages of the *Cuadernos de todo*. It is also possible to see how, from the outset, her own preoccupations are constantly interlaced with her reading and writing.

From *Cuaderno 3* Martín Gaite starts using the notebooks in a different way. Thus, her work in progress starts filling the pages. Looking at the function of the *cuadernos* as a writer's workshop, examining the different entries she wrote in these books (with regard to the subsequent creation of *El cuento de nunca acabar*, *El cuarto de atrás*, *La Reina de las Nieves*, and so on) it is possible to see the connection between her personal circumstances and her fictional characters' preoccupations and development. *El cuento de nunca acabar* is a good example of how Martín Gaite's thoughts were interwoven with her biography, ending in a work where the idea of narration is discussed through the author's personal experiences. Reading *Cuadernos de todo*, it is also possible to understand the evolution and complexity of some of her published works, which were developed over many years. Indeed, there are frequent links between the first notebooks and the ideas which the author used in her later novels. Such links lead into one of the ideas studied here, the development of the characters of the novels as mirrors of the author.

'Cuenta pendiente' (1979) is a project Martín Gaite started after her parents' death in 1978, one of the most traumatic experiences of her life. It reveals a more intimate side of the author as the subjects of her writing are her parents as well as her own memories and dreams after their death. The loss of her mother was also the moment for Martín Gaite to start thinking about herself an older woman. This period sees the start of more reflective type of writing which is closely related to the kind of writing Martín Gaite's protagonists of the novels of the 1990s will engage in. Most of these female protagonists write in their mature years, after having lost their mothers (or parents) and in some cases once they have themselves become mothers. As Didier comments:

> La présence de la mère prend inévitablement pour les femmes un autre sens que pour les hommes, puisque leur mère est leur exacte matrice, leur préfiguration. D'autant plus sensible que l'âge de l'autobiographie est souvent celui de la maturité, et du moment où elles saisissent la ressemblance avec leur mère, ayant alors l'âge qu'elle avait lors de leur enfance.[5]

> [The mother's presence inevitably has a different meaning for women than for men, since their mother is their definitive mould, she prefigures (or foreshadows) them. Indeed, it is all the more so since autobiographies are often written at a mature age, at a time when women recognize their resemblance to their mother, when they are the same age she was during their childhood.]

As the author wrote in a note to the publication of her 'Bosquejo autobiográfico' in *Agua pasada*: 'para un lector que no conozca mi biografía reciente, donde lea "soledad" y "muerte", puede estar seguro de que mi vivencia de esas dos nociones era aún bien incompleta'.[6] Having written in her *cuadernos* on the subject of her parents' death, Martín Gaite did so again a few years later after losing her daughter in 1985, another death that the author found difficult to overcome. The deaths of her two main interlocutors, her mother and her daughter, left her with a great emptiness which she seems to be transferring to her characters' lives, giving them her own questions and doubts about life and family relationships. It was thanks to her writing that Martín Gaite managed to get over that emptiness: 'estoy sola, más sola de lo que he estado nunca en mi vida, rodeada de silencio … sin creerme mucho nada de lo que pasa ni de lo que veo. Tal vez por eso mismo necesite apuntarlo'.[7] These lines are perhaps the best example of Martín Gaite's use of the *Cuadernos de todo* as a psychoanalytic tool, which I explored through the idea of writing as *tabla de salvación* or the writing cure.

---

[5] Beatrice Didier, *L'Écriture-femme* (Paris: Presses Universitaires de France, 1981), p. 26.
[6] Carmen Martín Gaite, 'Un bosquejo autobiográfico', in *Agua pasada* (Barcelona: Anagrama, 1993), pp. 11–25 (p. 11).
[7] Carmen Martín Gaite, *Cuadernos de todo*, ed. and intro. Maria Vittoria Calvi (Barcelona: Areté, 2002), p. 611.

Being in America allowed Martín Gaite to gain the necessary solitude and isolation and put the necessary distance between her and people who knew of her recent loss. In addition, this complete isolation helped her look into herself and find reasons to write. The author's sister comments on how:

> Cuando murió Marta se fue a América, empujada por mí, porque ella no quería, pero yo casi la obligué a que se marchara. Eran seis meses y pensé que, como allí nadie había conocido a mi sobrina, no sé cómo explicarte, podía ser un corte en su vida del que, a lo mejor, venía un poco de salvación.[8]

Since 1980, Martín Gaite had encountered in the United States many 'rooms of her own' where, as well as finding solitude and suffering bereavement, she found herself and lived some of her most fulfilling moments. The American notebooks are also a clear illustration of the use of the notebooks as diaries, written nearly every day, and in this respect are different from the other notebooks that had been written in her home country. The *cuadernos americanos* show moments of happiness and optimism in the writer's life, which contrast with the pages written in Spain. However, even though it is possible to find pages written in times of difficulty in the *Cuadernos de todo*, the use of diaries as therapeutic tools is made more clear in her novels.

I have analysed Martín Gaite's novels of the 1990s, and the use of diaries, letters and life-writing to understand the characters' past, make sense of their present and take charge of their future. For this to happen her characters had to go through very difficult times which made them reflect on their present life: they all had to go through a crisis to feel the urge to examine their past lives. The need to re-encounter (and understand) the mother, even after her death, is also fundamental for Martín Gaite's characters. Dreams and recording them help to understand the mother, establishing through those dreams a more open communication. Martín Gaite's characters, just like herself, find communicating with the dead in their dreams a way to continue having them as part of their life. The themes studied in Martín Gaite's first *cuadernos* are also developed in these novels making a parallel between the author and her characters. It is

---

[8] Cited in Juan Carlos Soriano, 'Ana María Martín Gaite: "Nadie, ni siquiera yo, conoció del todo a Carmiña"', *Turia: Revista Cultural*, 83 (2007), 267–79 (p. 274).

also possible to see the way she 'gives' her protagonists some of her own characteristics, especially the need to write in moments of desperation.

In the 1990s Martín Gaite seems to be looking for answers about the meaning of life, after the death of her daughter, and this quest is again projected into the protagonists of her novels:[9] they all search their past to understand their present situation, taking writing as their own *tabla de salvación* – Martín Gaite gives pen and paper to every one of them. From Mariana and Sofía who need to make sense of the moment of separation in their youth to Amparo who travels back to her home town in Spain to understand her present life, each protagonist of her novels of the 1990s uses writing as their way to reach that understanding. They all are going to go back to their early years before they reached maturity to see what circumstances took them to the place they find themselves in. They examine family relationships, the separations from their mothers and the need to make peace with them. Through this understanding they are able to develop and grow.

While Mariana, Sofía and Leonardo all write in the present with an urgency to write down their thoughts, reflections and experiences, Agueda and Amparo do not write their lives *until* they have lived the circumstances which they will reveal in the novels. Agueda writes two years after the episodes she relates took place, while Amparo, although taking notes of some of the episodes she is living, leaves the actual writing of her life (her script) for the future. As time passes, the need to write in order to survive becomes less urgent and indeed, it is possible to see Martín Gaite in *Cuadernos de todo* (at least in the published work) writing less and less as the years pass. From *Cuaderno 35*, the last of her *cuadernos americanos*, written in 1985, there is no continuation of her diaries. The last chapter or *cuaderno* in the published work is *Cuaderno 36*, which consists of notes taken in 1992. After that, the *notas fugaces* at the end of the collection give examples of notes taken in 1990, 1997 and a final note of 1999. The last note in *Cuadernos de todo* is a farewell from the author: 'Escribo desde el más allá. ... No sé dónde estaré enterrada, pero estaré en un sitio desde el que no podré hablar, y los que vienen a llorarme no pueden hablar por mí'.[10] Whether the author (or her sister) decided to destroy the notebooks written in the last decade of her life or whether the decision was simply not to publish them is something that

---

[9] It should be noted that *La Reina de las Nieves* and *Nubosidad variable* are both dedicated to Marta.
[10] Martín Gaite, *Cuadernos*, p. 669.

remains unknown at this moment.[11] Similarly, the protagonists of the last two novels, *Lo raro es vivir* and *Irse de casa*, even though they still search for an understanding of their past, do not have the need to note their findings in order to be able to continue. The writing is left for the future.

The importance of life-writing in Martín Gaite's 1990s novels is fundamental for an understanding of her biography. Analysing the novels and her *Cuadernos de todo* in conjunction, it is possible to draw a series of parallels which before the publication of the *Cuadernos* would have been more difficult to form.

This work has attempted to develop a new path in Martín Gaite studies by examining in detail many of the aspects of her *Cuadernos de todo* and linking them to her work, especially her novels of the 1990s. José Teruel and Maria Vittoria Calvi are, of course, the critics who carried out the preliminary work analysing Martín Gaite's fiction in relation to her notebooks in some of their articles and introductions. Here, though, I have undertaken a much more comprehensive study of the *Cuadernos de todo* and their relation to character development in the late novels, focusing on diaries, letters and life-writing as self-reflective writing and therapy. I have shown the extent to which the various forms of personal writing that Carmen Martín Gaite cultivated throughout her career have been harnessed for the development of the characters and the dramatic and thematic content of her later novels, as well as the way her characters took the idea of the writing cure further than the author ever did in her own *cuadernos*.

---

[11] In a short introductory note, Calvi comments that *Cuaderno 36* is 'El último *Cuaderno de todo* de cierta extensión ... que se ha incluido en la presente edición' (*Cuadernos*, p. 631).

BIBLIOGRAPHY

Abbott, H. Porter, *Diary Fiction: Writing as Action* (Ithaca, NY: Cornell University Press, 1984).
Alas, Leopoldo, *La Regenta* (Barcelona: Manuel Cortezo, 1884).
Alborch, Carmen, *Solas: Gozos y sombras de una manera de vivir* (Madrid: Temas de Hoy, 2006).
Aldecoa, Josefina, *Confesiones de una abuela* (Madrid: Temas de Hoy, 1998).
——, *En la distancia* (Madrid: Santillana, 2004).
——, *Porque éramos jóvenes* [1986] (Barcelona: Anagrama, 1996).
Alemany Bay, Carmen, *La novelística de Carmen Martín Gaite* (Salamanca: Ediciones de la Diputación, 1990).
Álvarez Vara, Ignacio, 'CMG con NYC de fondo', in Carmen Martín Gaite, *Visión de Nueva York* (Madrid: Siruela/Círculo de Lectores, 2005), pp. 125–30.
Andersen, Hans Christian, 'The Snow Queen: A Tale in Seven Stories', in *The Christian Andersen Fairy Tales*, trans. Tina Nunnally (London: Penguin, 2004).
Arkinstall, Christine, 'Towards a Female Symbolic: Re-Presenting Mothers and Daughters in Contemporary Spanish Narrative by Women', in *Writing Mothers and Daughters: Renegotiating the Mother in Western European Narratives by Women*, ed. Adalgisa Giorgio (Oxford: Berghahn Books, 2002), pp. 47–84.
Ballesteros, Isolina, *Escritura femenina y discurso autobiográfico en la nueva novela española* (New York: Peter Lang, 1994).
Baranda Leturio, Nieves and Lucía Montejo Gurruchaga (eds), *Las mujeres escritoras en la historia de la Literatura Española* (Madrid: UNED, 2002).
Beauvoir, Simone de, *The Second Sex*, trans. and ed. H. M. Parshley (London: Picador, 1988).
Bettelheim, Bruno, *Psicoanálisis de los cuentos de hadas* (Barcelona: Editorial Crítica, 1977).
Blanchot, Maurice, 'El diario íntimo y el relato', *Revista de Occidente, El diario Íntimo: Fragmentos de diarios españoles (1995–1996)*, 182–3 (1996), 47–54.
Borau, José Luis, 'Al día siguiente', *Turia: Revista Cultural*, 83 (2007), 249–60.
Bosch, Lolita, *La persona que fuimos* (Barcelona: Mondadori, 2006).
Bou, Enric, 'El diario: Periferia y literatura', *Revista de Occidente, El diario Íntimo: Fragmentos de diarios españoles (1995–1996)*, 182–3 (1996), 121–62.
Brown, Joan Lipman, 'The Challenge of Martín Gaite's Woman Hero', in *Feminine Concerns in Contemporary Spanish Fiction by Women*, ed. Roberto C. Manteiga, Carolyn Galerstein, and Kathleen McNerney (Potomac, MD: Scripta Humanistica, 1988), pp. 86–98.

———, *Secrets from the Back Room: The Fiction of Carmen Martín Gaite* (Valencia: University of Mississippi, 1987).
Caballé, Anna, 'La autobiografía escrita por mujeres: Los vacíos en el estudio de un género', in *Las mujeres escritoras en la historia de la literatura española*, ed. Nieves Baranda Leturio and Lucía Montejo Gurruchaga (Madrid: UNED, 2002), pp. 141–52.
———, 'Ego tristis (El diario íntimo en España)', *Revista de Occidente, El diario Íntimo: Fragmentos de diarios españoles (1995–1996)*, 182–3 (1996), 99–120.
———, 'Memorias y autobiografías escritas por mujeres (siglo XIX y XX)', in *Breve historia feminista de la literatura española (en lengua castellana) 5: La literatura escrita por mujer (Del s. XIX a la actualidad)*, ed. Iris Zavala (Barcelona: Anthropos, 1998), pp. 111–37.
——— (ed.), *Lo mío es escribir: La vida escrita por las mujeres, I* (Barcelona: Lumen, 2004).
——— (ed.), *La vida escrita por las mujeres, II: Contando estrellas* (Barcelona: Lumen, 2004).
——— (ed.), *La vida escrita por las mujeres, III: La pluma como espada* (Barcelona: Lumen, 2004).
——— (ed.), *La vida escrita por las mujeres, IV: Por mi alma os digo* (Barcelona: Lumen, 2004).
Calvi, Maria Vittoria, 'El autobiografismo dialógico de Carmen Martín Gaite', *Turia: Revista Cultural*, 83 (2007), 223–35.
———, *Dialogo e conversazione nella narrativa di Carmen Martín Gaite* (Milano: Archipelago, 1990).
———, 'Introducción', in Carmen Martín Gaite, *Cuadernos de todo*, ed. and intro. Maria Vittoria Calvi (Barcelona: Areté, 2002), pp. 9–16.
———, 'Introducción', in Carmen Martín Gaite, *El libro de la fiebre*, ed. and intro. Maria Vittoria Calvi (Madrid: Cátedra, 2007), pp. 9–83.
———, 'Presentación de los *Cuadernos de todo* en Salamanca', *Espéculo: Revista de Estudios Literarios* (Madrid: Universidad Complutense, 2003), available at: <http://www.ucm.es/info/especulo/cmgaite/c_todo.html>.
Campbell, Federico, *Conversaciones con escritores* (Mexico D.F.: CONACULTA, Dirección General de Publicaciones, 2004).
Camprubí, Zenobia, *Diario I: Cuba (1937–1939)* (Madrid: Alianza, 1991).
———, *Epistolario I: Cartas a Juan Guerreo Ruiz 1917–1956*, ed. Gabriela Palau de Nemes and Emilia Cortés Ibáñez (Madrid: Publicaciones de la Residencia de Estudiantes, 2006).
Camus, Albert, *The Outsider*, trans. Joseph Laredo (London: Penguin, 2000).
Carbayo Abengózar, Mercedes, *Buscando un lugar entre mujeres: Buceo en la España de Carmen Martín Gaite* (Malaga: Servicio de Publicaciones de la Universidad, 1998).
———, 'Significación social de las novelas de Carmen Martín Gaite en cuanto al desarrollo de la conciencia feminista en la España del siglo XX', in *El papel de la literatura en el siglo XX. I Congreso Nacional Literatura y Sociedad*, ed. Fidel López Criado (A Coruña: Servicio de Publicaciones, 2000), pp. 361–75.
Cardinal, Marie, *Las palabras para decirlo* (*Les Mots pour le dire*), trans. Marta Pessarrodona (Barcelona: Noguer, 1976).

Casewit, Curtis W., *The Diary: A Complete Guide to Journal Writing* (Allen, TX: Argus Communications, 1982).
Casorran Marín, María José, *Estudio crítico de 'El cuarto de atrás'* (Zaragoza: Mira Editores, 2006).
Castrejón Sánchez, María, 'Lo raro es vivir', in *Carmen Martín Gaite*, ed. Alicia Redondo Goicoechea (Madrid: Ediciones del Orto, 2004), pp. 185–97.
Castro, Rosalía de, 'Carta a Eduarda', in *Obras completas*, I, ed. Marina Mayoral (Madrid: Turner, 1993), pp. 655–9.
Catelli, Nora, 'El diario íntimo: Una posición femenina', *Revista de Occidente, El diario Íntimo: Fragmentos de diarios españoles (1995–1996)*, 182–3 (1996), 87–98.
Celaya, Beatriz, 'El amor es una tara: *Cuadernos de todo*, de Carmen Martín Gaite', *Neophilologus*, 91 (2007), 221–41.
Chacel, Rosa, *Alcancía: Ida* (Barcelona: Seix Barral, 1982).
——, *Alcancía: Vuelta* (Barcelona: Seix Barral, 1982).
——, *Cartas a Rosa Chacel*, ed. Ana Rodríguez-Fischer (Madrid: Cátedra, 1992).
——, *De mar a mar: Epistolario Rosa Chacel – Ana María Moix*, prologue and ed. Ana Rodríguez Fischer (Barcelona: Península, 1998).
——, *Memorias de Leticia Valle* [1945] (Barcelona: Bruguera, 1980).
Chisholm, Kimberly, 'Maternal-Filial Mirroring and Subjectivity in Carmen Martín Gaite's *Lo raro es vivir*', in *Carmen Martín Gaite: Cuento de nunca acabar/Never-ending Story*, ed. Kathleen M. Glenn and Lissette Rolón Collazo (Boulder, CO: Society of Spanish and Spanish-American Studies, 2003), pp. 109–27.
Choderlos de Laclos, Pierre, *Dangerous Acquaintances* (*Les Liaisons dangereuses*), trans. Richard Aldington (London: Routledge, 1979).
Chodorow, Nancy J., *Feminism and Psychoanalytic Theory* (New Haven, CT: Yale University Press, 1989).
——, *The Power of Feelings: Personal Meaning in Psychoanalysis, Gender and Culture* (New Haven, CT: Yale University Press, 1999).
——, *The Reproduction of Mothering: Psychoanalysis and the Sociology of Gender* (Berkeley: University of California Press, 1999).
Chown, Linda, *Narrative Authority and Homeostasis in the novels of Doris Lessing and Carmen Martín Gaite* (New York: Garland, 1990).
Cibreiro, Estrella, '*El mismo mar de todos los veranos* y *Nubosidad variable*: hacia la consolidación de una identidad femenina propia y discursiva', *Letras Peninsulares*, 13 (2000), 581–607.
Ciplijauskaité, Biruté, *Carmen Martín Gaite (1925–2000)* (Madrid: Ediciones del Orto, 2000).
——, *La construcción del Yo femenino en la literatura* (Cádiz: Servicio de Publicaciones de la Universidad, 2004).
——, *La novela femenina contemporánea (1970–1985): Hacia una tipología de la narración en primera persona* (Barcelona: Anthropos, 1994).
Cixous, Hélène, *The Writing Notebooks*, ed. and trans. Susan Sellers (London: Continuum, 2004).
Cott, Jonathan (ed.), *Cuentos de hadas victorianos*, trans. Carmen Martín Gaite (Madrid : Siruela, 1993).

Cruz, Jacqueline, 'Replegando la voz: Carmen Martín Gaite y la cocina de la escritura', in *Sexualidad y escritura (1850–2000)*, ed. Raquel Medina and Bárbara Zecchi (Barcelona: Anthropos, 2002), pp. 249–69.
Cruz-Cámara, Nuria, *El laberinto intertextual de Carmen Martín Gaite: Un estudio de sus novelas de los noventa* (Newark, DE: Juan de la Cuesta, 2008).
——, '*Nubosidad variable*: Escritura, evasión y ruptura', *Hispanófila*, 126 (1999), 15–25.
Didier, Beatrice, *L'Écriture-femme* (Paris: Presses Universitaires de France, 1981).
——, *Le Journal intime* (Paris: Presses Universitaires de France, 1976).
Encinar, Ángeles, Eva Löfquist and Carmen Valcárcel (eds), *Género y géneros II: Escritura y escritoras iberoamericanas* (Madrid: Servicio de Publicaciones de la UAM, 2006).
Escartín Gual, Montserrat, 'Noticias de Carmen Martín Gaite y *Retahílas*', in Carmen Martín Gaite, *Retahílas*, afterword by Montserrat Escartín Gual [1974] (Barcelona: Destino, 2003), pp. 169–232.
Espina, Concha, *Esclavitud y libertad: Diario de una prisionera* (Valladolid: Reconquista, 1938).
Etxebarria, Lucía, *Un milagro en equilibrio* (Barcelona: Planeta, 2004).
Fagundo, Ana María, *Literatura femenina de España y las Américas* (Caracas: Editorial Fundamentos, 1995).
Falcón, Lidia, *Los derechos civiles de la mujer* (Barcelona: Nereo, 1963).
——, *Los derechos laborales de la mujer* (Madrid: Montecorvo, 1964).
Fernández, Celia and María Ángeles Hermosilla (eds), *Autobiografía en España: Un balance. Actas del Congreso Internacional celebrado en la Facultad de Filosofía y Letras de Córdoba del 25 al 27 de octubre de 2001* (Madrid: Visor, 2004).
Fernández, Laura, 'Lolita Bosch explora «la intimidad» en un libro autobiográfico', *El Mundo*, 6 October 2006, available at: <http://www.elmundo.es/papel/2006/10/06/catalunya/2034149.html>.
Fernández Cubas, Cristina, *Cosas que ya no existen* (Barcelona: Lumen, 2001).
Folguera, Pilar (ed.), *El feminismo en España: Dos siglos de historia* (Madrid: Pablo Iglesias, 1988).
Foucault, Michel, 'Self Writing', in *Ethics, Subjectivity and Truth: The Essential Works of Michel Foucault 1954–1984*, ed. Paul Rabinow, trans. Robert Hurley et al. (London: Penguin, 1997), pp. 207–22.
Freixas, Laura, *Adolescencia en Barcelona hacia 1970* (Barcelona: Destino, 2007).
——, 'Auge del diario ¿íntimo? en España', *Revista de Occidente, El diario Íntimo: Fragmentos de diarios españoles (1995–1996)*, 182–3 (1996), 5–14.
—— (ed.), *Madres e hijas* (Barcelona: Anagrama, 1996).
——, *Último domingo en Londres* (Barcelona: Plaza & Janés, 1997).
Freud, Sigmund, *La interpretación de los sueños* (Barcelona: Planeta Agostini, 1985).
Fromm, Erich, *The Fear of Freedom* (London: Routledge, 1961).
Gala, Antonio (ed.), *I love NY: Diez autores en busca de una ciudad* (Madrid: Planeta, 2002).

García, Adrián M., *Silence in the Novels of Carmen Martín Gaite* (New York: Peter Lang, 2000).
Garlinger, Patrick Paul, *Confessions of the Letter Closet: Epistolary Fiction & Queer Desire in Modern Spain* (Minneapolis: University of Minnesota Press, 2005).
——, 'Diálogo crítico sobre Carmen Martín Gaite', *Revista de Estudios Hispánicos*, vol. 36, no. 1, 2002, 143–4.
Gazarian Gautier, Marie-Lise, 'Conversación con Carmen Martín Gaite en Nueva York', in *From Fiction to Metafiction: Essays in Honor of Carmen Martín Gaite*, ed. Mirella Servodidio and Marcia L. Welles (Lincoln, NE: Society of Spanish and Spanish-American Studies, 1983), pp. 25–33.
Genette, Gérard, *Narrative Discourse*, trans. Jane E. Lewin (Oxford: Basil Blackwell, 1980).
——, *Paratexts: Thresholds of Interpretation*, trans. Jane E. Lewin (Cambridge: Cambridge University Press, 1997).
Gilroy, Amanda and W. M. Verhoeven (eds), *Epistolary Histories: Letters, Fiction, Culture* (Charlottesville: University of Virginia Press, 2000).
Ginzburg, Natalia, *Nuestros ayeres*, trans. Carmen Martín Gaite (Barcelona: Círculo de Lectores, 1996).
——, *Querido Miguel*, trans. Carmen Martín Gaite [1989] (Barcelona: Acantilado, 2003).
Giorgio, Adalgisa (ed.), *Writing Mothers and Daughters: Renegotiating the Mother in Western European Narratives by Women* (Oxford: Berghahn Books, 2002).
Glenn, Kathleen M., 'Collage, textile and palimpsest: Carmen Martín Gaite's *Nubosidad variable*', *Romance Languages Annual*, 5 (1993), 408–13.
——, '*Nubosidad variable*', *Hispania*, 76 (1993), 297–8.
——, 'Voz, marginalidad y seducción en la narrativa breve de Carme Riera', in *Literatura y feminismo en España (S.XV–XXI)*, ed. Lisa Vollendorf (Barcelona: Icaria, 2005), pp. 339–52.
—— and Lissette Rolón Collazo (eds), *Carmen Martín Gaite: Cuento de nunca acabar/Never-ending Story* (Boulder, CO: Society of Spanish and Spanish-American Studies, 2003).
Goldsmith, Elizabeth (ed.), *Writing the Female Voice: Essays on Epistolary Literature* (London: Pinter, 1989).
Gómez de Avellaneda, Gertrudis, *Autobiografía y cartas (hasta ahora inéditas) de la ilustre poetisa Gertrudis Gómez de Avellaneda* (Huelva: Imprenta de Miguel Mora, 1907).
——, *Diario de Amor* [1914] (La Habana, Cuba: Letras Cubanas, 1993).
——, *Diario Intimo* (Buenos Aires: Ediciones Universal, 1945).
González Couso, David G., *Los perfiles Gallegos de Carmen Martín Gaite* (Almería: Procompal, 2008).
——, *Una propuesta de lectura para 'Caperucita en Manhattan'* (Almería: Procompal, 2008).
Gruber, Doris, *Literarische Konstruktion und geschlechtliche Figuration: Das Erzählwerk Carmen Martín Gaites und Juan Goytisolos im Kontext des Frakismus* (Berlin: Edition Tranvía, 2003).

Guardiola Tey, María Luisa, '*Lo raro es vivir*: Propuesta vitalista de Carmen Martín Gaite a finales del siglo XX', in *Género y géneros II: Escritura y escritoras iberoamericanas*, ed. Ángeles Encinar, Eva Löfquist and Carmen Valcárcel (Madrid: Servicio de Publicaciones de la UAM, 2006), pp. 133–42.

Gudmundsdóttir, Gunnthórunn, *Borderlines: Autobiography and Fiction in Postmodern Life Writing* (Amsterdam: Rodopi, 2003).

Guillén, Claudio, *Múltiples moradas: Ensayo de Literatura Comparada* (Barcelona: Tusquets, 1998).

Ibsen, Henrik, *The Lady from the Sea*, trans. Michael Meyer (London: Rupert Hart-Davis, 1960).

Jordan, Barry and Rikki Morgan-Tamosunas (eds), *Contemporary Spanish Cultural Studies* (London: Arnold, 2000).

Jurado Morales, José, 'La narrativa de Carmen Martín Gaite, la esencia misma del ensayo', in *Actas del VIII Simposio Internacional sobre Narrativa Hispánica Contemporánea: Novela y Ensayo* (El Puerto de Santa María: Fundación Luis Goytisolo, 2000), pp. 95–108.

——, *Del testimonio al intimismo: Los cuentos de Carmen Martín Gaite* (Cádiz: Servicio de Publicaciones de la Universidad, 2001).

——, *La trayectoria narrativa de Carmen Martín Gaite (1925–2000)* (Madrid: Gredos, 2003).

Kafka, Franz, *The Diaries of Franz Kafka 1910–1913*, ed. Max Brod (London: Secker & Warburg, 1948).

Kent, Victoria, *Cuatro años en Paris (1940–1944)* (Buenos Aires: SUR, 1947).

Klein, Melanie, *Love, Guilt and Reparation and other works 1921–1945* (London: Virago, 1988).

Kristeva, Julia, 'Women's Time', in *The Kristeva Reader*, ed. and intro. Toril Moi (New York: Columbia University Press, 1986), pp. 187–213.

Laverge, Gabriel de, Viscomte de Guilleragues, *Cartas de amor de la monja portuguesa Mariana Alcoforado*, trans. and intro. Carmen Martín Gaite (Madrid: Hiperión, 2000).

Lepore, Stephen J. and Joshua M. Smith (eds), *The Writing Cure: How Expressive Writing Promotes Health and Emotional Well-Being* (Washington DC: American Psychological Association, 2002).

Levine, Linda, 'Carmen Martín Gaite's *El cuarto de atrás*: A Portrait of the Artist as Woman', in *From Fiction to Metafiction: Essays in Honor of Carmen Martín Gaite*, ed. Mirella Servodidio and Marcia L. Welles (Lincoln, NE: Society of Spanish and Spanish-American Studies, 1983), pp. 161–72.

Lewis, C. S., *A Grief Observed* (London: Faber & Faber, 1961).

——, *Una pena en observación*, trans. Carmen Martín Gaite (Madrid: Trieste, 1988).

Lindo, Elvira, 'Nueva York un amor correspondido', in *I love NY: Diez autores en busca de una ciudad*, ed. Antonio Gala (Madrid: Planeta, 2002), pp. 267–97.

Lluch Villalba, María de los Ángeles, *Los cuentos de Carmen Martín Gaite: Temas y técnicas de una escritora de los años cincuenta* (Pamplona: Ediciones Universidad de Navarra, 2000).

Longhurst, Alex, 'Culture and Development: The Impact of 1960s "desarrollismo"', in *Contemporary Spanish Cultural Studies*, ed. Barry Jordan and Rikki Morgan-Tamosunas (London: Arnold, 2000) pp. 15–28.

López Cabrales, María del Mar, *Palabras de mujeres: Escritoras españolas contemporáneas* (Madrid: Narcea, 2000).

López Criado, Fidel, *El papel de la literatura en el siglo XX. I Congreso Nacional Literatura y Sociedad* (A Coruña: Servicio de Publicaciones, 2000).

Luna, Verónica, 'Diario, memorias y crónica', *Correo del Maestro* 122 (2006), available at: <http://www.correodelmaestro.com/anteriores/2006/julio/anteaula122.htm>.

MacDonald, George, *La princesa y los trasgos*, intro. and trans. Carmen Martín Gaite, illus. Pablo Álvarez de Toledo (Madrid: Siruela, 1995).

McLaren, Margaret A., *Feminism, Foucault and Embodied Subjectivity* (Albany, NY: State University of New York Press, 2002).

Mansfield, Katherine, *Journal of Katherine Mansfield* [1927], ed. John Middleton (London: Persephone Books, 2006).

Manteiga, Roberto C., Carolyn Galerstein and Kathleen McNerney (eds) *Feminine Concerns in Contemporary Spanish Fiction by Women* (Potomac, MD: Scripta Humanistica, 1988).

Martens, Lorna, *The Diary Novel* (Cambridge: Cambridge University Press, 1985).

Martín Gaite, Carmen, *A Fondo*, interview 1981, available at: <http://video.google.com/videoplay?docid=8932946931150749996>.

——, *Agua pasada* (Barcelona: Anagrama, 1993).

——, *A palo seco (Monólogo en un acto)* (Alarcón, Madrid: Foto Cine, 1985).

——, *A rachas* (Madrid: Libros Hiperión, Editorial Ayuso, 1976).

——, *Las ataduras* [1960] (Barcelona: Barral, 1978).

——, *El balneario* [1955] (Madrid: Alianza, 1993).

——, 'Un bosquejo autobiográfico', in Joan Lipman Brown, *Secrets from the Back Room: The Fiction of Carmen Martín Gaite*, pp. 193–206; repr. in Carmen Martín Gaite, *Agua pasada* (Barcelona: Anagrama, 1993), pp. 11–25.

——, *La búsqueda de interlocutor* (Barcelona: Anagrama, 2000).

——, *La búsqueda de interlocutor y otras búsquedas* [1973] (Barcelona: Destinolibro, 1982).

——, *Caperucita en Manhattan* (Madrid: Siruela, 1990).

——, *El castillo de las tres murallas*, illus. Juan Carlos Eguillor [1981] (Barcelona: Lumen, 1991).

——, *El conde de Guadalhorce, su época y su labor* (Madrid: Colegio de Ingenieros de Caminos, Canales y Puertos, 1977).

——, *Cuadernos de todo*, ed. and intro. Maria Vittoria Calvi (Barcelona: Areté, 2002).

——, *El cuarto de atrás* [1978] (Barcelona: Destino, 1996).

——, *El cuento de nunca acabar* [1983] (Barcelona: Anagrama, 1988).

——, *Cuentos completos* [1978] (Madrid: Alianza, 1989).

——, 'De su ventana a la mía', in *Madres e hijas*, ed. Laura Freixas (Barcelona: Anagrama, 1996), pp. 39–44.

——, *Desde la ventana: Enfoque femenino de la literatura española* [1987] (Madrid: Espasa Calpe, 1992).

——, *Dos cuentos maravillosos* (Madrid: Siruela, 1992).
——, *Entre visillos* [1958] (Barcelona: Destino, 2002).
——, *Esperando el porvenir: Homenaje a Ignacio Aldecoa* (Madrid: Siruela, 1994).
——, *Fragmentos de interior* [1976] (Barcelona: Destino, 1996).
——, *La hermana pequeña* (Barcelona: Anagrama, 1999).
——, *Irse de casa* (Barcelona: Anagrama, 1998).
——, *El libro de la fiebre*, ed. and intro. Maria Vittoria Calvi (Madrid: Cátedra, 2007).
——, *Macanaz, otro paciente de la Inquisición* (Madrid: Taurus, 1975).
——, *Nubosidad variable* [1992] (Barcelona: Anagrama, 2002).
——, *Obras completas*, I, ed. and intro. José Teruel (Barcelona: Galaxia Gutenburg/Círculo de Lectores, 2008).
——, *Obras completas*, II, ed. José Teruel (Barcelona: Galaxia Gutenburg/Círculo de Lectores, 2009).
——, *Obras completas*, III, ed. José Teruel (Barcelona: Galaxia Gutenburg/Círculo de Lectores, 2010).
——, *Los parentescos* [2001] (Barcelona: Anagrama, 2003).
——, *El pastel del diablo* (Barcelona: Lumen, 1985).
——, *Pido la palabra* (Barcelona: Anagrama, 2002).
——, *Poemas* (Barcelona: Plaza & Janés: 2001).
——, *El proceso de Macanaz: Historia de un empapelamiento* (Madrid: Moneda y Crédito, 1970).
——, 'El punto de vista, Edward Hopper: *Habitación de hotel*', *Conferencia impartida el día 14 de diciembre de 1996 en el Museo Thyssen-Bornemisza de Madrid* (Madrid: Museo Fundación, Colección Thyssen-Bornemisza, 1997).
——, *Lo raro es vivir* [1996] (Barcelona: Anagrama, 1999).
——, *La Reina de las Nieves* [1994] (Barcelona: Anagrama, 2002).
——, 'Retahíla con nieve en Nueva York', in *From Fiction to Metafiction: Essays in Honour of Carmen Martín Gaite*, ed. Mirella Servodidio and Marcia L. Welles (Lincoln, NE: Society of Spanish and Spanish-American Studies, 1983), pp. 19–24; repr. in Carmen Martín Gaite, *Agua pasada* (Barcelona: Anagrama, 1993), pp. 26–32.
——, *Retahílas*, afterword by Montserrat Escartín Gual [1974] (Barcelona: Destino, 2003).
——, *Ritmo lento* [1963] (Barcelona: Anagrama, 1984).
——, *Tirando del hilo (Artículos 1949–2000)*, ed. and intro. José Teruel (Madrid: Siruela, 2006).
——, *Usos amorosos del dieciocho en España* (Madrid: Siglo XXI de España Editores, 1972).
——, *Usos amorosos de la postguerra española* (Barcelona: Anagrama, 1987; 1994).
——, *Visión de Nueva York* (Madrid: Siruela/Círculo de Lectores, 2005).
Martinell Gifre, Emma (ed.), *Al encuentro de Carmen Martín Gaite: Homenajes y bibliografía* (Barcelona: Departamento de Filologia Hispanica, Universitat de Barcelona, 1997).
—— (ed.), *Carmen Martín Gaite* (Madrid: Ediciones de Cultura Hispánica, 1993).

―――, 'Entrevista con Carmen Martín Gaite', *Espéculo: Revista de Estudios Literarios* (Madrid: Universidad Complutense, 1998), available at: <http://www.ucm.es/OTROS/especulo/cmgaite/entr_cmg.htm>.
―――, '*Fragmentos de interior*', in *Carmen Martín Gaite*, ed. Alicia Redondo Goicoechea (Madrid: Ediciones del Orto, 2004), pp. 161–71.
―――(ed.), *Hilo a la cometa: La visión, la memoria y el sueño* (Madrid: Espasa Calpe, 1995).
―――, *El mundo de los objetos en la obra de Carmen Martín Gaite* (Cáceres: Universidad de Extremadura, 1996).
―――, 'Prólogo', in Carmen Martín Gaite, *Desde la ventana: Enfoque femenino de la literatura española* (Madrid: Espasa Calpe, 1992), pp. 9–21.
Martínez Cachero, José María *et al.* (eds), *Mostrar con propiedad un desatino: La novela española contemporánea* (Madrid: Eneida, 2004).
Masanet, Lydia, *La autobiografía femenina española contemporánea* (Madrid: Editorial Fundamentos, 1998).
Matute, Ana María, *Primera memoria* [1959] (Barcelona: Destino, 1996).
Medina, Raquel and Bárbara Zecchi (eds), *Sexualidad y escritura (1850–2000)* (Barcelona: Anthropos, 2002).
Medio, Dolores, *Diario de una maestra* [1961] (Barcelona: Destino, 1985).
Mistral, Silvia, *Éxodo: diario de una refugiada española* (México: Minerva, 1940).
Moi, Toril, *Sexual/Textual Politics* (London: Methuen, 1985).
Montero, Rosa, *Crónica del desamor* (Barcelona: Debate, 1979).
―――, *La función Delta* [1981] (Barcelona: Plaza & Janés, 1995).
―――, *La loca de la casa* [2003] (Madrid: Santillana, 2004).
Montseny, Federica, *El éxodo: pasión y muerte de españoles en el exilio* [1969] (Barcelona: Galba, 1977).
―――, *Mis primeros cuarenta años* (Barcelona: Plaza & Janés, 1987).
Moreno Sardá, Amparo, 'La réplica de las mujeres al franquismo', in *El feminismo en España: Dos siglos de historia*, ed. Pilar Folguera (Madrid: Pablo Iglesias, 1988), pp. 85–110.
Muñoz Molina, Antonio, *Ventanas de Manhattan* (Barcelona: Seix Barral, 2004).
Ochoa, Debra J., 'Martín Gaite's *Visión de Nueva York*: Collages of Public and Private Space', in *Beyond the Back Room: New Perspectives on Carmen Martín Gaite*, ed. Marian Womack and Jennifer Wood (Oxford: Peter Lang, 2011), pp. 81–97.
O'Leary, Catherine and Alison Ribeiro de Menezes, *A Companion to Carmen Martín Gaite* (Woodbridge: Tamesis Books, 2009).
Paatz, Annette, 'Perspectivas de diferencia femenina en la obra literaria de Carmen Martín Gaite', *Espéculo: Revista de Estudios Literarios* (Madrid: Universidad Complutense, 1998), available at: <http://www.ucm.es/OTROS/especulo/cmgaite/a_paatz1.htm>.
―――, *Vom Fenster aus gesehen? Perspektiven weiblicher Differenz im Erzahlwerk von Carmen Martín Gaite* (Frankfurt: Vervuert, 1994).
Palma Borrego, María José, 'La autobiografía psicoanalítica femenina o el "relato de cura" femenino', in *Autobiografía en España: Un balance. Actas del Congreso Internacional celebrado en la Facultad de Filosofía y Letras*

de Córdoba del 25 al 27 de octubre de 2001, ed. Celia Fernández and María Ángeles Hermosilla (Madrid: Visor, 2004), pp. 533–40.
Paoli, Anne, *Personnages en quête de leur identité dans l'oeuvre romanesque de Carmen Martín Gaite* (Aix-en-Provence: Publications de l'Université de Provence, 2000).
Pardo, María, 'La vida vislumbrada', in *La vida escrita por las mujeres III: La pluma como espada*, ed. Anna Caballé (Barcelona: Lumen, 2004), pp. 15–40.
Pardo, Rosa, 'El feminismo en España: Breve resumen, 1953–1983', in *El feminismo en España: Dos siglos de historia*, ed. Pilar Folguera (Madrid: Pablo Iglesias, 1988), pp. 133–40.
Pardo Bazán, Emilia, 'Apuntes autobiográficos', in *Obras Completas*, III, ed. Harry L. Kirby, Jr. (Madrid: Aguilar, 1973), pp. 698–732.
——, *Cartas a Benito Pérez Galdós*, prologue and ed. Carmen Bravo Villasante (Madrid: Ediciones Turner, 1975).
Paredes Núñez, Juan, *5 Narradores de posguerra* (Granada: Universidad de Granada, 1987).
Parker, Margaret, 'Revisiting Spain as Liberation from the Past in *Irse de casa* and *A Woman Unknown*: Voices from a Spanish Life', *South Central Review*, 18 (2001), 114–26.
Pereda, Rosa María, 'Carmen Riera: "Yo me sé la receta para un 'best-seller' de mujeres": Se presentó su novela "Una primavera para Domenico Guarini"', *El País*, 3 February 1982, available at: <http://www.elpais.com/articulo/cultura/ORTEGA/_SOLEDAD_/NO_USAR/Carmen/Riera/receta/best-seller/mujeres/elpepicul/19820203elpepicul_6/Tes/>.
Perez, Janet. 'Structural, Thematic, and Symbolic Mirrors in *El cuarto de atrás* and *Nubosidad variable* of Martín Gaite', *South Central Review*, 12 (1995), 47–63.
Perry, Ruth, *Women, Letters and the Novel* (New York: AMS Press, 1980).
Pittarello, Elide, 'Artesanías autógrafas de Carmen Martín Gaite', *Journal of Interdisciplinary Literary Studies*, 5 (1993), 101–18.
Puente Samaniego, Pilar de la, *La narrativa breve de Carmen Martín Gaite* (Salamanca: Plaza Universitaria Ediciones, 1994).
——, '*Nubosidad variable*', *Anales de Literatura Española Contemporánea*, 18 (1993), 404–6.
Puértolas, Soledad, *Con mi madre* (Barcelona: Anagrama, 2001).
——, *Recuerdos de otra persona* (Barcelona: Anagrama, 1996).
Ramos, Alicia, 'Conversación con Carmen Martín Gaite', *Hispanic Journal*, 1 (1980), 117–24.
Redondo Goicoechea, Alicia, 'Las autoras frente al espejo: Imágenes y modelos', in *Lo mío es escribir: La vida escrita por las mujeres, I*, ed. Anna Caballé (Barcelona: Lumen, 2004), pp. 11–53.
—— (ed.), *Carmen Martín Gaite* (Madrid: Ediciones del Orto, 2004).
——, 'Introducción literaria: Teoría y crítica feministas', in *Feminismo y misoginia en la literatura española. Fuentes literarias para la historia de las mujeres*, ed. Cristina Segura Graíño (Madrid: Narcea, 2001), pp. 19–46.
Regàs, Rosa, *Diario de una abuela de verano* [2004] (Barcelona: Planeta, 2006).
——, *Ginebra* [1987] (Barcelona: Seix Barral, 2002).

Riera, Carme, *Cuestión de amor propio* (Barcelona: Tusquets, 1988).
——, *La mitad del alma* (Madrid: Alfaguara, 2004).
——, *Tiempo de espera* (Barcelona: Lumen, 1998).
Rilke, Rainer Maria, *Cartas francesas a Merline*, trans. Carmen Martín Gaite (Madrid: Alianza Editorial, 1987).
Rivera, Maria Milagros, 'Egregias señoras: Nobles y burguesas que escriben', in *La vida escrita por las mujeres, IV: Por mi alma os digo*, ed. Anna Caballé (Barcelona: Lumen, 2004), pp. 17–22.
Rodríguez Fischer, Ana, 'Prólogo', in Rosa Chacel, *De mar a mar: Epistolario Rosa Chacel – Ana María Moix*, prologue and ed. Ana Rodríguez Fischer (Barcelona: Península, 1998), pp. 9–17.
Rolón Collazo, Lissette, *Figuraciones: Mujeres en Carmen Martín Gaite, revistas femeninas y ¡Hola!* (Madrid: Iberoamericana, 2002).
Scanlon, Geraldine M., *La polémica feminista en la España contemporánea: 1868–1974* (Torrejón de Ardoz, Madrid: Ediciones Akal, 1986).
Schiwy, Marlene A., *A Voice of Her Own: Women and the Journal-Writing Journey* (New York: Fireside, 1996).
Segura Graíño, Cristina (ed.), *Feminismo y misoginia en la literatura española. Fuentes literarias para la historia de las mujeres* (Madrid: Narcea, 2001).
Seoane, María Cruz, 'La historia y las historias en la obra de Carmen Martín Gaite', *Turia: Revista Cultural*, 83 (2007), 214–22.
Servén, Carmen, 'La amistad entre mujeres en la narrativa femenina: Carmen Martín Gaite (1992) y Marina Mayoral (1994)', *DICENDA: Cuadernos de Filología Hispánica*, 16 (1998), 233–43.
Servodidio, Mirella and Marcia L. Welles (eds), *From Fiction to Metafiction: Essays in Honour of Carmen Martín Gaite* (Lincoln, NE: Society of Spanish and Spanish-American Studies, 1983).
Simón Palmer, María del Carmen, 'La mujer y la literatura en la España del siglo XIX', *Centro Virtual Cervantes*, available at: <http://213.4.108.140/obref/aih/pdf/08/aih_08_2_069.pdf>.
Smith, Sidonie and Julia Watson, *Reading Autobiography: A Guide for Interpreting Life Narratives* (Minneapolis: University of Minnesota Press, 2001).
Soldevila Durante, Ignacio, '*Irse de casa*, o el haz y el envés de una aventurada emigración americana', in *Carmen Martín Gaite*, ed. Alicia Redondo Goicoechea (Madrid: Ediciones del Orto, 2004), pp. 199–206.
Soliño, María Elena, *Women and Children First: Spanish Women Writers and the Fairy Tale Tradition* (Potomac, MD: Scripta Humanistica, 2002).
Soriano, Elena, *Testimonio materno* (Barcelona: Plaza & Janés, 1986).
Soriano, Juan Carlos, 'Ana María Martín Gaite: "Nadie, ni siquiera yo, conoció del todo a Carmiña"', *Turia: Revista Cultural*, 83 (2007), 267–79.
Soto Fernández, Liliana, *La autobiografía ficticia en Miguel de Unamuno, Carmen Martín Gaite y Jorge Semprún* (Madrid: Editorial Pliegos, 1996).
Teruel, José, 'Un contexto biográfico para *Caperucita en Manhattan* de Carmen Martín Gaite', in *Género y géneros II: Escritura y escritoras iberoamericanas*, ed. Ángeles Encinar, Eva Löfquist and Carmen Valcárcel (Madrid: Servicio de Publicaciones de la UAM, 2006), pp. 143–51.
——, 'Introducción', in Carmen Martín Gaite, *Obras completas*, I, ed. and

intro. José Teruel (Barcelona: Galaxia Gutenburg/Círculo de Lectores, 2008), pp. 9–54.

——, 'El rescate del tiempo como proyecto narrativo: *El cuarto de atrás* y otras consideraciones sobre Carmen Martín Gaite', in *Mostrar con propiedad un desatino: La novela española contemporánea*, ed. José María Martínez Cachero *et al.* (Madrid: Eneida, 2004), pp. 191–209.

Torre Fica, Iñaki, 'Discurso femenino de autodescubrimiento en *Nubosidad variable*', *Espéculo: Revista de Estudios Literarios* (Madrid: Universidad Complutense, 2000), available at: <http://www.ucm.es/info/especulo/cmgaite/ina_torre.html>.

Torres Torres, Antonio, 'La perspectiva narrativa en *Nubosidad variable* de Carmen Martín Gaite', *Anuario de Estudios Filológicos*, 18 (1995), 499–506.

Trueba Lawand, Jamile, *El arte epistolar en el renacimiento español* (Madrid: Támesis, 1996).

Tusquets, Esther, *Confesiones de una vieja dama indigna* (Barcelona: Bruguera, 2009).

——, *Correspondencia privada* (Barcelona: Anagrama, 2001).

——, *Habíamos ganado la guerra* (Barcelona: Bruguera, 2007).

——, *El mismo mar de todos los veranos* (Barcelona: Lumen, 1978).

Uxó, Carlos, 'Cinco años de estudios sobre Carmen Martín Gaite: 1998–2002', in *Carmen Martín Gaite*, ed. Alicia Redondo Goicoechea (Madrid: Ediciones del Orto, 2004), pp. 215–26.

——, 'Revisión crítica de los estudios sobre su obra', *Espéculo: Revista de Estudios Literarios* (Universidad Complutense de Madrid), 1998, available at: <http://www.ucm.es/info/especulo/cmgaite/c_uxo1.htm>.

Vollendorf, Lisa (ed.), *Literatura y feminismo en España (S.XV–XXI)* (Barcelona: Icaria, 2005).

Welles, Marcia L., 'Carmen Martín Gaite, *Nubosidad Variable*', *Revista Hispánica Moderna*, 47 (1994), 256–9.

Winnicott, Donald W., *The Family and Individual Development* (London: Tavistock/Routledge, 1989).

——, 'Transitional Objects and Transitional Phenomena', *International Journal of Psycho-Analysis*, 34 (1953), 89–97.

Womack, Marian and Jennifer Wood (eds), *Beyond the Back Room: New Perspectives on Carmen Martín Gaite* (Oxford: Peter Lang, 2011).

Woolf, Virginia, *A Room of One's Own* and *Three Guineas* (London: Penguin, 1993).

Wright, Elizabeth (ed.), *Feminism and Psychoanalysis: A Critical Dictionary* (Oxford: Blackwell, 1996).

Zambrano, María, *Delirio y destino: Los veinte años de una española* [1989], ed. Rogelio Blanco Martínez and Jesús Moreno Sanz (Madrid: Editorial Centro de Estudios Ramón Areces, 1998).

Zatlin Boring, Phyllis, 'Carmen Martín Gaite: A Feminist Author', *Revista de Estudios Hispánicos*, 3 (1977), 323–38.

Zavala, Iris M. (ed.), *Breve historia feminista de la literatura española (en lengua castellana) 5: La literatura escrita por mujer (Del s. XIX a la actualidad)* (Barcelona: Anthropos, 1998).

INDEX

A palo seco 3
Abbott, H. Porter 25, 26, 139, 140, 145, 200
Agua pasada 2, 2 n. 3, 3 n. 5, 6, 27 n. 55, 34 n. 84, 67 n. 89, 68, 75 n. 126, 76, 116 n. 27, 120 n. 52, 149 n. 47, 202
Alborch, Carmen 119, 130 n. 99, 132, 136
Aldecoa, Josefina 4, 24
Andersen, Hans Christian 91, 92, 138, 153–9, 160
Las ataduras 1, 7
'Las ataduras' 27
autobiography 16, 20, 44, 46, 85, 153, 182 n. 8

El balneario 1, 86, 87, 115
Beauvoir, Simone de 21, 60, 64, 65 n. 73, 73, 120, 129
Bettelheim, Bruno 158, 159, 159 n. 90
Blanchot, Maurice 23
Borau, José Luis 4, 8, 97 n. 252, 98, 100
Brown, Joan Lipman 3, 3 n. 5, 28, 32, 106 n. 305
La búsqueda de interlocutor 2, 13, 31, 39, 57

Caballé, Anna 16, 20, 42
Calvi, Maria Vittoria 4, 7 n. 14, 8, 9, 9 n. 16, 12, 50, 52 n. 13, 54, 55, 69 n. 97, 75 n. 127, 76 n. 128, 88, 89, 205, 205 n. 11
Camprubí, Zenobia 21, 22
Camus, Albert 138, 154, 155
Caperucita en Manhattan 1, 2, 3, 7, 9 n. 16, 13, 109, 111, 123, 138, 170 n. 40
Carroll, Lewis 84, 87, 90, 90 n. 216
Cartas de amor de la monja portuguesa Mariana Alcoforado 11, 17 n. 13

El castillo de las tres murallas 2, 35, 126 n. 79, 138
Castro, Rosalía de 19, 39
Catelli, Nora 15, 18
Chacel, Rosa 20, 20 n. 26, 22, 54
children's literature 2, 8, 138
  children's stories 2, 120, 138, 153 n. 65
  fairy tales 41, 138, 153, 156, 158
Chodorow, Nancy J. 66, 123, 124, 125, 130 n. 104, 132, 135, 162, 163, 172, 173, 174, 176, 183
cinema 8, 68, 100, 101, 192
  cinematic 190, 192
  cinematographic 180
  film and film-script 3, 39, 85, 96, 120, 180, 182, 187, 188, 189, 192, 193, 195, 196, 197, 198
Civil War 22, 60, 86
Cixous, Hélène 55, 56
El conde de Guadalhorce, su época y su labor 30, 75, 83
consumerism 11, 59, 71, 174 n. 62
Cuadernos de todo, 3, 5, 8, 9, 10, 11, 12, 13, 14, 21 n. 29, 26, 27, 30, 32 n. 78, 34 n. 86, 36, 37, 41, 42, 43, 48, 50–111, 115, 132, 133, 137 n. 1, 138, 142, 143, 144 n. 24, 147, 148 n. 43, 163, 164, 165 n. 16, 170 n. 40, 171, 175 n. 68, 176, 177, 190, 191, 192 n. 56, 200, 201, 202, 203, 204, 205, 205 n. 11
El cuarto de atrás 2, 5, 6, 7, 23, 28 n. 59, 33, 34 n. 83, 35, 52, 53, 57, 63, 74, 79, 81, 83–8, 90 n. 216, 91, 102, 105, 106, 109, 115, 144 n. 24, 147, 182 n. 8, 184, 196, 201
'Cuenta pendiente' 13, 93–5, 121 n. 57, 143, 162 n. 6, 201
El cuento de nunca acabar 2, 8, 11, 27, 35, 36, 37, 50, 52, 54 n. 23, 57, 58, 74,

75, 76–81, 83, 87, 102, 103, 104, 125, 128, 156, 168, 201

death 2, 12, 13, 20, 21, 23, 27 n. 55, 32, 33, 35, 43, 44, 44 n. 128, 51, 58, 59, 60 n. 46, 67, 74, 88, 93, 94, 95, 96, 106, 107, 108, 109, 111, 114, 121, 121 n. 57, 134, 137, 138, 141, 144, 148, 152, 155, 157, 159, 160, 161, 162, 163, 164, 169, 174, 175, 178, 184, 185, 186, 195, 197, 201, 202, 203, 204
Desde la ventana 2, 6 n. 12, 11, 37, 38, 39, 81 n. 162, 99
diary and diaries 5, 9, 10, 11, 12, 13, 15–49, 50, 51, 53, 54, 58 n. 42, 73, 75, 76, 77, 90, 91, 94, 95, 100, 103, 106, 107, 110, 111, 112, 113, 114, 115, 116, 118, 121, 121 n. 57, 126, 129, 133, 137, 139, 140, 144, 145, 146, 148, 151, 153, 164, 168, 198, 199, 200, 203, 204, 205
diary-writing 10, 96
Didier, Beatrice 46, 48, 80, 199, 200, 202
Dos cuentos maravillosos 2
dreams 6, 13, 35, 39, 43, 51, 85, 94, 95, 106, 111, 122 n. 62 and 63, 134, 142, 143, 157, 162, 162 n. 6, 171, 175, 178, 194, 201, 203

Entre visillos 1, 4, 6, 7 n. 14, 27, 99, 115, 162 n. 6, 180, 182, 182 n. 8, 191, 198, 200
Esperando el porvenir 2, 6 n. 12
Etxebarria, Lucía 24

family and family relationships 9, 10, 13, 60, 61, 64, 66, 68–71, 82, 89, 99, 103, 125, 141, 144, 159, 161, 181, 186, 187, 190, 194, 201, 202, 204
feminism 61, 62, 110
Foucault, Michel 10, 26, 46, 55, 72, 199
Fragmentos de interior 2, 33, 34 n. 83, 74, 81, 83, 192
Franco, Francisco 23, 33, 58, 86, 109, 114, 161 n. 2, 182, 191
freedom 23, 26, 28, 46, 50, 61, 66, 70, 76, 80, 93, 98, 136, 138, 139, 147, 152, 156, 160, 178, 191, 197
Freixas, Laura 21, 22, 23, 24, 54 n. 25
Freud, Sigmund 122 n. 63, 131 n. 106
Fromm, Erich 73, 146, 147, 152

Galicia 7, 27, 32, 140, 148 n. 43, 152
Genette, Gérard 145, 181
Ginzburg, Natalia 11, 116 n. 27, 117, 153 n. 66, 170 n. 40
Gómez de Avellaneda, Gertrudis 19, 20

La hermana pequeña 3
history 2, 11, 18, 22, 30, 32, 36, 57, 64, 84, 165, 169, 177, 180
homosexuality 131, 131 n. 106, 132, 184

identity 7 n. 14, 47, 139
interlocutor 13, 20, 25, 27, 37, 38, 39, 42, 52, 56, 57, 78, 79, 85 n. 188, 95, 113, 118, 119, 123, 135, 136, 141, 142, 144, 149, 153, 167, 168, 189 n. 46, 202
Irse de casa 2, 12, 43, 111, 152 n. 60, 164, 172, 180–98, 205

Kent, Victoria 22
Klein, Melanie 66
Kristeva, Julia 61, 62

letter and letters 9, 10, 11, 12, 13, 15–49, 51, 72, 77, 83, 88, 92, 103, 108, 109, 111, 111 n. 330, 112, 113, 114, 116 n. 25, 117, 119, 127, 128, 129, 130, 133, 135, 137, 138, 139, 140, 141, 148–53, 155, 156, 157, 160, 164, 168, 173, 174, 182, 184, 185, 186, 188, 197, 198, 199, 200, 203, 205
Lewis, C. S. 11, 44
life-writing 9, 10 n. 24, 11, 12, 93, 178, 180, 182, 193, 197, 199, 200, 203, 205
Lindo, Elvira 97 n. 254

Macanaz
  see *El proceso de Macanaz*
Madrid 29, 32, 34, 58 n. 42, 59, 60 n. 46, 81, 94, 96, 97, 98, 100, 104, 114, 130, 135, 146 n. 33, 150, 161, 161 n. 2, 165 n. 15, 172, 190
Mansfield, Katherine 21, 48, 53, 77, 120
marriage 13, 60, 60 n. 46, 68, 69, 73, 83, 119, 134, 152, 190
Matute, Ana María 22
Medio, Dolores 22
memory 10 n. 23, 91, 103, 136, 137, 158, 188
mirror and mirrors 4, 13, 48, 49, 114,

117, 134, 136, 139, 145, 153, 153 n. 66, 171, 189 n. 46, 194, 199, 201
Mistral, Silvia 22
Moi, Toril 65 n. 73
Montero, Rosa 7, 24, 120 n. 48
Montseny, Federica 22, 23
motherhood 9, 11, 59, 65, 66–8, 74, 162, 175, 176, 179, 201
  parent-child relationship 66, 67, 182
Muñoz Molina, Antonio 97 n. 254

New York 3, 8, 39, 59, 75 n. 126, 94, 96–110, 111, 128, 181, 182, 184, 186, 188, 195, 197
Nubosidad variable 2, 5, 12, 13, 34, 36, 39, 42, 43, 45, 48, 56, 67, 88, 89, 90, 108, 109, 112–36, 137, 138, 139, 140, 145, 148, 148 n. 42, 149, 153, 153 n. 66, 157, 162, 165, 170 n. 40, 172, 174 n. 62, 175, 189 n. 46, 196, 200, 204 n. 9

Pardo Bazán, Emilia 20
Los parentescos 1, 5, 8, 115
El pastel del diablo 2, 7, 138
Pido la palabra 6, 6 n. 12
Poemas 5
El proceso de Macanaz: Historia de un empapelamiento 2, 30, 31, 36, 74, 81, 83, 166, 168, 177, 178
Puértolas, Soledad 7, 24

Lo raro es vivir 2, 5, 12, 31, 43, 67, 122 n. 63, 144 n. 24, 161–79, 205
reflection and reflections 10 n. 23, 11, 28, 35, 37, 39, 42, 43, 48, 52, 54, 55, 60, 64, 65, 70, 72, 73, 76, 77, 103, 105, 108, 110, 134, 138, 139, 144, 161, 163, 164, 166, 169, 175, 177, 197, 199, 204
  reflective writing and self-reflective writing 10, 13, 15, 30, 34, 35, 41–7, 48, 49, 110, 118, 200, 205
  self-reflection 38, 139
Regàs, Rosa 24
La Reina de las Nieves 2, 7 n. 14, 12, 13, 30, 34, 43, 48, 52, 67, 84, 89, 90–3, 108, 122 nn. 62–3, 123, 137–60, 161 n. 1, 162, 164, 172, 174 n. 62, 179, 189 n. 46, 200, 201, 204 n. 9
Retahílas 2, 5, 32, 35, 63, 65, 66, 74, 81–3, 85, 85 n. 188, 115, 147, 175, 184
Riera, Carme 24, 24 n. 38, 25, 129, 151 n. 56
Ritmo lento 1, 2, 29, 30

Salamanca 1, 3, 84, 192
Sánchez Ferlosio, Chicho 165 n. 15
Sánchez Ferlosio, Rafael 60 n. 46
sex and sexuality 68, 69, 92 n. 223
Smith, Sidonie and Julia Watson 9 n. 19, 10 n. 24, 116
solitude 27, 39, 41, 42, 43, 57, 58, 59, 70, 72, 73, 80, 81, 82, 96, 98, 99, 104, 107, 110, 111, 128, 130, 132, 133, 134, 138, 139, 144, 147, 169, 189 n. 46, 203

Teruel, José 6, 8, 9 n. 16, 12, 13, 200, 205
therapy 12, 29, 41, 46, 47, 111, 160, 205
  psychotherapy 113 n. 3
  writing cure 9, 12, 13, 41–9, 93, 108, 199, 202, 205
Tirando del hilo (Artículos 1949–2000) 6, 9 n. 16
Tusquets, Esther 24, 119

Usos amorosos del dieciocho en España 2, 30, 36, 70
Usos amorosos de la postguerra española 2, 39, 40, 41, 68, 69, 84, 85, 86, 109

Visión de Nueva York 5, 96–104, 107

Winnicott, Donald W. 66, 124, 151, 163
women's writing 10, 15, 16, 47, 99
  women writers 19, 47, 77

Zambrano, María 22